SOME IMPORTANT OPERATIONS

IN BEE MANAGEMENT

Northern Bee Books

SOME IMPORTANT OPERATIONS

IN BEE MANAGEMENT

by

T. S. K. Johansson and M. P. Johansson

Northern Bee Books

Originally published by International Bee Research
Association

Registered office:
International Bee Research Association
16 North Road
Cardiff CF10 3DY (UK)

This edition is a reprint of the original 1978 edition
Reprinted and published 2010 by Northern Bee Books

ISBN 978-1-904846-48-2

and obtainable from:

International Bee Research Association
16 North Road
Cardiff CF10 3DY (UK)

and Northern Bee Books
Scout Bottom Farm
Mytholmroyd
Hebden Bridge HX7 5JS (UK)

Printed by in the United Kingdom by
Lightning Source UK Ltd., Milton Keynes

FOREWORD

This book starts where many books on beekeeping leave off. Each chapter is devoted to a subject of great importance to the beekeeper in getting the best return from his bees. It shows what beekeeping practice and scientific research have found out, all over the world, and gives meticulous directions to the beekeeper based on these findings. The reader is provided with full details of the sources of information, and most of these publications can be purchased from IBRA as photocopies. He is also told where to find a summary of them in English.

Dr. and Mrs. Johannson have always been popular authors with readers of *Bee World*, and it is the great demand for reprints of their articles this has led to the publication of this book. The various chapters of *Some important operations in bee management* were originally published in Bee World between 1971 and 1978. Dr. and Mrs. Johansson were made joint Honorary Members of the International Bee Research Association in 1977, in recognition of their services. Dr. Johannson was appointed Associate Editor *Bee World* in 1964. Further *Bee world* articles are now planned on the routine examination of colonies, management schemes, preparation of bees for overwintering, swarm control, requeening, and moving bees.

The material in this book is written for an international readership, and experience in most of the temperate regions of the world is taken into account, especially in the USA and Canada, Britain and Ireland, continental Europe, Australia and New Zealand. The authors themselves live in New York City, and have their bees in upstate New York at East Berne, 38 km south-west of Albany, where winters can be long and hard. Both are professors of biology, at Queens College and Queensborough Community College, New York, respectively.

Experience has shown that there will commonly an interval of twenty five years between a discovery and its wide application in beekeeping practice. I sincerely hope that this book is shorten such delays, to the great benefit of beekeepers all over the world.

1 August 1978

Eva Crane
Director, International Bee Research Association

Foreword to the 2010 Reprint

Although the book was originally published thirty-two years ago it is still highly relevant to those who wish to further their apicultural skills and perhaps even increase their profits from beekeeping. Little can be added to Dr Eva Crane's original foreword, as it is indeed a book designed to take beekeepers beyond the basics. Such a practical and comprehensive book, international in its coverage and appeal, will always be in demand. The International Bee Research Association is pleased that Jeremy Burbidge of Northern Bee Books has undertaken this reprint.

Sarah Jones
Executive Director IBRA

HOW TO FOLLOW UP INFORMATION GIVEN IN THIS BOOK

Most chapters include a list of references to publications referred to in the text, either by number or by author and year. Many of the references are summarized in English in the journal *Apicultural Abstracts,* published by the International Bee Research Association, and the location of the summary in the journal is given at the end of each reference. For instance, 483/68 shows that the summary is no. 483 in the 1968 volume of *Apicultural Abstracts;* 483L/68 would indicate that the full bibliographical reference is given there, but no summary, or a very short one. In Chapters 1, 2 and 6, numbers such as 483/68 are given in the text, and there is no list of references at the end.

Almost all the publications referred to in the book are in the Library of the International Bee Research Association. Photocopies of them can be purchased by sending a photocopy order form, with the undertaking (necessary because of copyright laws) that the photocopy supplied will be used only for private study, and not for resale. Forms are supplied by IBRA free on request, and they set out the scale of charges.

ACKNOWLEDGMENTS

Chapters were first published in *Bee World,* and some subsequently as separate reprints:

Chapter			Reprint
1.	*Bee World*	57 : 47-50 (1976)	—
2.		57 : 96-100 (1976)	—
3.		51 : 23-35 (1970)	M57
4.		50 : 89-100 (1969)	M55
5.		54 : 149-175 (1973)	M72
6.		57 : 137-143 (1976); 58 : 11-18, 49-52 (1977)	M92
7.		58 : 105-118, 135, 161-164 (1977)	M91
8.		59 : 11-17, 54-64 (1978)	—
9.		52 : 146-156 (1971)	M61
10.		48 : 133-143 (1967)	M51

The drawing on the cover, by Carl Preuss, is published here for the first time, by the courtesy of Joe Parkhill of Arkansas, USA.

CONTENTS

CHAPTER 1

HANDLING BEES

1. Introduction

The guidelines below are based on a wide variety of publications, and should apply to most conditions in temperate latitudes.   The authors and the editor would welcome suggestions towards a similar set of guidelines for working in tropical and subtropical conditions with *Apis mellifera* (including *A. m. adansonii*), and *Apis cerana*.

Many beekeepers would admit that they began by being very fearful of the bees they were going to work with.   But any person who will follow a few simple principles can learn to handle bees, receiving a minimum of stings in the process, which are unlikely to inconvenience him.   A few people are hypersensitive to bees; anyone who experiences an allergic reaction, with sneezing, a feeling of suffocation, an outbreak of rash and blistering of the skin, should arrange with a physician for tests.   If these show that he is hypersensitive to bees then he should not keep them.

2. Behaviour of bees

a. Under suitable hive conditions (see 3 below) bees are remarkably tolerant of manipulations by the beekeeper.

b. Colony conditions which tend to make bees difficult to handle (see also 7 below) include: queenlessness; supersedure; drone-laying queen; sudden cessation of the nectar flow; a very large population; presence of many old bees; unsuitable weather (see 3); robbing; previous alerting of the colony by disturbance of any kind.

c. When a hive is opened, many bees are often in the air; some may settle on you, but they are unlikely to sting unless injured or alerted.

d. Smoke "disorganizes" a colony and makes it easier to handle, although the full mechanism is still not understood.

e. "Guard" bees at the hive entrance react to any interference or disturbance (see 6*e*).

3. When to manipulate bees

a. In temperate regions, those beekeepers who can choose their own time should work on a warm, dry, windless, sunny day between 10 and 16 hours (10 am–4 pm); most of the older bees are then out foraging.

b. Nevertheless, do not postpone a necessary manipulation which would be difficult to do if the weather changes for the worse.

c. Avoid cold, windy or showery days when the forager bees are all in the hive.

d. Avoid periods with electric disturbances in the atmosphere.

e. Do not manipulate hungry colonies until you have fed them; bees' reaction to smoke is to engorge honey (or syrup).

4. How long to keep a hive open

There are three separate dangers from prolonged exposure: chilling the brood; dis-
organizing the colony; robbing (especially unsealed) honey.

a. In good weather the surface of a comb containing brood may be exposed for a
few moments, but not longer unless the air temperature is near brood-nest temperature
(35°C).

b. The boxes that constitute a hive may themselves be separated from each other
for say half an hour, provided each is kept covered up except when being inspected.

c. Combs containing honey will attract robbers; do not put such combs down
except inside a hive box that can be covered up. Boxes containing sealed honey
may be left 5–10 minutes if covered on top and made bee tight below.

d. Disorganization or robbing will itself alert the operator that he has had the hive
open too long. Chilling of brood will give no such warning.

5. Dress and personal hygiene

a. Always wear a veil to protect the face (especially eyes and mouth) and to prevent
bees getting entangled in the hair. On hot days, soaking the veil in water at intervals
helps to keep the operator cool. If bees get inside your veil, walk away from the hive
before opening up the veil to remove them. Bees are unlikely to follow you into a
building or into woodland or bushes.

b. Check that all clothing is bee-tight, i.e. that there are no gaps through which bees
can gain access to the body.

A white cover-overall (boiler-suit) with a veil zippered to it provides maximum
protection against bees. If the veil is separate, check that bees cannot get in under
it.

Boots—with string, elastic bands or cyclists' clips round the trousers—will
prevent bees gaining access to the legs and crawling up them.

Gloves prevent the hands getting sticky with propolis. Make a bee-tight joint
between the sleeve and the glove (or bare arm).

c. Avoid clothes of dark rough-textured material (this applies also to socks if
exposed).

d. Bees are alerted to sting by the smell of the alarm pheromone (isopentyl acetate),
which is itself released during stinging or when bees are crushed. It is therefore
important to prevent *any* stings. If this is not possible, mask the alarm scent by puffing
smoke over the area concerned, or by rinsing hands and hive tool in water, etc.

e. When you are going to work with bees, do not use any scented cosmetic materials
(e.g. hair preparation, perfume, powder), as some scents may act similarly to the alarm
pheromone. Many authors say that the sweat of humans or horses, and other body
odours, make bees more likely to sting.

6. Manipulation techniques

a. Make all movements smooth and deliberate, not jerky or rough. Do not bump
or jar hives or frames.

b. Light the smoker 10 minutes in advance, to ensure a steady flow of cool smoke
when you need it.

c. Always work at the side or back of the hive. Stay out of the flight path as
much as possible.

d. As far as possible keep boxes of frames and/or bees covered up, to reduce the number of flying bees and to prevent robbing. "Manipulating cloths" are useful; they are as wide as a hive box and slightly longer, with a rod inserted across each short end to weight the cloth down.

e. First blow 3 or 4 puffs of smoke into the hive entrance. This will start the bees engorging honey; the number reaches a maximum after 2 minutes and remains high for at least 10 minutes (85/69, 904/70*).

f. Slowly pry off the hive cover from the frames, while gently puffing smoke beneath it. Do not jerk it off.

g. Place the hive cover upside down on the ground, so that hive boxes can be put on it.

h. The first frame to pry out is that next to the end frame in the top hive box (body, chamber), or some other frame not stuck with burr comb.

i. Replace the frames to occupy their original positions, since some combs may have irregularities.

j. Pry up the top super with the hive tool, and puff a little smoke through the gap before lifting the super off.

k. If supers are heavy, place them on an empty hive box or two, to facilitate later removal.

l. Resmoke at intervals with a gentle horizontal puff to keep the bees below the tops of the frames. Experience will dictate the most effective interval on any one occasion. Do not wait too long, or the colony may get out of control (see 7h).

m. Kill any persistent guard bee that annoys you by following you around.

n. Scrape burr comb into a can and keep this covered. Do not throw scraps of comb on the ground, because it may then incite robbing.

o. Open hives as briefly as possible and only when necessary.

Dzierzon asserted in 1853 that frequent examinations did not affect foragers; more recent experiments have shown the same (620/64).

During a major nectar flow there may be a 20–30% production loss on the day of manipulation, indicating that bees in the hive are affected even if foragers are not (759/65).

On a windless day, if the ambient temperature is 20°C or higher, opening the hive is not harmful if bees cover the brood (177/57).

Frequent opening of a hive (as in queen rearing) increases the likelihood of nosema infection (351/68).

p. Specific operations (some experimental) may use other agents than smoke for subduing bees, for instance: spraying with water or dilute sugar syrup; anaesthetizing with chloroform, ether or carbon dioxide; fumigating with carbolic acid (not recommended since it is carcinogenic) or benzaldehyde; reducing the body temperature with dry ice or refrigeration.

7. Manipulating difficult colonies

a. Before manipulating, move the hive about 12 metres from its stand, perhaps near a weak colony that needs extra bees. Make the move in the evening or in the middle of a nice day when the bees are flying well. Stuff the entrance temporarily with grass, wet rags, or a screen, to prevent the bees escaping while the hive is being moved. If

* Such numbers refer to entries in *Apicultural Abstracts;* 620/64 is no. 620 in the 1964 volume.

the hive is too heavy to lift, first remove supers and set them aside with covers and/or screens underneath and on top of them.

b. Place another hive on the old stand with empty frames (and foundation or starters if desired), and preferably one frame with honey and pollen, but no brood from the troublesome colony.

c. Undertake manipulations during the next day or two, when the foragers have returned to the old location, leaving young nurse bees (less disposed to sting) in the hive.

d. Either requeen the hive at the new stand, or provide a new queen at the old stand.

e. If it is necessary to keep colonies that are difficult to manipulate, there are benefits in using a bee house.

f. Use a cage round the hive, to prevent the access of robber bees during manipulations; this is also useful for public demonstrations.

g. If you do get stung, scrape the sting out immediately with the finger nail, without squeezing the poison sac; while this continues to contract venom is pumped into the wound. In the event of an anaphylactic reaction, adrenalin or other treatment must be administered without delay. Such reaction is fortunately very rare.

h. In exceptional circumstances, so many bees become alerted that effective operation is no longer possible. If a colony gets out of control in this way, reassemble the hive as quickly as possible, leaving no gaps by which robbers can enter. Leave the apiary, removing any uncovered combs, and do not open other hives there until the next day.

CHAPTER 2

UNITING COLONIES

1. Introduction

Basic techniques are described here for the weekend or hobby beekeeper who may not be able to unite colonies under ideal conditions, any more than the commercial bee-keeper with hundreds or thousands of hives to manage. Possible alternatives are therefore mentioned along with known basic principles, so that other techniques may be devised to suit unique situations.

It may be desirable or necessary to unite two or more colonies:

to combine small colonies into one larger colony (e.g. queen-rearing nuclei);

to unite a colony without a queen to one with a queen;

to unite a colony with laying workers (but *not* with a drone-laying queen) to a queenright colony;

to unite a swarm to an established colony.

2. General procedures and precautions

(*a*) If the queen is not removed (24 hours in advance of uniting) from one of the two colonies, the resultant united colony will eventually choose one of the queens, but there is risk that she may be damaged in the fighting, resulting in queenlessness. It is better if the beekeeper removes one of the queens, and he can decide which one is less worth keeping.

(*b*) Bees in small colonies are prone to " ball " (smother) their queen during or following manipulations: in the spring, or when the weather is poor, stores are short, or robbers are present. The end of the season, after drones are eliminated, is another critical time when manipulations should be performed with as little disturbance as possible.

(*c*) Two colonies which must be united during a dearth of nectar should be fed with 1 : 1 sugar syrup for a day or two beforehand.

(*d*) If the weaker colony is moved to the site of the stronger one, there will be less drifting back to the old stand.

(*e*) Bees will not return to their old stand if they have been moved from a stand at least 3 km or 2 miles away.

(*f*) There will be little or no fighting if the stronger colony is placed on top of the weaker colony. But a small colony thrown in front (or placed on top) of a strong colony without precautions will provoke a vigorous defence on the part of the strong colony.

(*g*) Colonies should be watched after uniting, and if fighting occurs the bees should be sprayed with water, to stop it.

(*h*)   A box with a queen-excluder top placed over the hive entrance will serve as a dead-queen trap, for checking whether the queen has been accepted. (For other queen traps, see 151L/73*.)

(*i*)   Bees added to another colony spread out and undertake activities appropriate to their age group. Neither house bees nor foragers are necessarily interrupted in their activities (135/56).

3.   C. C. Miller's newspaper method of uniting

This is generally advocated as the safest method, particularly when robbing is prevalent in spring, or after the nectar flow has ceased.

(*a*)   Move one or both hives towards the other, through 1-1½ m (3-5 ft) at the end of each day when the bees can fly. The bees orient to the new position before they are moved again, and both colonies' flying bees are retained. In early spring or autumn, the colonies can be moved twice as far after a good flight.

(*b*)   When the colonies are close together, loosen the bottom (floor) board and the hive roof, well before uniting will take place, so that the manipulation can then be accomplished with a minimum of disturbance.

(*c*)   In the evening, or on a cool day when the bees are not flying (say 10°C, 50°F), remove the cover of the hive with the weaker, queenless colony (at the stand to be used), and place a single-thickness sheet of newspaper on top of the frames.

(*d*)   Punch several holes in the paper with a match, stick, nail, or pencil, or cut slits with the hive tool (use two sheets of newspaper and two holes if colonies are of different or difficult races).

(*e*)   Place the queenright and stronger colony on top of the newspaper. The bees enlarge the holes and mingle very gradually, without fighting. Small pieces of paper outside the entrance, and absence of dead bees below the entrance, signify success.

(*f*)   In very hot weather additional ventilation can be provided by placing a match stick at each corner between the two hive bodies.

(*g*)   Some beekeepers put a queen excluder over the newspaper, to slow down the mingling of the bees. The excluder is removed a day or two later.

(*h*)   A double screen of wire-cloth (e.g. a ventilated super clearer) can be used in place of newspaper and may ensure that the queen will not be damaged by balling.

(*i*)   After about a week the frames can be rearranged.

(*j*)   If there are supers of honey, a second sheet of newspaper and an excluder should be placed over the top of the upper brood chamber, and the supers placed on top.

4.   Direct uniting

This can be done safely only during a rapid, heavy nectar flow, and in the middle of the day when most forager bees are out of the hive.

(*a*)   Move the queenless colony to the queenright colony, as queenless bees more readily remain at the new site. Any bees that return to the old stand will join nearby colonies.

(*b*)   Place the queenright colony on top of the queenless colony. A queen excluder placed between the two colonies will slow down the mingling of the bees.

(c)   Some beekeepers advocate alternating the combs from the two colonies as they are placed in a new hive box, and spacing the frames widely apart at first so that the bees are exposed to light. Smoke gently at intervals.

(d)   Quick, horrendous action follows:
kill one of the queens ;
place brood of both in one hive body with the other queen and some of her bees;
shake all the other bees in front, and sprinkle or spray them with sugar solution;
puff smoke at the entrance.
If successful, there will be much confusion but no fighting.

(e)   Another useful technique is to remove brood combs and the adhering bees (even an entire hive body) to another colony. Unite the remainder of the colony to a neighbouring colony. Whichever queen is considered the better should be retained.

(f)   At the end of the season colonies can be joined with little loss of flying bees, because these fly infrequently and will orient to the new position.

5.   Uniting by disorientating the bees

A device has been described that consists of a queen excluder and a reverse bend which connects two or more hives (U.S. Patent 3,426,374, 978/70).

6.   Uniting by anaesthetizing bees

Ether is reported to permit the uniting of colonies, even during severe weather, e.g., in a room held at 10-12°C (108/50).

7.   Uniting a nucleus to a queenless colony

(a)   A small nucleus in an empty super can be placed on newspaper over the colony, and the frames later incorporated with the queenless colony below.

(b)   A nucleus can be added directly to a colony made queenless the day before, by spraying the bees with a thin (1 : 1) sugar syrup and placing any brood from the nucleus adjacent to the brood of the colony. If there is not a good nectar flow, the bees in the colony should be sprayed with syrup until they are gorged.

8.   Uniting two or more nuclei or small colonies

(a)   The frames of two small colonies can be placed into one brood nest, separated by at least one comb without bees.

(b)   A colony can be made up of several small nuclei by alternating frames from the nuclei in a hive box. The frames should be widely spaced at first, and the bees smoked gently at intervals. The colony is given a final smoking before the hive is closed.

(c)   G. H. Vansell sprayed the bees with water until it ran freely out of the hive entrance, and then stacked up the nuclei one on top of the other.

(d)   G. M. Doolittle devised a box-plan for uniting queenless nuclei :
puff a little smoke into the entrance, and strike 5 or 6 blows on the top of the hive :
wait at least two minutes for the bees to gorge with honey (or spray them with syrup) ;
shake the bees off the frames into a box 22 × 20 × 35 cm (9 × 8 × 14 inches) screened on the top and bottom. A hole 6 cm (2½ inches) in diameter in the top screen is fitted with a funnel to receive the bees;

shake in additional nuclei (as many as 5 or 6);

the funnel is removed, the hole closed, and a queen introduced by bumping the collected bees to the bottom of the box and dropping her amongst the bees through a smaller hole;

the box is stored in a cool dark place, until the bees are hived by dumping them in front of their new hive as if they were a natural swarm.

9. Uniting swarms to colonies

(a) A swarm (or "driven" bees) can be added directly to a recently hived swarm or a small colony (nucleus) by shaking it in front of the hive.

(b) To add a swarm to a strong established colony is more difficult:

cage the queen of the colony;

shake all the bees from the combs in front of the hive;

throw the swarm on top of the bees;

smoke the entrance as the bees go into the hive.

(c) Alternative to method (b) above:

establish the swarm in a hive alongside the colony;

after 3 days dequeen the swarm and unite it to the colony by the newspaper method;

if the queen from the swarm is to be used for requeening the colony, the union should be made a week or so after she is laying satisfactorily.

10. Uniting a queenless colony to an established colony

(a) Early in the season, a queenless colony can be shaken in front of an adjacent colony without much risk of fighting.

(b) In August-September the presence of strange bees may cause the colony to kill its queen. (This may also occur when bees are dumped from honey supers on to the brood-chamber frames.

(c) A queenless colony can be added to a colony that has just swarmed (12/128).

(d) Bees from a queenless colony can be shaken into a travelling box (package bee container) and then thrown into an empty super placed on a newspaper over the receiving colony. The travelling box is first given a sharp bump, causing the bees to fall on to the bottom of the box, and they can then be " poured " out easily.

(e) If removing one queen the day before the colonies are united will promote success, making both colonies queenless will further reduce the chance of failure, even with the most difficult races (Cyprian, Syrian). In the former situation the selected queen may be caged in the queenless colony about mid-day, and the bees united in the evening. In the latter the selected queen is returned in the evening.

11. Uniting laying-worker and queenright colonies

(a) When it is not possible to procure a fertilized queen, or efforts to introduce one are unsuccessful, the laying-worker colony can be united to a strong queenright colony using the newspaper method.

(b) A small laying-worker colony whose bees are all of foraging age can be fed sugar syrup, and moved some distance from its stand in the middle of the day, and the bees shaken off the combs there. They will be accepted into other colonies as returning foragers. The hive is removed, and the frames are given to other colonies.

(c) The frames of laying-worker brood, with their bees, are exchanged for brood frames from a " normal " colony with some nurse bees. The laying worker(s) will probably be destroyed in the queenright colony, and a day later the laying-worker hive can be given a queen.

(d) On a day when there is a good flight, give the laying-worker colony a frame of emerging brood, and cage the queen to be introduced alongside this frame of brood. Exchange the positions of the laying-worker hive and one containing a normal colony. The bees of the queenright colony returning to their former stand will probably destroy the laying workers, and any laying workers returning to their former stand will be destroyed by the normal colony.

(e) An " infallible " Canadian-US method for eliminating laying workers is described as follows :

> Remove the laying-worker hive 200 metres away (not less than 100).
> Shake and brush all bees off the combs and the hive on to a sheet on the ground.
> Return the combs, without a single bee on them, to a new hive placed on the stand where the laying-worker hive stood.
> Only the laying workers and a few very old or very young bees will remain on the sheet.
> A laying queen can then be introduced to the new hive at the old stand.

12. Adding forager bees only to a colony

(a) If an adjacent hive is turned to face a different direction, flying bees from it will enter the hive facing in the original direction.

(b) A hive may be gradually moved close to one in which it is desired to increase the number of flying bees, and left there for a short period. The hive which has been moved is removed again on a day when the foragers are flying actively. This can be repeated as often as necessary to obtain the desired population of flying bees for honey production.

(c) During either of the above manipulations, a sudden weather change which induces foragers to return empty may stimulate aggressive behaviour.

CHAPTER 3

ESTABLISHING AND USING NUCLEI

The small, young colonies of bees referred to by beekeepers as nuclei, or more familiarly nucs, should form part of every beekeeping establishment, whether it is a large commercial enterprise, a garden apiary, or one used for teaching. Many beekeepers share the aesthetic experience of their first hive started up with a small, quiet colony building exquisitely delicate combs. Such nuclei are easy and pleasant to handle—whereas the "monstrous, boiling colonies" inhabiting piled up boxes of dark comb, which sometimes later take their place, are definitely not. This article collects together much information on nuclei, and encourages the practice of keeping them, for good and sufficient reasons which are set out, as well as for pleasure. Some notes on the history of nuclei are included on page 27.

Introduction

The *Concise Oxford Dictionary* includes among the explanations of "nucleus (plural, nuclei)" the following: "central part or thing round which others are collected, kernel of aggregate or mass, beginning meant to receive additions". Webster's *New International Dictionary*, published in New York, allows nucleuses as an alternative plural, and adds the beekeeping usage: "a small mass of bees and combs or brood, used in forming a new colony or in rearing queens". Beekeepers often refer to a nucleus as a "division", because it is divided off from an existing colony; the German term *Ableger* is that used in horticulture for a slip taken from an existing plant for propagation. Since swarming is the *bees'* method of dividing a colony in two, the *beekeeper's* division is commonly referred to as "artificial swarming". Before the First World War, nuclei were widely used in the United States and Canada for establishing colonies. Fear of the transmission of diseases then reduced the demand, and the package bee business developed, packages purchased from shippers in the southern States replacing the nuclei used earlier. Since the cost of packages has now risen steeply, whereas the price obtained for honey has not, rearing bees for his own needs has become a profitable use of a beekeeper's equipment today.

Nuclei are an essential part of modern apiary management; they are also more suited for many educational purposes than full colonies, and give pleasure and confidence to beginner beekeepers—who may be put off beekeeping for ever by having to handle monstrous boiling colonies on many brood chambers.

Farrar has successfully championed the large hive for maximum honey production where the honey flow is brief, copious and occurs early in the season. But other conditions may require other management, and even Farrar concedes that there is less difference between the performance of small and large colonies in longer seasons:

"During a 2 weeks' honeyflow, a full-strength colony with 60 000 bees will normally produce 50 percent more honey than four small colonies each with 15 000 bees. Under a longer flow, the four small colonies will increase in population because of their higher relative brood production, thus narrowing the difference in yield between one strong colony and the four small colonies. There is no advantage, however, in keeping small colonies just because their storing efficiency increases; it is better management to have all colonies strong at maximum efficiency throughout the flow."

For non-commercial beekeepers, the disadvantages of manipulating large colonies may seem an excessive price for a larger honey surplus. Jean-Prost found his *Méthode 60* superior for the lavender flow in France. He used 4 colonies to make 3–7 nuclei from each one during May and June, and then gradually reunited them in time for the major honey flow in August. The differences in brood production, morale, comb building etc. of nuclei may make them an important ingredient in profitable beekeeping where large colonies are a detriment.

Statutes in many countries prohibit keeping bees in hives that cannot be inspected for disease, so the discussion that follows is written from the point of view of using movable-frame hives.

Procedures for making nuclei

1. General methods

A nucleus includes at least one comb of emerging brood and one of honey and pollen. The adhering bees provide some adults to perform hive duties, but to ensure adequate numbers, bees are shaken from at least two additional brood combs. These can be taken from several colonies if no single colony is sufficiently strong to withstand loss of the required bees. Experience will provide a basis for judging when enough bees have been added to cover the brood, or scales can be used to weigh out a precise quantity. One-half to one pound of bees [say 250–500 g] should be sufficient ($\frac{1}{2}$–1 litre or quart). It is astonishing to see what progress a small colony can make when conditions are favourable. Doolittle counted 81 workers and a queen in an overwintered colony which by the end of the season had produced 5 pounds [2·3 kg] of surplus honey and was in excellent condition for wintering. Giving stores and emerging brood to tiny colonies will secure more rapid and certain development.

Bees can be shaken from combs into a wire-bottomed box, sprinkled with sugar syrup, forced to settle to the bottom of the box by jarring it sharply, and then ladled out with a scoop or measure of some sort. If the bees are shaken on to a queen excluder when collected, drones will be sifted out, older bees will fly back to the parent hive, and a queen shaken off in error will be detected. Instead of scooping the bees out of the box, the frames of brood can be placed above the collecting box so that the bees will move up and cover the combs, ready to be placed in the nuclei. Another alternative is to place the frames above a queen excluder on a populous hive. This eliminates the need to shake bees off their frames—not a pleasant chore in rainy weather.

Older, oriented bees will return to the hives from which they were taken, unless these are more than say 2 miles [3½ km] away. Plugging up the entrance with grass helps to keep more bees with the nucleus. Some of the grass will gradually be removed, and the remainder should be cleared away by the beekeeper after 24 hours. Queenless bees confined 12–24 hours are less likely to return to their parent hive; the presence of capped brood also helps to hold the bees. If there is no brood, wire screening can be used to close the entrance of the hive, which should be kept in a cool shady place for 2 days, while the bees are fed dilute sugar syrup (or water if they have combs of honey). Just before removing the screen, the hive is placed on its hive stand.

An alternative is to move the screened nucleus to a new location at least two miles away before opening the entrance. After several days it can be returned to its previous site, and few bees, if any, will return to the parent hive. If the bees added to the nucleus are shaken or brushed on to the front of the hive, the older, oriented bees will fly back to their colony immediately. The younger bees will remain, and a more dependable judgment can be made as to whether there are enough bees in the new colony.

Additional bees and frames of emerging brood given to a nucleus enable the colony to build up faster. However, unsealed brood should be kept to a minimum (and preferably avoided altogether), as the nucleus is too small to feed and care for very many larvae.

Whatever method is used to set up nuclei, their hive entrance should be reduced to an opening 3 × ⅜ inches [8 × 1 cm]. If the nectar flow slows down and bees begin robbing, it should be even smaller. A hole ½–¾ inches (12–19 mm] in diameter can be successfully defended by a single bee, and a screened opening at the back of the hive or on the bottom will provide ventilation. It is best to make up nuclei late in the day so that the little colonies can become organized before bees return to the parent hive and "report" the hive as a source of food to be robbed out. If several nuclei are to be made from a single colony, at least 1 frame (preferably 2) of brood should be left in the old hive with the queen.

There is an enormous advantage in using standard deep or shallow frames for making nuclei, because brood, honey and pollen can then be obtained directly from regular hives. However, hive boxes can be constructed to fit 3, 4, or 5 frames, or a standard 10-frame box can be divided into *bee-tight* compartments [see Birch], each with a separate opening. Atwater devised a single-frame hive with a removable side so that when paired with another, a third frame could be inserted. He also used divided frames allowing for twin nuclei in each hive. These combs could be used in a regular hive and the nuclei wintered. A nucleus that can be attached to the side of the hive does not interfere with manipulation of the parent colony, and bees from the parent colony can move freely back and forth through a hole bored in the hive side. This ensures a sufficiency of bees for the nucleus, and in the Tropics provides protection against ants [*Glean. Bee Cult.* 49 : 20–22 (1921); 64 : 93 (1936)].

Multiple hives for nuclei may be advantageous in cold regions, and the need to make and store special equipment is eliminated. Drifting of bees is inhibited by placing entrances as far from one another as possible, and by using bees from a different colony (preferably from a different apiary) in each compartment. Pieces of oilcloth, heavy plastic fabric or canvas used as "inner covers" can be peeled back carefully, without the use of smoke which might disturb the colony and incite balling of the queen. The side pieces are fastened along one edge, and the centre ones left loose. In all circumstances, the hive space should be appropriate to the quantity of bees in the nucleus and sufficient for 2–3 layers of bees between the frames to keep the brood warm.

2. Queenless colony

A colony made queenless 10–15 days previously will have sealed brood and queen cells, plus adult bees which are more alert in marking new locations and less likely to return to the old location. As many nuclei can be made as there are combs with queen cells, or cells that can be cut from the combs and placed in cell protectors or otherwise attached to combs.

3. Swarm or supersedure colony

A colony from which a swarm has issued, or which is preparing to swarm, is ideal for making nuclei, as most of the brood is sealed, and there will be queen cells due to emerge in a few days. If the swarming trait is to be discouraged, the queen should be replaced at the earliest opportunity, or the cells destroyed and a laying queen or a queen-cell from a non-swarming stock introduced. A good stock that is superseding its queen would be a more desirable source.

4. Excluded brood

A super with frames of young uncapped brood, and honey and pollen, placed above a queen excluder 10-15 days before nuclei are to be made, will provide an abundance of sealed brood and young nurse bees for stocking the nuclei. If the queen excluder is replaced by a double screen, a screened inner cover or a solid board, 24 hours after the frames of brood have been raised, the bees will be isolated from the queen below, and will produce queen cells from young larvae on the combs of brood, provided that conditions are favourable. Warmth from the lower colony will ensure optimum conditions for maturation of the brood and queen cells in the nucleus above the double screen. Where high temperatures are a hazard, the fanners in the large colony will help to prevent overheating in this upper super. This method may be the least troublesome of all, particularly for the weekend beekeeper, or whenever it is uncertain that the strict schedule required for queen rearing can be met, but it is not always successful, so several units should be set up to assure at least a few cells.

Mating queens from brood excluded above a parent colony was first reported by C. C. Miller and recognized by Doolittle as a possible solution to his "hobby" of seeking a method of mating queens without the need of forming nuclei. He used pieces of queen-excluding zinc to form compartments at each side of a super, with sufficient room for two frames in each and an opening at the back to allow virgins to fly out to mate. If supersedure was desired, the queen-excluder could be removed after a young queen had filled the box with brood and was judged satisfactory. The possibilities of the method fascinated Doolittle:

> "I think that no one will deny that the plan as given in this book, of rearing Queens at pleasure, and having them fertilized in the same hive with a laying Queen, is quite a step in advance of what we were 25 years ago, in this part of our beloved pursuit. The doing of this, without in the least interfering with the working of any colony, must, it seems to me, commend itself to every apiarist."

One commercial beekeeper, Charles Mraz, routinely makes a nucleus on each hive, above a solid inner cover whose front rim has been removed to provide an entrance. He stuffs this front entrance with grass to confine the bees and, in cold weather, takes special care to use only a moderate amount of brood with enough adult bees to prevent the brood getting chilled.

This past season, we tried a variation proposed by Bentley which does not require finding the queen but does require placing half a strong two-storey colony *underneath* another strong colony.*   In May our largest colonies were enormous and our middling colonies still heavy with honey after an extremely long, difficult winter requiring some modification of Bentley's plan.   Nuclei were made up from a colony with honey, pollen and some eggs and young brood (but mostly capped brood), and placed on a normal floor board.   This bottom board was placed on the top box of a second colony, where bees were still using the upper entrance (in winter the bottom entrance becomes clogged with dead bees and debris, so the hole bored in the top box is the only flight entrance).   When this top entrance was closed with a cork, the bees soon found the entrance to the nucleus on the new bottom board above them and joined this colony.

The new colony was thereby assured of sufficient bees, and warmth from below increased the chance of survival during the cold spring weather.   Ten days later we found queen cells sufficient to set up 19 new colonies.   Doolittle's concluding sentence to his chapter on "How to form nuclei" might apply to *this* method, but it seems irrelevant to the fourth and last method in his chapter: "At all times when bees are working in upper stories, I consider the last plan the best yet known".

5.   Double excluder

E. S. Miller's method provides for an automatic adjustment of bee populations between the isolated nucleus and the host colony underneath.   Instead of a double screen, the nucleus is placed on an inner cover (clearer board) with a piece of zinc queen-excluder fastened over the bee-escape hole.   A queen-excluder confines the queen in a brood chamber below.   A super or two of honey, between the brood chamber and the nucleus, improves chances of queen cells being drawn.   In theory, the bees come through the excluder to the nucleus so slowly that the amount of queen substance does not inhibit queen-cell production.   Good weather for manipulation is less critical than with other methods, but good conditions are still essential for mating flights.

6.   Shake swarm (or shook swarm)

Doolittle shook bees from one or two frames through a funnel into a screened box between 10 and 11 a.m., left them in a shady place until 2 p.m., and then introduced a queen (reared in a nursery) by setting the box down suddenly, causing the bees to fall to the bottom, and putting her in amongst them.   He used virgins as old as 8 days.   At sunset, he hived the bees with at least one frame of sealed and emerging brood and one of honey and pollen.   Hedberg is an enthusiastic advocate of this system as a superior method for producing nuclei with the least fuss.   For success he underscores the importance of keeping bees under stress for the 3 hours before the queen is introduced, and of feeding them generously with 60% sugar syrup.   [See also Kramer and Zecha.]

---

* Rauchfuss in Colorado attained the same end by raising a box of brood above an inner cover with queen-excluder zinc covering the hole.   After 8 days, the box containing eggs was known to contain the queen, so it would be set on a new stand. The bees at the old stand would produce a new queen.   An editorial in the journal, half as long as the article, praised the ingenuity, simplicity and importance of the method for apiculture.

7.   Source of queens

A queen can be provided most readily by introducing a laying queen from another colony, or a queen cell, when the nucleus is made up.   Colonies receiving queen cells should not be disturbed for at least 10 days, by which time the queen should have emerged.   Barring adverse circumstances such as poor flying conditions which would have prevented mating, she should be laying eggs three weeks after the nucleus was made up; if not, she should be discarded.   Adequate space for egg laying must be provided well in advance of its being required by the queen.

Virgin queens that have emerged from queen cells in nursery colonies and are older than 24 hours are the most difficult to introduce.   Intervals varying from 3 to 72 hours after establishment of the nucleus are recommended before attempting introduction.   Some authors recommend dropping the virgin amongst the bees immediately after these are shaken into a box.   A newly emerged queen can be introduced with impunity, as the bees pay her little attention, but once she begins to behave like a queen, it is quite another matter.   On the other hand, queens in full lay are readily accepted.

Uses of nuclei

1.   Establishment, increase and replacement of colonies

Acquiring a three- or four-frame nucleus is an ideal way for a beginner to establish a colony.   It may be possible to make arrangements with a local beekeeper to purchase nuclei from him; occasionally they are advertised for sale.   A nucleus established above a colony can be used for making increase as well as for replacing an undesirable queen in the colony below, as was the practice of A. I. Root by 1874 or earlier [*Glean. Bee Cult.* 73 : 378, 400 (1945)].   If the nucleus is placed on a new stand, it can be built up rapidly by adding frames of capped brood taken from populous colonies.   At the same time, this procedure serves as a swarm control measure for the large colony.

2.   Introduction of shipped queens

Queens purchased from breeders and introduced directly into full-size colonies are often superseded after a poor initial egg-laying performance.   If they are placed in a nucleus on arrival, they can recover from the stress of being shipped, and gradually regain an egg-laying capacity sufficient to inhibit production of supersedure cells by the colony into which they are introduced.

3.   Surplus queens

Surplus queens kept in nuclei are a reservoir for emergencies.   Giving the frames of honey or brood produced in a nucleus to weak colonies avoids congestion in the nucleus.   When no longer needed, nuclei can be united, built up into full-size colonies, or added to weak colonies.   It is also possible to overwinter them if conditions are not too severe or if they can be given special care [see Arnt; Johansson & Johansson; Telschow].

4.   Swarm control

Removing brood and bees from strong colonies to make nuclei will serve to inhibit preparations for swarming, by decreasing the colony population.

Moderate-size colonies are also pleasanter to work with. If a colony has already drawn queen cells in preparation for swarming, it is ideally suited for making nuclei. The danger of losing a swarm is reduced, and any nuclei that do not develop sufficiently can be reunited later to provide a strong colony for wintering [see Mraz].

5. Drawing worker comb

Strong, populous colonies produce quantities of drone or storage cells, whereas small colonies or nuclei will pull mainly worker cells, even if not provided with foundation. Combs that have been damaged, or from which patches of drone cells have been cut out, can therefore be given to nuclei to repair.

6. Observation colonies

A small, growing population of bees has the amiable characteristics of quietness and gentleness that are essential for extended study and observation. Anyone wanting to learn about bees should establish a small colony on "starters" (pieces of comb foundation or sheet of thin wax 1 inch or 2 cm wide) instead of full sheets of foundation in the frames, so that comb building, brood and stores can be seen as in the natural state. A nucleus can also be established in a glass-walled observation hive for convenient viewing. If it is put into a large glass-sided case without frames, the process of natural comb building can be watched from the start.

7. Breeding

The life span of a queen selected for breeding will be extended if she is placed in a nucleus where the demands for egg production are considerably reduced, and the eggs can be used for rearing daughters. If the nucleus is given the opportunity to draw comb in which eggs are then laid, such comb can be used for various queen-rearing methods including the Miller method.

8. Queen rearing

Starting queen cells and mating queens in strong nuclei is an ideal method of testing the queens and their progeny. After a new queen has laid a compact area of brood, she can be introduced to a full-size colony, and a new queen cell given to the mating nucleus after 4-6 hours. Queens laying irregular patches of brood should be discarded.

9. Queen mating

Mating nuclei are in such wide use, and so much has been said and written about them, that they deserve a section of their own.

Mating nuclei

American practice

Commercial queen breeders in the southern United States place sealed queen cells in small ("baby") nuclei where the queen emerges; she mates from the nucleus and is allowed to lay eggs for a few days before being removed for shipment to a customer. Even a few dozen bees will suffice for this purpose, but generally $\frac{1}{2}$ pint of bees is used [1 cup or 250 cc] to ensure maintenance of adequate temperatures during cool weather. A square measure is used to dip the bees out of a screened box of bees (brought from an out-apiary, to ensure that the bees will stay with the nucleus). After the queen is mated and laying, a strip of excluder is placed over the entrance hole to prevent absconding. If the bees do abscond, it is important to collect the swarm, because other virgin queens may join the cluster. Some European mating hives are equipped with a circular plate over the entrance which can be rotated to give an opening of the desired size, or complete closure.

On first use, a piece of brood comb is fastened in one frame until the little colony can begin drawing combs in the other frames. Some nucleus boxes have a hole in the top to permit insertion of a queen cell and replenishment of the feeder without disturbing the colony. The presence of brood creates conditions favourable for acceptance of a new queen cell and prevents absconding when the queen goes off on her mating flight. If a cell is introduced at the time the queen is removed, a cell protector prevents the bees from tearing into the side of the cell; but if the nucleus has been queenless for several hours and is well fed, there is usually no need for one.

A check for emergence of the queen can be made a few days after introduction of the cell. Two weeks after emergence is the earliest that one can expect to find eggs, but in three weeks all queens should be laying, if weather conditions for mating flights are favourable. The queen is left to lay eggs for 4 or 5 days before another queen cell is introduced.

There are now many variations of mating hives, made up according to local practices; in the United States they have not been available from supply dealers for many years, and queen rearers make their own. The economy in bees and ease in finding queens with small mating hives are real advantages, even though the tiny colonies in them require close attention. Jay Smith (1931) tried 16 different sizes of mating hive and adopted one with three section-boxes and a feeder. Smith emphasized that feeding sugar syrup is a critical factor in acceptance of queen cells by a newly established nucleus, even during a good honey flow, because the little colony is deficient in field bees. Generous feeding prevents their tearing down the queen cell and absconding, but it can be discontinued later if there is a heavy honey flow. These small nuclei may even store honey, in which case their combs may be replaced with empty frames furnished with starters, from which they will build comb with worker cells. At other times the nuclei should be fed twice weekly, so that reserve stores will always be on hand. If the colonies become crowded, some of their brood can be given to weaker colonies or used to establish additional nuclei; this will help to prevent too rapid a consumption of food followed by absconding when stores run down.

Feeders

Various feeders for nuclei have been devised. Pratt waxed the bottom of his hive and fed syrup through the entrance with a bulb and pipette, but this was not practical in dry climates because the joints separated. One alternative was to put syrup in grooves cut in the bottom board (as in Alexander's feeder) or to insert a shallow pan provided with a float or wood shavings to prevent drowning of bees. The Root hive used a feeder mortised in one side with a small hole through which the bees gained entrance. Benton's feeder was an integral part of the hive, and its lid could be raised to check on its contents without disturbing the colony. Other feeders were hung on the outside of the hive with an entrance hole aligned with a similar hole in the wall of the hive.

Robbing

Robbing is a serious threat to any nucleus, and especially to these miniatures, necessitating special precautions. If the feeder is a division-board (frame) type at the *back* of the hive, any robbers must go through the whole cluster. Entrances should be small, with provision for easy closure and adequate screened openings on the bottom or back for ventilation if closure is necessary. Honey should not be used for feeding, since its odour is attractive to any bees. Filling of feeders and other work should be done quickly, so that robbers do not gain entrance to the hives. Since smoke is not used when working nuclei, this signal for robbers to assemble is avoided. If nuclei cannot be kept in an apiary separate from large colonies, it might be useful to have a portable screened enclosure for use when robbing becomes a problem.

European mating hives

Honey producers who rear queens to improve stock or requeen will not generally bother with small mating hives, as the use of standard frames in separate nuclei or above regular colonies is much less trouble all round. Notwithstanding, European supply houses list a variety of hives for mating nuclei. Some are available as a pair in an insulated box which is supported on a stake driven into the ground. One of the reasons for a continued demand for such hives is that beekeeping associations operate mating stations in isolated areas where selected stocks of drones are maintained for mating with queens sent by members. Travelling boxes holding several of these nuclei are available for shipping by public transport.

Development of miniature mating hives

Henry Alley (1883) usually receives credit for developing the first small mating nucleus, and he was certainly the first to use it extensively. Unfortunately, his frames did not fit within the regular Langstroth frame, precluding the use of a working colony to draw out the combs and fill them with brood and stores. He did tier up the little boxes, but could not winter them. Pratt (1901) devised a smaller hive with section-boxes $4\frac{1}{4} \times 4\frac{1}{4}$ inches [10·8 × 10·8 cm] for combs; this was a great improvement since six of these hives could be inserted into a standard frame and placed in a stock colony. He later modified his hive to use two frames, but the tiny colonies required too much attention to be widely accepted. One strong colony can provide for 5 standard-frame nuclei or 25–50 "baby" nuclei.

Frank Benton's mating hive [see Phillips] used a larger, sturdier frame (three to a standard frame), and this was adopted by the A. I. Root Co. and others on a wide scale, two frames being used at each side of a "twin" mating-box. Benton had devised metal projections for the top-bars which could be pulled out when the frame was hung in the nucleus but pushed out of the way when it was fitted into a standard frame to be given to the stock colony. It became known as the Root hive, but credit to Benton is given by E. R. Root in an article entitled

"The Pratt nuclei" [*Glean. Bee Cult.* 33 : 1243–1244 (1905)]. A photograph of Benton with his hive appears on page 866 of the same volume. Discussion of nuclei by Benton in his own manual is surprisingly abbreviated.

Another clue to the origin of miniature hives is found in a publication by Wilhelm Wankler [see also Ludhorff]. Wankler, a watchmaker, had developed tools for making artificial queen cells and transplanting larvae for queen rearing, after learning of Rev. Weygandt's efforts in 1880. He exhibited his apparatus at an exhibition in Frankfurt in 1883 and records that Benton was present at the exhibition, asked questions about the method, and purchased a complete set of equipment. Perhaps it was Benton who brought over the inspiration that culminated in the development of Doolittle's grafting method for rearing queens? Wankler also used miniature mating boxes with frames that fit into regular frames, and Benton may have patterned his own hive after these. However, there are earlier antecedents: C. C. Miller saw some used by Adam Grimm in 1863, and A. I. Root used one devised by D. A. Jones (Benton's Canadian business partner) in 1882 [*Glean. Bee Cult.* 34 : 947 (1906)] but did not appreciate its value. Jones and Benton went to Europe in 1879 in search of new races of bees for importation to the United States and Canada, and Benton had offered Italian queens for sale as early as 1875.

The origin and development of the use of nuclei in beekeeping

With movable-frame hives

A 66-page chapter on "artificial swarming" appeared in Langstroth's book (1853), as a major argument for the superiority of the movable-comb hive in managing swarming. Apparently Langstroth was the first to use the term nucleus: "These small colonies I shall call *nuclei*, and the system of forming stocks from them, my nucleus system . . .". Langstroth would have had access to the 1828 or 1847 edition of Webster which gave two meanings for nucleus: "1. properly the kernel of a nut; but in usage, any body about which matter is collected. 2. the body of a comet, called also its head; which appears to be surrounded by light." Certainly the first implies the potential for growth, and both could apply to a cluster of objects such as bees hanging on comb. J. Phin defined and described the method of making nuclei in his "Dictionary of practical apiculture" (*New York*, 1884).

T. W. Woodbury [see Neighbour, p. 80] claimed to have originated this system, but Bevan (1838) states: "This is a mode of multiplying bees which is said to have been long in use, though the knowledge of it seems to have been confined to certain localities. The only written accounts [della Rocca, Wheler?] of the practice that I have seen refer to it as being in use at Candia, Syra, and other islands of the Archipelago, from whence the knowledge of it probably found its way into some of the Sicilian Islands, Lusatia, etc. Swammerdam . . . was acquainted with the practice of producing artificial swarms, but only by means of natural queens."

With the earlier movable-comb hives

In his third edition (footnote p. 210) Langstroth referred to Wheler's account (1682) of colony division using the ancient Greek movable-comb hive [see also

Wildman, p. 96]. A comb containing eggs from an established colony was put into a new hive, which was then placed on the site of a strong colony whose flying bees would populate the new hive and rear a queen on the brood comb.

With fixed-comb hives

Swammerdam's instructions reveal that, when he wrote his manuscript in Holland (1673–1674), beekeepers were already using an intensive system of division into nuclei:

> "That the office of rearing up the Worms, or the young brood of the Bees, is really intrusted to the common or working Bees alone, and that all their care, and every thing they do, is directed to that end, this signal observation shews plainly, which was communicated to me by a certain breeder of Bees yet living, who is thoroughly skilled in the management of them. He told me, that by a certain and infallible method, a prodigious number of females, vulgarly called kings, might be procreated, and that from hence, in the space of one year, three or four times more swarms might be obtained, than otherwise is usual in our cold climate. It is done in this manner, viz. in the month of April, when on inverting a hive you shall find some eggs or Worms in the peculiar cells destined for the females, take out the elder female, together with some few Bees, and put them into another hive apart; these will settle in this new place, build their cells, lay their eggs, and raise up a progeny: then sometime afterwards look again into the first hive, and if you find there a female newly come our [out?], sprung from the egg left before in the hive, take this likewise in the manner mentioned above, out from thence, and, in company with some other Bees, put her into a hive of her own, that she may bring forth there. If in the same manner you shall manage afterwards the rest of the females, which shall be one after another produced from the eggs deposited in the first hive, in the space of one fruitful summer, from a single hive, you will thus be able to get ten, nay, sometimes fourteen females, each together with a stock of Bees, their subjects as it were, that is so many swarms. It must be observed that this can only be done in a fruitful year, for at other times the Bees not only will not multiply fast enough, but they will not be able to provide a quantity of wax and honey to subsist themselves during the winter: care must also be taken to prevent that first hive from swarming, since each female, which with its working Bees is taken out from thence in the manner here mentioned, should be looked upon as constituting a separate swarm."

Gelieu (1816) used the method devised by Schirach for German beekeepers whereby combs of honey and newly hatched larvae were placed in a screened box 10 inches [25 cm] square along with 1000–1500 bees [½ litre or 1 pint], which were confined for three days and released on the fourth. After 15 days, the queen was found and caged in a new hive, which could be substituted on the stand of a non-swarming colony. Most beekeepers in Europe and America at that time were using straw skeps or wooden box hives, and increasing their colonies by the more primitive system of capturing natural swarms or "drumming" out artificial ones.

Critical factors in the use of nuclei*

1. Prevent robbing by larger colonies
    A. Reduce the entrance

    B. Do not use smoke

    C. Use sugar syrup rather than honey for feeding

    D. Separate nuclei from large colonies by flight barriers or, preferably, by distance

2. Ensure optimum conditions

    A. Use partially shaded locations, or provide shade

    B. Maintain temperature for brood development by using sufficient bees

    C. Ventilate with screened openings

    D. Maintain stores of honey and pollen

3. Give colonies proper management

    A. Control excessive population build-up

    B. Provide adequate comb space in which the queen can lay

    C. Give capped brood to prevent the colony absconding with the queen on her mating flight

    D. Prevent balling of the queen by avoiding the use of smoke

4. Feed sugar syrup

    A. Supply dilute syrup during periods of confinement

    B. Feed generously when introducing a queen or queen cell

    C. Feed regularly except during a good nectar flow

* In hives without movable frames the colony can build combs as required (provided there is space), but the beekeeper cannot give the colony combs of honey or brood, so factors 2D and 3A–C would not usually apply.

Colonies kept in frame hives cannot accommodate their needs for comb unless the beekeeper adds additional boxes of combs or frames in advance of the need (factors 3A, 3B). The hive advocated by Haccour (1967) for use in underdeveloped regions is intermediate in nature, since additional boxes can be given to a colony in which it builds its own comb as needed.

References

ABBOTT, C. P. (1947) Queen breeding for amateurs. *Petts Wood, Kent : Bee Craft*

ALLEY, H. (1883, 1885) The beekeeper's handy book: or twenty-two years' experience in queen-rearing. *Wenham, Mass. : published by the author*

ARNT, W. L. (1943) Wintering fall nuclei. *Am. Bee J.* 83(9) : 346

ATWATER, E. F. (1906) The baby-nucleus idea not new. *Glean Bee Cult.* 34(14) : 946–947

BENTLEY, R. (1960) Increase with queen rearing. *Am. Bee J.* 100(5) : 190–191

BENTON, F. (1896) The honey bee. *Washington : Government Printing Office*

BEVAN, E. (1838) The honey bee. *London : Van Voorst* 2nd ed.

BIRCH, H. W. (1944) Adjustable bee-tight division board. *Glean. Bee Cult.* 72(6) : 268–269

DEANS, A. S. C. (1963) Beekeeping techniques. *Edinburgh : Oliver & Boyd*

DOOLITTLE, G. M. (1889) Scientific queen-rearing. *Chicago : Thomas G. Newman & Son*

DZIERZON, J. (1882) Dzierzon's rational bee-keeping. *London : Houlston & Sons* trans. from German by H. Dieck & S. Stutterd, ed. C. N. Abbott

FARRAR, C. L. (1968) Productive management of honey-bee colonies. *Am. Bee J.* 108(3) : 95–97

GELIEU, J. de (1816) Le conservateur des abeilles. *Mulhausen : Chez Jean Risler et Comp.*

——— (1829) The bee preserver. *Edinburgh : John Anderson Jr.* trans. of above

GIRAUD-PABOU & FILS (1902) Traité pratique de l'élevage de reines

HACCOUR, P. (1967) Beekeeping with the "Maroka" hive. *XXI Int. Beekeep. Congr.* : 413–417

HEDBERG, I. (1938) How to make a shakeswarm. *Glean. Bee Cult.* 66(9) : 554–556 [See also "Drottningodling". *Kristianstad : Sveriges Biodlares Riksförbund* (1938, 2nd ed. 1951)]

JEAN-PROST, P. (1960) L'apiculture méridionale. *Hyères : published by the author* 2nd ed.

JOHANSSON, T. S. K. & JOHANSSON, M. P. (1969) Wintering. *Bee Wld* 50(3) : 89–100

KRAMER, U. (1908) Die Rassenzucht der Schweizer Imker und die amerikanischen Zuchtmethoden. *Freiburg : Paul Wässel* 3rd ed.

LAIDLAW, H. H., JR. & ECKERT, J. E. (1950) Queen rearing. *Hamilton, Ill. : Dadant & Sons Inc.*

LANGSTROTH, L. L. (1853) Langstroth on the hive and the honey-bee. *Northampton : Bridgman & Company;* also 3rd ed. (1865)

LUDHORFF, O. (1934) A noted German queen breeder. *Glean. Bee Cult.* 62(1) : 40–41

MILLER, A. C. (1915) Queen-mating nuclei. *Glean. Bee Cult.* 43(9) : 361–366

MILLER, C. C. (1911) Fifty years among the bees. *Medina, Ohio : A. I. Root Co.*

MILLER, E. S. (1932) Mating queen from a top story. *Am. Bee J.* 72(10) : 403

MRAZ, C. (1963) Swarm control for commercial beekeeping. *Glean. Bee Cult.* 91(4) : 206–209, 245

NEIGHBOUR, A. (1865) The apiary; or, bees, bee-hives, and bee culture. *London : Kent & Co.; Geo. Neighbour & Sons*

PELLETT, F. C. (1918) Practical queen rearing. *Hamilton, Ill. : American Bee Journal*

PHILLIPS, E. F. (1905) The rearing of queen bees. *Washington : Government Printing Office*

PHILLIPS, G. W. (1905) Errata to modern queen rearing. *Medina, Ohio : A. I. Root Co.* 3rd ed. [See also *Glean. Bee Cult.* 34(1) : 17–18 (1906)] Another ed. rev. M. T. Pritchard (1924)

RAUCHFUSS, F. G. (1921) Swarm control. *Glean. Bee Cult.* 49(5) : 266–267, 275

ROCCA, L'ABBÉ DELLA (1790) Traité complet sur les abeilles. *Paris : Chez Bleuet Père*

ROOT, E. R. (1905) Pratt's "Baby nuclei". *Glean. Bee Cult.* 33(7) : 361, 470

SLADEN, F. W. L. (1913) Queen-rearing in England. *London : Madgwick, Houlston & Co. Ltd.* 2nd ed.

SMITH, J. (1923) Queen rearing simplified. *Medina, Ohio : A. I. Root Co.*
——— (1931) Small nuclei for mating queens. *Glean. Bee Cult.* 59(3) : 145–148; (4) : 214–217

SNELGROVE, L. E. (1949) Queen rearing. *Bleadon : I. Snelgrove*

SWAMMERDAM, J. (1758) The book of nature. *London : Seyffert* [trans. by T. Flloyd of "Biblia naturae sine historia insectorum" (1735)]

SWARTHMORE [E. L. PRATT] (1901) The Swarthmore system of queen-rearing. *Am. Bee J.* 41(24) : 373–374
——— (n.d.) Nuclei miniatures. *Paris : E. Bondonneau*
——— (n.d.) L'élevage industriel des reines. *Paris : E. Bondonneau*
——— (1903) Forming section-box nuclei. *Glean. Bee Cult.* 31(1) : 19–21

TELSCHOW, G. (1962) Wintering extra queens. *Glean. Bee Cult.* 90(11) : 667, 697

WANKLER, W. (1903, 1906, 1924) Die Königin. *Freiburg : Theodor Fisher*

WHELER, SIR GEORGE (1682) A journey into Greece. *London : for W. Cademan*

WILDMAN, T. (1768) A treatise on the management of bees. *London : printed for the author and sold by T. Cadell*

ZECHA, H. (1960) Die Zucht von Königinnen insbesondere mit Hilfe der "Federleiste". *Bienenvater* 81(4) : 109–111

CHAPTER 4

WINTERING

"Bees do not freeze to death in winter—they starve." *Herman Rauchfuss, Sr.*

The authors have kept bees since 1951 near Albany in New York State, at an altitude of 1500 feet [450 m], where winter conditions would be considered severe. Continuous snow cover for four months is usual, and it is not uncommon to have some snow as early as October and as late as May. Winter temperatures may drop to -20° F [-29° C], alternating with occasional warm days when the bees can take flights. The average growing season is 130 days (range 92-188).

Dr. and Mrs. Johansson have used recommended wintering practices, as well as variations of their own, and attempt to offer a detached review, examining some of the contradictions between theoretical and practical aspects of this perennial problem. The article concludes with a summary, "Ten points for successful wintering" (page 41), and most of these points are of general application.

Non-metric units can be converted as follows: 1 pound = 0.45 kg; 1 foot = 30 cm; 1 inch = 2.5 cm.

Biological basis

Frequently the first question put to a beekeeper by the curious layman is: "What do you do with your bees in the winter?" Answers will reflect local practices of management, but agree on the biological facts—unlike our own mammalian, homiothermic, constant metabolism, the bee is an insect endowed with a poikilothermic (cold-blooded, variable) metabolism, but nevertheless in their colony honeybees can maintain a minimum temperature. Nearly 300 years ago Swammerdam wrote: "We should particularly observe here, that there is such a wonderful heat in the hives, even in the midst of winter, that the honey does not concrete or lose its original fluid consistence, nor is gathered into grains or crystals, unless in hives in which the bees happen to be fewer than usual. The Bees, when they are fruitful, nourish, cherish, and warm their offspring in the midst of winter, and preserve a mutual heat amongst each other. But I do not know that this is the case in any other insects, for even the Hornets themselves, as well as Wasps, Bumble Bees and Flies, are all rigid and motionless in the winter; and in all that season neither move nor change place, nor do they take any nourishment, nor discharge any faeces."

Honeybees form a cluster on the combs when the temperature in the hive falls below 14°C. Heat provided by the consumption of honey enables the cluster to maintain a temperature of 24–30° at the centre and 6–9° at the surface. (Boxes of bees we placed in a deep-freeze to kill them released enough heat to start thawing the other material stored in the box!) The difficulties of measuring temperatures in a constantly changing cluster have yielded a wide range of results in reported studies.

Honeybees instinctively store reserves of food far beyond that necessary for survival in extreme seasonal and climatic conditions, whether of humidity or temperature. The security of excess stores for survival during environmental stress has obviously been a selective mechanism in the evolution of the honeybee. But circumstances may prevent accumulation of sufficient food, and even in tropical rain forests there is an annual period of nectar dearth when as many as one-third of the colonies may starve for lack of stores.

Insulation principles

Many wintering schemes for bees are applications of our own ideas of comfort. In summer and winter we try to keep the rate of heat radiation within suitable limits by using technological devices such as fans or heaters, and insulation. Insulation is worthless as such if moisture is allowed to penetrate it, as anyone knows who has walked in snow with wet woollen socks or worked in wet gloves during cold weather. In modern house construction, humidity is controlled by installing a continuous vapour barrier between the interior of the house and the insulation, and providing ventilation above the ceiling insulation. Unless the prodigious quantity of moisture produced from cooking, bathing and laundry is removed with fans, or by exchange of air from the outside through open windows, it will condense on the cold surfaces of walls and windows.

Within the hive, a minimum temperature is maintained in the cluster by the bees' metabolism of honey; this process releases carbon dioxide and water as end products of the respiratory process. Without adequate provision for ventilation, the water will condense on any cold surfaces of hive insulation, walls, furniture, and covers, resulting in soggy insulation, wet combs and sodden hive furniture. A waterproof covering (such as asphalt roofing paper or plastic) on an unventilated hive is much like a rubber raincoat worn during physical exercise. The relative humidity inside the coat soon reaches 100%. Those who keep bees in dry climates cannot imagine what a discouraging experience (visual and olfactory) it is to open up a mouldy hive dripping with moisture.

It is important to bear in mind these basic features of insulation and moisture control when considering various recommendations for wintering, in order to avoid applying the right rationale to the wrong procedure or vice versa. Considerable discussion still prevails as to how the risks in maintaining colonies over the winter season can be reduced, and each winter a few vigorous colonies in seemingly optimal condition will be lost whereas some in marginal condition will survive.

Methods

In the heyday of beekeeping, the late 1800s, there was one dominant theme running through the copious literature on methods of wintering: bundle them up with insulation, or keep them in ventilated cellars. Typical recommendations are to be found in the beekeeping texts and bulletins of E. F. Phillips, who would not tolerate suggestions that bees wintered about as well without special treatment as with it. But gradually the experience of beekeepers who wintered bees without elaborate protection made an impression*. A. C. Miller's proposals in 1903 for successful wintering can now be found in current articles: "The formula is, plenty of bees, sound queen, abundant stores, *early preparation*, and black wrapping [to absorb heat]".

In northern Europe beekeepers customarily winter their hives in bee houses or exterior cases with quilts or other insulating material. In opposition to this practice, by which colonies are given little space, stores and air—and insulated to conserve heat—in England it is common to provide plenty of space, stores and air, but no packing. In the United States, bee houses have not generally been used, but it was once common practice to place four hives together in outer cases, the spaces around each hive being packed with sawdust or other insulating material, or alternatively to move the hives into cellars. Wintering in cellars required close attention, as the bees became restless when the temperature rose, and their removal to the open air was mandatory. The use of elaborate double-walled insulated hives, extensive packing or bee cellars is currently not recommended.

In northern regions of Canada and United States, hives are often wrapped for winter in heavy tarred building paper or roofing (slater's) felt, fastened with asphalt or quick-drying roofing cement to form a loose sleeve. A corrugated box made of water-resistant paper is also used. Insulating material—such as hay, dry leaves, sawdust or shavings—is frequently placed on the inner cover, the ends of the paper folded over it, and the outer cover forced down on top. Small openings are cut in line with the upper and lower hive entrances and held in place with a strip of lath. Such covering protects the hive from weathering, and the black paper will absorb warmth from the sun. The temperature of the air surrounding the cluster is about 2°F [1°C] higher than in a hive without such wrapping. The paper reduces air leakage through the hive and so may be helpful in locations exposed to intense winds.

A moisture-absorbing layer at the top of the hive helps to prevent the mess of mouldy combs and equipment. The use of a straw mat, burlap sacking or a piece of rigid polyurethane insulation, placed between the inner cover and the hive roof, has been advocated. One beekeeper wraps a queen excluder in several thicknesses of newspaper and places this over the inner cover. Hive roofs have been made in which corrugated cardboard, sheets of newspaper or other insulating material were sandwiched between the metal lid and the wood below. For the beekeeper with relatively few colonies, boxes or old hive bodies to hold straw, leaves or other absorbent material can be made up; the bottom is covered by screening or by an inner cover with a screened bee-escape hole, and provision is made for ventilation above the "chaff". With ingenuity, other alternatives might be devised using scrap materials. But for a commercial beekeeper, the additional work and equipment involved may be a suspect luxury.

Insulation can cause considerable distress to a colony. On a cold sunny day the temperature in an insulated hive covered with black paper may be raised

---

* The fundamentals of wintering were extensively discussed between 1938 and 1949. See *Glean. Bee Cult.* 45(10) : 750–751, 753–763; 67(1) : 48–49; 68(9) : 550–552, (10) : 609–612, 638–653, (11) : 673–678, 682–683, 720, 684–685, 718, 693–695, (12) : 758–759; 70(9) : 521–522, 554–556, (10) : 602–603, 637, 615–619, 636, (11) : 690–693, (12) : 742–745; 71(1) : 34–35, 225–226; 72(9) : 398–399, (10) : 433–436, 462, 438–441, (11) : 480–481, 501, (12) : 519, 567, 533, 557; 73(1) : 17, (10) : 418–421, 428–431; 75(2) : 87; 77(10) : 624–628.

sufficiently for a large colony in it to produce enough heat (by consuming honey) to raise the temperature sufficiently to make some bees leave the hive; they may then become chilled, be unable to return, and so perish. On the other hand, insulated walls may retard the absorption of heat on occasional warm days in winter, resulting in a temperature lag of 6–8 hours or more if there is much honey in the hive. It is essential that the bees are enabled to respond to warm, sunny winter days by taking a flight to empty their intestines of accumulated faeces. Dr. Phillips, the chief proponent of packing, heard a level-headed plea by G. Allen in 1918 for "unbiased, unprejudiced" investigation of the problem. Allen reported that after a month of cold, bees were flying freely from hives that were not packed or top-packed only, whereas the substantially packed hives had only a few bees flying: "The next day might have been too cold again".

The disadvantages of insulation are of course less where hives are accessible to the beekeeper in bee houses or in outer cases that can be opened, so that the insulating material can be removed when the weather makes this desirable.

Ventilation

During a long winter, dead bees and debris from cappings usually clog the bottom entrance to the hive, so an upper opening is imperative. A ½-inch auger hole, say 2 inches to one side of the handhold on the front side of the top box, will be sufficient for bee traffic in winter. Such a hole is useful in all hive boxes at the height of the season, for providing direct bee access to the brood chambers as well as for ventilation. In the autumn, every hole except that in the top box can be plugged with a cork. A hole of this size does not provide adequate winter ventilation, but a larger one may permit mice to enter. Additional ventilation can be provided in other ways, e.g. by laying a medium-sized nail between the hive body and inner cover. Australian beekeepers use specially designed "cavity" ventilated covers.

Location

Ideally, colonies should be exposed to sunlight and located midway on a slope facing south. The hives should be placed on a stand off the ground, to prevent danger of flooding during spring thaws or rains.

Windbreaks

Colonies in hives without packing, but provided with a windbreak, are better off than colonies in hives exposed to the prevailing wind and given two layers of wall-board insulation. An ideal natural windbreak is a dense stand of trees or brush; this will deflect the wind upwards and slow it down for a distance some twenty times the height of the windbreak. On the edge of an undisturbed wooded area there is usually a gradual reduction in wind speed from the lowest point of the windbreak to the highest. If a natural hedgerow is not available, a good wind barrier can be provided by vegetation such as corn stalks, or a 6-foot wooden fence with 2-inch spaces between the boards, or snow fencing. However, a windbreak is valuable the year around, so an apiary site with permanent protection is to be sought, or developed by planting ornamental or fruit trees.

Colonies that have built their combs in the open do surprisingly well and may survive the winter, particularly if they are provided with a roof and a shield against prevailing winds. Combs enclosed with only glass or cardboard sides have been successful. One colony in an apiary wintered successfully in a bushel peach basket, when colonies in hives died!

Cellar wintering

Comparatively few beekeepers now winter their colonies in cellars in North America, but this was common practice after 1840, and in northern parts of the Soviet Union cellar wintering is still fairly usual. American practice is as follows. Each colony is confined to one hive body and fed as much sugar syrup as it will take (sugar : water 1·5 : 1 if done early, or 2 : 1 if late), up to a total weight of 50 or 60 pounds. If not fed early, the syrup is inverted to prevent granulation in the combs. The colonies are moved into the cellar after their last flight in November, and left until pollen and nectar are available in the spring.

The cellar must be dry (but not so dry that the bees get desiccated and thus become restless), dark, free of disturbance, and with means for ventilation. Often a special cellar is constructed solely for wintering bees, but a cellar beneath a dwelling is also used if insulated against warmth from the house. If the temperature in the cellar rises above 50°F [10°C], means to reduce it to the optimum 38–45°F [3–7°C] should be at hand, so that the bees will not become restless and consume large amounts of food, predisposing them to dysentery. Colonies cannot be put into a cellar and forgotten. Some bee-keepers used to carry the hives out and place them on their summer stands during a warm day in mid-winter so that the bees could have a cleansing flight. As beekeepers acquired larger holdings it was impracticable to provide cellar space at out-apiaries, or to give them the close attention required. Fortunately, bees not only survive without such elaborate accommodation but are actually better off out of doors exposed to the warmth of the winter sun.

Colony condition

In early September, a colony should have at least five combs of brood, to provide bees for the winter cluster and a working force in the spring. Small colonies should be combined into units of about 30 000 ± 5 000 bees (10 pounds), which will cover six or more frames in October. Where there is a late honey flow, unrestricted space for egg laying by the queen should be provided by replacing combs of honey in the brood chamber by empty ones.

C. C. Miller reported successful overwintering of double two-frame nuclei with a thin division board between them, even during seasons when winter losses were high. Payne and Rosene overwinter nuclei on top of large colonies, but it is important that moisture from one such colony does not collect in another; Gooderham wintered two nuclei in one hive body.

During the winter, the presence of dead bees on top of the snow banks around the hives is no cause for alarm; these bees are either dead bees carried out of the hive or old bees which flew out and died. At the first spring inspection, the accumulated mass of dead bees and trash on the bottom board must be scraped away.

Pollen stores (bee bread)

Spring colony build-up is limited by pollen rather than honey, since brood rearing begins as early as January and in some regions fresh pollen is not available until April or May. If two deep hive bodies are used for the brood chamber, considerable amounts of pollen may be stored in the combs of the lower chamber in autumn. Five or six combs of pollen are usually recommended. As the brood nest expands in spring, this pollen will be used to feed brood before fresh pollen is available and during periods of pollen dearth. Ideal bee pasturage has some plants in bloom throughout the entire flying season from which bees can collect pollen. Brushy, weedy fields may not provide a great honey surplus, but are valuable in providing a continuous sequence of minor pollen and nectar sources.

A really satisfactory substitute for pollen is essential in areas without early pollen sources. At present, a mixture of non-fat soya-bean flour, brewer's yeast, dried milk, dry egg yolks and sugar syrup is used. Some beekeepers use a trap to collect pollen, which is dried and stored for mixing with the above ingredients the following spring. Such a mixture is used at the rate of about 0.1 gram for every bee reared (1 pound for 3500 bees); as soon as natural pollen is available, bees ignore the substitute.

Pollen can be preserved by freezing soon after collection, but it will deteriorate quickly once it has thawed. An alternative method is to mix the pollen with half its weight of granulated sugar, pack the product in a container, and cover the top with a $\frac{1}{2}$-inch layer of sugar; it will then keep in good condition for about two years without being frozen, and can be added directly to the pollen substitute.

Honey stores

The recommended quantity of honey to be left as stores for winter has increased steadily with the years. In North America a minimum of 50 pounds would now be regarded as sufficient until March or April, with an additional 25 pounds for the eventuality of either an extremely cold, late spring or a mild winter. Active bees consume more honey, so ideally the colony is quiescent during the winter except for cleansing flights on occasional warm days. A colony uses 3–4 pounds of honey per month until brood rearing begins in January or February, and the rate of consumption then increases geometrically. During a cold rainy spring, when it is not possible to check colonies for stores, an extra 30 pounds left on in the fall would have eliminated much anxiety, and would be an inexpensive insurance at current wholesale prices for honey. The relatively high price for sugar makes syrup feeding unprofitable, even if the weather makes feeding possible. In the temperate north, the recommended practice is to leave 90 pounds or more for colony consumption during the winter and until the first nectar flow in the spring. This initial investment is never wasted, for any left after the winter is used for rearing more bees.

If bees are able to fly occasionally, they will winter successfully on almost any type of honey. If it is granulated they require water to liquefy it. Some honey (for instance from honeydew) has more residual matter than is usual, and this creates a problem if the weather does not permit cleansing flights for defaecation in January or February. Where the honey stores are not suitable for wintering, then the provision of 10–20 pounds of sugar syrup is considered essential.

Weighing colonies

Hefting a hive, by tipping it from the back with the front edge acting as a pivot, is a rather rough and unsatisfactory method of estimating the weight of stores. It is better to inspect the combs, counting a full standard Langstroth comb as 5 pounds of honey. To leave 10 pounds of excess stores is not a waste, but to leave even slightly too little will end in catastrophe. The most dependable method is to weigh the hive. A spring balance, tied to a hook which is used to tip up one edge of the hive, gives a reading which is about half the gross weight. The weight of the furniture will vary according to type; a conversion factor for calculating the actual amount of honey can be determined by weighing several sample hives. A standard ten-frame Langstroth two-storey hive with a total gross weight of 160 pounds would have approximately 90 pounds of stores. The traditional time for weighing skeps used to be Michaelmas (September 29th).

Feeding

If the gross weight of a stock is not sufficient, heavy combs of surplus honey from another colony should be substituted for light combs to make up the difference—unless there is danger of spreading disease. J. Fixter recommended feeding cakes of granulated honey when honey in the comb is not available. Concentrated syrup (sugar : water 2 : 1 by weight or measure) can be fed rapidly when warm, by using ten-pound friction-top cans with 12–15 nail holes punched in the cover. The can is placed upside down over the hole on an inner cover (super clearer), or several cans are placed directly on the frames. Hives must be level, or the syrup will drip, so wedges of wood and a spirit level should be carried in the tool box. An empty super and a bee-tight roof are needed to protect the feeders from robber bees. The danger of robbing is reduced if feeding is done in the evening.

Feeding is usually an emergency measure when the nectar flow fails. One U.S. firm specializes in providing ex-quota sugar, at considerable savings to beekeepers who use at least 5 000–10 000 pounds or who can pool car loads. Feeding syrup is more common in Europe than in North America, because good prices for honey make it economically feasible to harvest most of the honey and to feed syrup for stores. European beekeepers use various types of wooden, plastic and metal feeders, holding anything up to 40 pounds of syrup.

Mouse guards

The brood box of a wintering honeybee colony is an ideal haven for mice. It is warm, protected, and stocked with food in the form of pollen, honey and bee carcases. Prevention of access to the hive by mice and other small rodents is thus an essential part of the preparations for wintering. Many European hives have standard entrance fittings with flight apertures too small for rodents to get through. Some of these have now come on the market in the United States, but of a type in which the galvanized plate is mounted on supports screwed into the hive body. This is unfortunate, since it is not certain which box will be on the bottom board until the hive has been checked in the fall.

Most beekeepers in the United States devise some sort of screening (hardware cloth) or entrance reducer, leaving openings narrower than the skulls of rodents likely to enter the hive. A local museum might be helpful in providing measurements of species indigenous to the area where the colonies are kept. In one such series, some skulls could be pushed through a $\frac{1}{2}$-inch gap. Recommended mouse barriers include: (1) $\frac{1}{2}$-inch auger hole, or hardware cloth with $\frac{1}{2}$-inch mesh; (2) holes $\frac{3}{8}$ inch square; (3) slots $\frac{1}{4}$ inch wide or wire screening with $\frac{1}{4}$-inch mesh; (4) screening 3 mesh/inch; (5) entrance reducer $\frac{5}{16} \times 4$ inches; (6) a bottom board reversed to provide an entrance $\frac{3}{8}$-inch high; or (7) corrugated tin. If wire screening is placed so that there is no cross thread along the bottom, the bees encounter less obstruction when dragging out debris. Unless the openings are large enough for drones, the mouse guards cannot be put on until after all drones are eliminated. If this is late in the fall, the guard may shut a mouse *in* rather than *out* of the hive.

Screening must be securely fastened, as predators like skunks can be most determined and ingenious about trying to get into the hive. Certainly something sturdier than push-pins should be used. A strip of hardware cloth, held tightly against the bottom entrance by a piece of lath nailed across the bottom board rails by two short box nails, is easy to put on and to take off in the spring. If the weather does not permit exchanging the bottom board when the guard is taken off, a long-handled scraper is helpful to drag out the accumulated debris.

If, in spite of all precautions, a persistent mouse gains entrance and builds a nest in the brood chamber, the damaged comb should be given to a nucleus or small colony. It will then be neatly repaired with worker cells, whereas a large colony would probably fill the hole with drone comb.

Recommendations to put poisoned wheat on the inner cover or into top packing, under the hive stand, or inside the hive, should be sharply rejected. Such practices are dangerous to wildlife (and in some States it is illegal to poison any wildlife); they also encourage the current adverse publicity for honey which associates pesticide damage to bees with the possibility that the honey harvested may be contaminated (in this instance with strychnine). The best long-term mouse control may be to set out baited mouse traps (peanut butter and oat flakes) or anti-coagulant bait in boxes or empty hives arranged so that other wildlife or pets cannot enter them.

Disease

A colony may survive the stress of a difficult winter only to fall prey to *Nosema* or some other micro-organism commonly present in bee populations, and prone to "flare up" when conditions are favourable for its propagation. When bees are confined for long periods, and cannot defaecate in flight as is their usual habit, they are likely to deposit within the hive faeces containing micro-organisms which then touch off an epidemic in the colony—referred to as spring dwindling, May disease, etc. Condensation of moisture on cold surfaces of the hive produces a high humidity, which contributes to the deterioration of the environment within the hive.

In spite of reverses, a colony has remarkable powers of recuperation under good conditions. One such cluster, the size of a teacup in April, occupied five deep boxes by September, and produced 100 pounds of surplus honey as well as 60 pounds of honey for wintering. Ordinarily, small colonies are united in the spring to secure more efficient populations.

Winter-kill

We must be prepared to view the incidence of winter losses as having at least some element of chance. Every northern beekeeper has found dead colonies in spring with heavy stores and a cluster of dead bees on empty combs far from the honey. The most apparent explanation for their death may be the incidence of a long cold spell during which the bees use up the honey in the immediate vicinity of the cluster. As the temperature drops, more bees crawl into empty cells; so the cluster contracts, moving still further away from the edge of the honey. If a colony happens to have eaten all the honey on one side of the hive, the bees may be out of reach of new stores, and will starve unless the outside temperature moderates in time*. There does not seem to be any way of avoiding this set of circumstances, which in areas with long periods of intense cold may account for a persistent winter-kill of the order of 10–15%. These deaths are not necessarily avoided by heavy packing, but Geiger in Manitoba and Haydak in Minnesota believe that in their climates winter *wrapping* will reduce winter losses by half. It is not surprising that in northern areas overwintering has been considered one of the most difficult problems of management; it has probably received more attention through the years than any other single subject. But the practice of killing colonies in the fall and starting afresh with package bees in the spring has produced a new generation of beekeepers with virtually no knowledge or experience of wintering problems. Beekeepers who need huge colonies early in the spring to collect a profitable surplus may have to accept chance catastrophies of winter losses. In regions where the honey crop is secured at the end of the growing season, there is of course no advantage in large colony populations early in the season.

If beekeepers producing package bees and queens select for strains of bees that produce large populations early in the spring and feed heavily with sugar syrup to rear bees for shaking into the packages, the characteristics of the bees may well not be suitable for the natural conditions prevailing in the diverse areas where the colonies made from the packages are to be kept. For instance the queen may continue egg laying at the end of the season at a higher rate than is optimal for good wintering.

Acclimatized stock

Promotional material about hybrid bees does not at present include an objective statement of their characteristics. It would be desirable to know whether a

---

* It is interesting that Langstroth, commenting on W. W. Cary's practice of cutting winter passages in combs, considered his movable-frame hive a handicap unless suitable winter passages were provided. A. C. Hooker suggested using a sharp tin tube for cutting such passages through the comb. Combs built when foundation is not provided often have such passage holes. There may be an optimum number of bees least likely to get into this predicament, and at the same time be sufficiently large to survive the winter. Villumstad reported a higher percentage mortality in large than in small colonies.

stock has been tested for resistance to difficult wintering conditions. Wisconsin rabbits take to their burrows when the temperature drops to $+10°F$ [$-12°C$], whereas those in South Dakota remain active down to $-10°F$ [$-23°C$]. Cattle-breeding associations have shown the value of widely based testing programmes to select the best stock on the basis of performance. The large size of the sample required for significant results shows that any similar effort in bee-keeping could not be undertaken by universities or experimental stations with modest apiaries. It would have to be a continuing programme using both the research facilities of experimental stations and routine testing on a large scale through the co-operation of some thousands of beekeepers.

The first question is whether breeding programmes are really practical, since naturally mated queens receive sperm from a number of drones. Is it realistic to expect queen breeders to establish the stringent conditions of isolation necessary to guarantee pure matings? Is there objective evidence that present breeding programmes have produced superior stock except in terms of the egg production of the queens? Under what conditions or in what regions are specific, selected traits an advantage?

Left on his own, each beekeeper selects the stock that survives and flourishes under the conditions of his own locale. The ability to withstand the rigours of long cold spells, susceptibility to nosema, etc., are certainly critical in successful wintering. We should be slow to abandon the good advice of Columella in A.D. 60: "We must especially be careful, that they be brought rather from the neighbourhood than from distant regions, because they use to be highly provoked with the strangeness of the climate".

Research

The work of Robert S. Filmer in New Jersey between 1937 and 1943 can be considered an objective model of investigation on the subject of wintering. He concluded there was no significant difference in honey production between packed and unpacked colonies which would warrant the expense and labour of packing. The unpacked colonies had more brood, built up faster, and began to fly earlier. During very severe winters and in the coldest climates, there may be some advantage in packing, but it is apparently a disadvantage in moderate climates. In large-scale commercial operations packing may in any case be too expensive, but locating apiaries so they have protection against piercing winds may be equally effective.

In the north, beekeepers who kill their colonies in the fall with cyanogas and start over in the spring with packages or nuclei from the south are finding this practice increasingly expensive; the cost of package bees is high, whereas the value of honey remains low. Beekeepers in northern Canada are therefore now reconsidering the proposition that overwintering their colonies may be economically more realistic and may ensure better bees in the spring. A drastic method was reported by Y. Hiratsuka in Japan to be successful in very cold climates: the colonies are placed in a cellar, each in a box provided with candy but *without combs*. Electric heating devices have been tried by many bee-keepers; they may be useful to ensure the survival of small colonies of inbred breeding stock, but are not a practical procedure for normal wintering.

Commercial beekeepers who are willing to experiment with sufficient numbers of colonies to get valid data can determine the most economical procedures for their particular area. Small academic or research apiaries are unlikely to keep enough colonies to obtain significant data (see Wedmore, 1946). The advice of a statistician concerning a valid experimental design might well be the first approach in securing answers to the questions posed.

Summary: ten points for successful wintering

1. Locate hives on a slope facing the sun with a windbreak against prevailing winds.
2. Place hives on stands out of danger of floods and seepage.
3. Remove the queen excluder, if used, so that the queen can move freely with the cluster.
4. Unite colonies which cover less than six frames in September.
5. Leave 60–100 pounds of honey and pollen [27–45 kg] in two deep or three shallow hive bodies, for stores until the first major spring nectar flow. Feed sugar syrup to colonies without this amount of food.
6. Provide a top emergency exit and ventilation.
7. Insert a dependable mouse guard before the rodents move into winter quarters.
8. If insulation is used, protect it by a vapour barrier from the moisture produced by the colony, and by adequate ventilation above.
9. In regions with extreme temperature variations in winter, either allow thorough ventilation or provide a moisture-absorbing layer above the combs, to ensure a reasonably dry hive.
10. Select hardy breeding stock acclimatized to local conditions.

Success depends on a balance of maximum dormancy, optimum bee population, minimum food consumption, occasional ameliorating temperatures when the colony can recluster on honey combs and take defaecating flights, and a measure of good luck. The challenge thrown out in the first volume of the *American Bee Journal* (1861) still taunts us: "He may be regarded as a master in bee culture, who knows how to winter his stocks in a healthy condition, with the least loss of bees, the smallest consumption of stores, and with the combs unsoiled".

References

ALLEN, G. (1918) Progress and cooperation. *Proc. Tennessee Beekprs Ass.* 13 : 93–98

BARRATT, G. (1930) Newer, simpler, and better beekeeping. *Am. Bee J.* 70(12) : 571

BAYLES, V. R. & PARKER, R. L. (1958) Winter protection of honeybee colonies in Kansas. *Am. Bee J.* 98(9) : 360–363

BRAUN, E. (1948) To winter or not to winter. *Glean. Bee Cult.* 76(10) : 614–618; see also *Am. Bee J.* 81(4) : 169–170, 178 (1941)

COLUMELLA, L. J. (1745) Of husbandry. [trans. M. C. Curtius] *London : A. Miller*

CORKINS, C. L. (1930) The metabolism of the honeybee colony during winter. *Bul. Wyo. agric. Exp. Sta.* No. 175; see also *Am. Bee J.* 72(10) : 400–402; (11) : 438–440 (1932)

CRANE, E. (1952) Science and practice. *Bee Wld* 33(9) : 152

DEYELL, J. (1962) A talk to beekeepers. *Glean. Bee Cult.* 90 : 623–625, 688

DOOLITTLE, G. M. (1885) Does a colony of bees ever freeze? *Am. Bee J.* 21(5) : 69; reprinted 75(1) : 27, 29 (1935)

FARRAR, C. L. (1952) Ecological studies on overwintered honey bee colonies. *J. econ. Ent.* 45(3) : 445–449

FILMER, R. S. [1943?] A study of the wintering problem in New Jersey. *New Jersey Agricultural Experiment Station Notes*

FIXTER, J. (1904) What kind of food to give colonies short of stores. *Glean. Bee Cult.* 32(4) : 183–184

GEIGER, J. E. (1967) Winter temperatures and the relative humidity in beehives. *Am. Bee J.* 107(10) : 372

GOODERHAM, C. B. (1945) Ottawa tests on wintering nuclei. *Glean. Bee Cult.* 73(11) : 454–455, 469, 482

HAYDAK, M. H. (1967) Wintering bees in Minnesota. *Am. Bee J.* 107(11) : 418

HIRATSUKA, Y. (1921) A method of wintering. *Bee Wld* 2(5/11) : 114–115

HOOKER, A. C. (1874) Implement for cutting winter passages. *Glean. Bee Cult.* 2(12) : 140

LANGSTROTH, L. L. (1861) A winter passage. *Am. Bee J.* 1(6) : 136

MILLER, A. C. (1903) Tarred paper for winter protection. *Glean. Bee Cult.* 31(12) : 534–535; see also *Am. Bee J.* 41(45) : 718 (1901)

MILLER, C. C. (1911) Fifty years among the bees. *Medina, Ohio : A. I. Root Co.*

MRAZ, C. (1962) Wintering bees in Vermont. *Glean. Bee Cult.* 90(11) : 658–660, 699; see also 75(10) : 577–583; 95(2) : 73–75

OWENS, C. D. & FARRAR, C. L. (1967) Electric heating of honey bee hives. *Tech. Bull. U.S. Dep. Agric.* No. 1377

PAYNE, A. G. (1960) Advanced method of wintering. *Am. Bee J.* 100(10) : 396–397

PHILLIPS, E. F. (1915, 1928) Beekeeping. *New York : Macmillan Co.*

ROSENE, S. (1958) Some suggestions for wintering. *Am. Bee J.* 98(11) : 438

SWAMMERDAM, J. (1758) The book of nature. [trans. T. ffloyd] *London : Seyffert*

VILLUMSTAD, E. (1960) [Food consumption, loss of bees, and formation of frost, in differently insulated hives.] *Birokteren* 76(4) : 57–60 [A.A. 469/62]

WEDMORE, E. B. (1946) Electric heating of bee hives and the scale proper to comparative experiments with stocks of bees. *London : British Electrical and Allied Industries Research Association;* see also *Bee Wld* 28(1) : 6–7 (1947)

——— (1947) The ventilation of bee hives. *Petts Wood, Kent : Bee Craft Books*

CHAPTER 5

METHODS FOR REARING QUEENS

"No person is an accomplisht apiarist until he is a thorough master of the queen-rearing part of the business."—*G. M. Doolittle*

Introduction

Although beekeepers do not rear queens without the aid of bees, it is now possible to produce queens in the laboratory without any contact with bees[66]. But it is much easier to let the bees raise queens, and the numerous methods reflect local practices and variations of individual beekeepers. Whatever the method, bees manage the care and feeding of the queen larva until it is "sealed" or "capped" in an elongated peanut-shaped queen cell. It is this cell which the beekeeper harvests—during the interval while the larva metamorphoses into a pupa and before the virgin queen emerges—and the term queen cell refers to the cell with the live immature queen in it.

Beekeepers may be reluctant to undertake the production of queen cells, but there are simple ways to obtain a few cells for replacement of undesirable queens or for increase, and it is a challenge to develop competency with more elaborate methods. Information on queen rearing in general beekeeping manuals is limited, and we hope that this compilation of information from specialized books and articles on queen rearing will stimulate more beekeepers to try this fascinating side-line of their craft.

Natural sources (supersedure and swarming)

It is possible to secure a few cells from a colony which is preparing to replace a failing or aged queen (supersedure). Only when queens are marked, or their wings clipped, are we aware of the frequency with which established colonies quietly supersede their queens without decrease in morale or honey production. If all supersedure cells are removed, the colony will make others, and the old queen does not disturb them. F. J. Wardell[133] was able to secure 263 such cells from one such colony during a season; Grimmond[56] reported 92 present at one time. However, if a new queen is allowed to emerge, she will attack the other cells, kill the young queens, and eventually replace the old queen.

Queen cells with reddish-brown tips, caused by bees removing most of the wax over the membranous cocoon, are "ripe" and the queens due to emerge (11–12 days after cell building began)[109]. The first virgin to emerge inhibits the emergence of the others, but they will start to emerge when the first queen is removed[68]. Queens reared in colonies about to supersede are fed more liberally by nurse bees than those forced to rear cells by the beekeeper[146].

Queen cells from colonies preparing to swarm are also usable, unless it is undesirable to perpetuate the swarming trait. Doolittle recommended manipulating colonies to stimulate the building of cells in preparation for swarming, as he was of the opinion that queens produced under "natural" conditions were superior to those produced by any other method[41]. He is supported by recent findings that queens from swarm cells have on the average more ovarioles than queens from emergency cells or from beekeeper-reared queens[20,152]. The following characteristics distinguish supersedure from swarm cells:

Queen cells	Supersedure	Swarming
Number	few (1–5)	many (3–30)
Position	tucked away in odd corners	protrude from face of comb
Age	approximately similar	widely variable
Contents of worker cells	eggs present	eggs absent

Woods proposes that his Apidictor can be used to distinguish differences in sounds from a colony 25 days prior to its swarming or supersedure[174].

"Artificial" queen cell production

All methods that stimulate the colony to build queen cells when the beekeeper wants them take advantage of the basic behaviour by which the colony produces emergency cells in the absence of a queen (the Japanese honeybee *Apis cerana japonica* is an exception[62]). The cells are capped 5-5½ days after hatching and can be given one each to queenless colonies or nuclei, where the virgin queens will emerge and fly to mate. Some authors suggest checking the colony for capped cells 3 days after dequeening and destroying any found, as these must have been produced from larvae older than 36 hours. Caste determination occurs shortly after this age, so intermediate forms might develop[4]. From the results of C. C. Miller's experiment it would be a rare occurrence[100].

Irrespective of the method, success depends upon: (1) an abundance of bees (if deficient, add frames of emerging worker brood a few days in advance, or shake bees off frames taken from other colonies); (2) a minimum of 2 full-depth (or 4 shallow) combs of honey; (3) an abundance of pollen; (4) a good nectar flow, or syrup (1 part sugar : 2 parts water) fed 3 days prior to manipulation and continued until the cells are capped. These conditions simulate the conditions in a colony preparing to swarm: an excessive number of bees, brood, nectar, and pollen for the space available[147a].

In queen rearing the time table for procedures must be followed strictly once it is begun, so the colonies used should be gentle as well as populous. The behaviour of large colonies is markedly different from that of small ones, and even in good weather a gentle colony may "boil up" and sting when the brood chamber is exposed. Under adverse conditions, aggressiveness in a colony can make work intolerable, if not impossible, and thus limit the choice of method to one that takes a minimum of manipulation and does not require finding the queen.

Disturbance of the colony resulting from manipulations affects foraging for only 10–60 minutes; the state of queenlessness itself has no effect[92]. Various methods used seem to be equally good, since the weight of virgins produced by them is the same,[137] but the opinion that naturally produced queens are superior to artificially reared ones has been often voiced[85,160]. One investigator contends that the evidence supporting this opinion results from the use of inadequate rearing methods[90]. The hobbyist or sideliner can afford to rear queens under ideal conditions[61]

The seasonal start of queen rearing is determined by the supply of mature drones to fly with the queens about a week after the queens emerge. According to F. W. L. Sladen (1920) drones are not mature enough to mate at 14 days old[46]. Kurennoi found some drones mature when 12 days old, but the greatest number were over 20 days old[80]. In temperate climates operations commencing with the appearance of dandelion or fruit bloom[101] are likely to ensure both drones and suitable weather for mating flights. Rearing should be completed before the hives are crowded with bees and require frequent checking for space and swarming preparations[72]. However, some queen-rearing procedures serve as effective swarm preventives, and the emergence of queens in the colony during the honey flow increases the amount of honey collected[77]. For the hobbyist, it may be more convenient to postpone queen rearing until late summer, as there seems to be no rationale for the traditional rite of early spring requeening[3]. In the north temperate region queens begun in early August are assured of being mated and tested before the earliest possible frosts, although some methods are less successful when used during periods of nectar dearth[1,47]. Since queens 2 or 3 years old perform better than younger ones, it is best to delay a decision to requeen until colonies have an opportunity to show their performance[67,141].

Dequeening

When the ancient Greeks wanted to increase the number of their colonies, they placed in a new hive some combs removed from one of their movable-bar hives[175]. The queenless bees would then produce queen cells from some of the worker larvae. This is the basic technique upon which various modifications of dequeening have been developed. Langstroth moved one queen around between three colonies[84]. Phillips used queen-excluder zinc to make three "divisions" in a hive body, but the disruption of shifting the queen from one side to the other did not always produce good results[122]. A more successful alternative was devised by Beyleveld using a hive mounted on a pipe. A queen-excluder slide was pushed in to make a portion of the colony queenless, and the hive was turned through 180° to get rid of the old, troublesome field bees[18]. The method described below does not require special hives or equipment.

1. Prepare an empty hive (1 brood box) whose entrance has been reduced to $2 \times \frac{3}{8}$ inches (50 × 10 mm) and closed with grass or window screening to help ensure that sufficient bees will stay with the little colony (nucleus) when the entrance is reopened after 2 days. Keep the hive cool and provide dilute syrup or water.

2. Remove from the parent colony and place in this empty hive:
   (a) the queen and the frame of brood on which she is found;
   (b) at least one frame of emerging brood, placed next to the frame with the queen;
   (c) at least two frames of honey and pollen (one on each side);
   (d) additional bees (from at least two other frames) shaken into the nucleus.

3. Complete the hive with drawn comb, or empty frames fitted with foundation, (one frame between 2(b) and 2(c) above). As more space is required for brood·or stores, the frames of honey should be moved out towards the sides.

4. If the queen is to be returned, place the nucleus behind the parent colony with the entrance in the opposite direction.

5. If the nucleus is moved more than say 8 km ($2\frac{1}{2}$ miles) away, the entrance can be opened up immediately and all the bees will remain with the new colony. After a week or more, it is closed again (at night), and returned to the home apiary. Very few bees will desert, but if it is not moved from the home apiary initially, field bees will return to the parent colony.

6. Since the nucleus will not have field bees for a few days, it should be fed thin syrup.

7. Queen cells will be built by the bees in the parent colony (from worker larvae 3 days old or younger); these should be removed by the 9th day after dequeening and the old queen returned, or the bees allowed to keep one or more of the cells for requeening. If the old queen is to be killed, she should not be disposed of until a new queen is mated and brood from her eggs is sealed. Alternatively, the old queen can be introduced to a queenless colony or an established nucleus.

8. The bees will seal uncapped brood placed above a queen excluder, and this will be ideal for making into nuclei after 9 days when the queen cells must be removed. The number of cells will vary from a few to 12 or more. If they happen to occur on several frames, each frame with its cell(s) can be used to set up a nucleus.

9. Alternative: Move the colony to one side of its stand, with the entrance at the back. On the parent stand, place an empty hive body containing a comb or two of honey, a frame of pollen, and a frame of eggs from the colony selected (be sure the queen is not on the frames). Fill the hive body with empty comb. The nucleus can be moved or united to the parent colony (provided with a rear entrance) before the major honey flow begins[156].

Induced supersedure

This method does not require elaborate manipulations or special equipment except for a queen excluder or two and a double division screen. The latter can be purchased, constructed[159], or made by stapling fine wire gauze (window screening) on both sides of a queen excluder, to prevent contact by bees. A strong colony is rearranged as indicated below, with a minimum of one deep frame of honey and one of pollen placed at each side of each box of brood:

A. Hive before sorting brood:

1. top cover
2. honey super
3. honey super
4. brood chamber
5. brood chamber
6. floor board (bottom)

B. Hive after sorting brood:

1. top cover
4. box containing combs with eggs and uncapped brood
   queen excluder no. 1
2. honey super
3. honey super
   queen excluder no. 2
5. box containing queen and capped brood
6. floor board (bottom)

Twenty-four hours after the brood has been arranged as in B, queen excluder no. 1 is removed and a double division screen put in its place. If the nurse bees that moved up into the top chamber (4) to care for the young brood then consider themselves queenless, there should be queen cells after another 24 hours, and the screen is again replaced by the queen excluder until the cells are removed within 9 days of starting the manipulation.

An alternative method uses a wooden inner cover with a piece of queen-excluder zinc covering the feed-hole both above and below[36,104,113,153]. This avoids switching screens and excluders (an advantage in regions with capricious weather) but is not always successful. Queen-excluder zinc has also been used to segregate a portion of the combs in the hive[11,122]. A horizontal double-screened board used by Chambers had excluder zinc in slots both above and below. A piece of metal was pushed in to cover the excluder and thus to separate the upper and lower chamber when starting cells in the upper (queenless) portion of the hive[34].

If a flight-hole is provided in the top brood box, a queen can be permitted to emerge, mate, and establish a second colony there, and this can be left in place for the two-queen system of management, or moved to a new site when strong enough to survive, or used for requeening. A virgin queen may be able to squeeze through the excluder, to kill the queen below, so it might be wise to substitute a solid board or double division screen before a queen emerges in the upper chamber, or to use one of these from the outset. The Bee Research Association conducted some research on modifications of the method[163].

Historical note: Separating the queen from the uncapped brood with a queen excluder is similar to Demaree's method of swarm control[40]. C. C. Miller took credit for first reporting that colonies may produce a new queen in a remote box of brood[103]. Doolittle advocated it as the ideal way to raise queens and squabbled with Alley over priority[42]. A letter written by Demaree in 1893 established that he was aware that bees would produce queen cells above an excluder with a queen below[87]. Long before others, A. A. Fradenburg had seen the advantage of using the upper storey of a hive to produce cells and queens, and thus to avoid making the colony queenless[50]. W. T. Cary suggested using two queen excluders[33].

It is curious that, on the page facing Fradenburg's claim to priority over Doolittle in an 1889 issue of *Gleanings in Bee Culture*, another claim appears[48,51]. W. E. Flowers had written to Heddon, Doolittle and Root in 1882, describing his infallible scheme for shaking bees on to frames of foundation and placing the brood in an upper storey with a queen excluder over the lower storey. He complained that his offer to write up the method met no response from Root, in spite of the fact that he could secure affidavits to verify the facts. It seems we should substitute "Flowers" for "Demaree, Doolittle, or Miller". The use of an upper storey for rearing and mating a queen has also been referred to as the Alexander method[6,26,134,157]. Recent work by A. K. Skriptschenko has shown the efficacy of placing the queen and bees on empty combs and foundation, for increased honey production[2].

Cells without locating queens

Directions to "find the queen" can be unacceptable when the hive is as tall as the beekeeper, or when the weather keeps the bees confined and they are quick to boil over and attack at the first exposure. The four methods described below may be useful in such circumstances.

R. Bentley: Place half the brood from a strong colony (at least 6 deep frames of brood) into an empty hive body, along with a minimum of 2 frames containing honey and pollen, and empty frames to fill out the box. Place this box (A2) on the floor board under another strong colony (B), with a solid inner cover separating the two. The upper colony is provided with a new entrance, using wooden wedges (e.g. strips of shingle), auger holes in the boxes, or upper entrances.

If, 5–8 days later, A1 on the original stand has no eggs, but does have queen cells, the queen is in A2 under colony B. If eggs are present, the queen is in A1 on the original stand. Twelve days after the colony was first divided, the queenless box (either A1 or A2) should be placed on a new stand some distance away, and B put in its place. If A2 is queenless, B will remain on its stand, but if A1 is queenless, B will be moved to the A position[16].

F. G. Rauchfuss: A much simpler alternative uses a box of brood above an inner cover with queen-excluder zinc over the feed-hole. After 8 days, the box containing eggs is known to contain the queen and can be set on a new stand. The bees at the old stand will then produce a new queen. If they do not already have queen cells, they will require at least one frame with eggs and newly hatched brood from which to produce them[127].

M. H. Stricker: See No. 9 in section on dequeening above.

Top entrance: This method is applicable to a colony in which an appreciable number of bees are using an entrance in the top hive body, as in spring after wintering with an auger hole as a top entrance. It is undertaken in the middle of a warm day when bees are flying freely. One or two combs of capped brood with small patches of eggs, and two or more frames of honey and pollen with the adhering bees, are placed in an empty hive body. The remainder of the hive body is filled with empty combs or frames to be drawn out (nuclei build worker cells readily). The parent hive is covered with a standard bottom board, and closing the space between it and the lower hive body. An inner cover with screening on each side of the hole (or a double division screen) may be used in place of a standard bottom board. Pieces of shingle or other wedges will elevate the nucleus enough to form an upper entrance. The nucleus is placed on top of this bottom board and covered. The top entrance to the parent hive is closed. Most of the flying bees oriented to this top hole will follow the bottom board into the nucleus, assuring a large enough population to keep the brood warm and to build queen cells.

The nucleus is checked for queen cells 5–7 days after establishment, and for eggs about a month later. At this time, if the nucleus is moved away without disorienting the bees, the procedure can be repeated. The nucleus with a laying queen may be used for a two-queen system, requeening, or increase. If for increase, the parent colony is moved to a new stand, and the nucleus placed on top of additional hive bodies at the original stand[70].

Quantity cell production

Until the 1880s, the only method for procuring queen cells was either to stimulate swarming conditions in the colony or to render it queenless. The cells produced by these methods (3–12 or more) are entirely satisfactory, but they are not always built where it is convenient for the beekeeper to cut them out, and the comb is damaged in the process. If the whole frame is put into a nucleus or colony there is no difficulty, but this limits the number of colonies that can be supplied with queen cells to the number of frames that chance to have cells on them.

To secure more than a few queen cells, it is necessary to use one of the following methods, in which comb containing eggs or young larvae is given to a colony in a way that enables the queen cells to be harvested easily. The additional cost of labour and equipment is compensated by higher yields of queen cells. Techniques for mass queen cell production are usually credited to four Americans (Alley, Doolittle, Pratt, Pridgen), although the basic information was established by European apiculturists. In 1568, 300 years before commercial exploitation, Nicol Jacob in Silesia published the observation that a queenless colony could rear a queen if it had eggs or young larvae in worker cells[162].

The interest in disseminating new races of bees, such as the Italians imported into the United States in 1860, and acceptance of bees by the post office in 1863, provided the stimulus for the American developments. But by 1872 postal authorities ruled to exclude bees from the mails, because of honey leakage and because personnel were stung. In frustration, A. I. Root and others (1873) mailed pieces of comb containing eggs from Italian queens, for introduction into colonies of black bees. Queens were successfully produced by this method, but better methods of propagation were needed. Suggestions began to appear in bee journals, which were developed into methods suitable for large-scale, commercial production of queens. W. J. Nolan summarized the history of this development which rose to a peak in 1881–1890 and again in 1911–1920[63,111].

Strips of brood comb (Alley method)

M. Quinby, in his *Mysteries of bee-keeping explained* (New York, 1853), described requeening queenless colonies by inserting a piece of comb with young larvae between the combs of his box hives, but he did not recommend this technique for producing queens routinely, as he believed the queens were of poorer quality than those produced under the swarming impulse. Support for this view by others has been noted above. Lukoschus suggests that differences in the position of queen cells on the comb (lower edge and/or sides in swarming or supersedure) results in temperature differences that have metabolic effects[93,94].

A. G. Shirach in Germany had advocated this method in 1771[63]. A. J. Cook in his *Manual of the apiary* (Lansing, 1876) recommended that pieces of worker comb be fitted into holes cut in the combs, as J. Dzierzon had done[28]; J. S. Harbison patented this process in 1859 (U.S. Pat. 26,431). D. H. Townsend fastened strips of worker comb underneath the top-bar of a frame, using tacks (drawing pins); J. M. Brooks fastened a strip to the bar with melted wax, after first trimming the cells down to the septum[83]. In 1883, H. Alley published his *bee-keeper's handy book*, pulling together these and other schemes he used in producing queens on a commercial scale, and his method was advocated by Jay Smith in a supplement to his own book[129,150].

Every other row of cells (in dark comb) containing eggs and larvae 1 day old is cut to form a strip, using a thin sharp knife kept warm in hot water and wiped dry before each cut. The cells on one side are trimmed to within 6 mm ($\frac{1}{4}$ inch) of the midrib; a match is twirled in every 2nd and 3rd cell, leaving the 1st cell of three as a potential queen cell. If more space is desired between cells, a greater number of eggs or larvae can be destroyed between those left intact.

The uncut side of the strip is dipped into melted beeswax (Alley used 2 parts rosin), 1 part beeswax [equal parts (1903).] which must not be so hot as to kill eggs and larvae, and attached to a suitable support. This may be: (1) the underside of a comb trimmed back from the bottom-bar about 8 cm (3 inches); (2) the underside of a wooden cross-bar nailed between the end-bars of a frame (a single nail permits tilting); (3) the underside of the bottom-bar of a shallow (or half) brood frame; or (4) the upper side of an opening 8–16 x 4 cm (3–6 x 1½ inches) cut out of a comb of honey (preferably with some open cells). The prepared comb is then placed in a starter cell building colony (see below).

The method has been refined, with holders for individual cells, and punches to cut out individual cells from comb[14,63,73,106,115,155,177]. R. M. Crawford prepared strips by embedding thin wooden slats into a sheet of foundation and then placing two such prepared sheets into a frame with the slats back to back. After the bees built out the cells and the queen laid eggs in them, the sheets of foundation were removed, and a pronged device used to destroy all but every third horizontal row of eggs. Each strip with a slat backing was then cut apart and fastened with thumb tacks (drawing pins) to the bottom-bar of a shallow frame. When the queen cells were completed, the strip was pried loose, and pruning shears used to cut the wooden slat between the cells, to separate them for introduction into a colony[37].

Whole brood comb (Miller method)

This method is likely to succeed at the first attempt, and under optimum conditions will produce sufficient cells for a small operation. The succinct description[112] of the method by "Obed." taken from *Bienenzeitung* about 1860 cannot be improved upon:

"If after depriving a colony of its queen, a horizontal cut be made through a brood-comb containing eggs and young larvae, and the upper section which remains attached to the top slat of the frame be reinserted in the hive, the bees will construct royal cells and raise queens from the larvae on the fresh-cut margin of the comb, even if no royal jelly be used to designate the place where royal cells are desired. This process invariably succeeds if the comb be placed in close proximity to the brood in the hive, and the bees be numerous enough to cover the brood-combs properly. If two or three days after, when royal cells have been partially built, another comb with eggs and young larvae be prepared in like manner and inserted, royal cells will be started on this likewise, and the queens reared therein will mature several days later than those on the former comb. This process may be extended with like success to the insertion of a third or a fourth cut comb, and successive rearings of queens thus secured. The apiarian must, however, be careful to remove and use these royal cells before the inmate of any one of them matures and emerges, or the destruction of the others would certainly follow. By seasonably rearing queens in this manner and placing them, or the royal cells containing them, in small boxes furnished with maturing worker-brood and a few hundred bees, the apiarian may readily multiply queens from a single hive, without interfering with the labours of other stocks; and the population of the hive used for this purpose may easily be kept up, by inserting from time to time, a few combs containing maturing worker-brood taken from other colonies"[112].

Damage to the brood comb can be avoided by trimming back the edge of a newly built comb to just-hatched or "hardly noticeable" larvae (as suggested by Anton Janscha in 1771), so the queen cells built along the edge are easy to remove[7]. This method was also suggested by A. J. Cook and publicized by C. C. Miller with modifications[102].

A half-sheet of wax foundation is fastened in the upper part of a frame with a single embedded top-wire. The frame is placed in the brood chamber of the colony selected for queen rearing, and after a week should have drawn-out cells containing eggs and newly hatched larvae. It is then removed and the bees brushed off, as the comb is too delicate to shake. A series of V-cuts are made along the (lower) edge of the comb with a sharp knife. This should be done in a warm, shady place so that the larvae are not harmed by exposure to the sun. The comb is placed in a queenless cell-building colony (see below); a check is made after 4 days, and cells touching one another are thinned out. In 9 or 10 days the cells can be harvested and distributed.

Narrow V-shaped strips of foundation may also be used, but a colony restricted entirely to worker comb may draw out drone instead of worker cells on worker foundation. To avoid this, remove all but two frames of brood, or provide empty frames in which the colony can produce drone or storage comb at will. If new comb drawn previously is used, newly hatched larvae may be present in 4 days rather than 1 week. M. Prichard placed an empty brood comb in a breeder colony for 6 days and then cut long horizontal strips of comb a few cm (about 1 inch) wide where there were eggs. The comb was then placed in a queenless colony to build queen cells along the upper edge of the openings in the comb[126].

Horizontal comb. I. Hopkins described the method but disclaimed the credit usually given to him (and also to Case) for its invention[60]. A thin knife is run along the sides of every 4th row of cells in a comb of eggs, the intervening 3 rows being removed down to the midrib. In the remaining 4th row every 2nd and 3rd egg is destroyed, leaving the 1st egg as a potential queen cell. The frame is placed face down in an empty hive body over a starter colony; notches need to be cut in the hive body to fit the projecting ends of the top bar. The whole is covered with canvas or cloth. J. Gray provided space for a cluster under the comb; he demonstrated his scheme in England in 1909[55]. Jordan used boxes to hold cut pieces of comb which were then placed in a frame[74a].

L. E. Snelgrove's "B.H.S." method combined the Barbeau punch system with the horizontal brood comb technique by Hiller, as a source of started queen cells; he used one empty frame under and another above such a comb to provide space in which the bees could build queen cells. The frames were covered with a canvas "quilt" and left for two days in an empty hive body above a colony made queenless and broodless[151].

The Stanley system provided cutters and plugs, and a plastic (Perspex) tip for use in a special hive cover much like Swarthmore's[123,155]. Fritz Bauckhage devised a simple pointed metal support on which to fasten a cell containing an egg or newly hatched larvae for attachment to the face of a comb[13a]. A simple triangle of tin can also be used.

Larval transplant (grafting)

In 1876, E. D. L. Larch used the term "grafting" for transferring a worker larva to a queen cell[83]. If strict rules of nomenclature were applied, the earlier "transposition" of J. L. Davis (1874) would have preference[83]. Grafting usually refers to the union of tissues, as in human skin or plant grafts. Since even the exchange of a whole organ is called a transplant, the removal of an entire organism should imply more than a "graft". However, the term transposition often implies a rearrangement of parts, as in grammar, music, mathematics, etc. The substitution of the term "transplant" for either transposition or graft would give a description closer to the actual process, and perhaps be more meaningful to the uninitiated.

In grafting (described in detail by Wm McKinley[96]), a worker larva 12–36 hours old is lifted out of its cell with a "grafting needle" and placed into a wax cell cup. Woyke supports the preference of commercial queen rearers for larvae less than 1 day old[176], but bees are less demanding[24]. Oettel observed that a colony chooses larvae that form a circle at the bottom of the cell[161]. Weiss found that queens reared from older larvae weighed less (those from eggs weighed least), but there was no significant difference between the numbers of their ovarioles[172].

On a small scale, queen cells harvested from old combs are highly acceptable to the bees; they were used by F. Huber in 1791 for repeating Schirach's investigations on producing queen cells from worker brood[83]. When offered a choice of natural or artificial queen cups, bees tear down the artificial ones[31]. Anticipating queen rearing, bees include queen cups when they draw out natural comb[8].

J. L. Davis transferred eggs, mailed to him by A. I. Root, into drone cells in queenless nuclei[83]. Wardell at Root's also used drone comb; he transplanted eggs into every 4th cell, first enlarging the opening slightly with a blunt stick[133]. J. D. Foosche reported using drone comb and exchanging larvae in queen cells[49]. Bees prefer larvae grafted into drone cells which have been used for brood rearing a few times—or not at all—to larvae grafted into comparable worker cells.

Queen cell cups

For large-scale production, machine-made wax cells and wooden cell receptacles can be purchased from supply houses or hand-dipped. There is no significant difference in acceptance[114]. Artificially made cell cups (8·9 mm) were preferred by bees to punched worker cells, but not if they were 7·8 mm in diameter[169]; experimental work in which larger cells were provided for rearing queens resulted in larger, heavier queens that laid eggs both earlier and later in the season[79]. When plastic cells are used, they should be sterilized before reuse to prevent disease transmission[76,95].

Hand-dipping of cell cups requires wooden dipping sticks, which can be bought from European supply houses or made from teeth of a wooden rake or pieces of dowelling 8–9 mm ($\frac{5}{16}$–$\frac{3}{8}$ inch), rounded and smoothed at one end. Wax is melted in a double boiler or can be placed in a pan of hot water. Bees will not accept cells made from scorched wax, and the wax should be refined with distilled or rain water. The stick is soaked in water and drained well before it is dipped about 12 mm ($\frac{1}{2}$ inch) into the just molten wax. It is lifted out quickly and redipped when the wax has set, although not as far as the first time. This is repeated 3–5 times, dipping a shorter distance each time. Cooling in water may speed the process, or a series of dipping sticks can be mounted in a holder so that several can be dipped together. The cell is carefully twisted off and mounted on a small block of wood with wax or softened propolis.

W. H. Pridgen mounted dipping sticks on a wheel and produced wax cell cups at the rate of 2000 an hour[125], and Rauchfuss used a similar machine[83]. Pratt's "Grace cell-compressor" pressed cups from solid plugs of cool wax *quickly* and the cups were less easily damaged. The melted wax was poured into wooden cups (length 12 mm, $\frac{1}{2}$ inch; diameter 9 mm, $\frac{3}{8}$ inch) with holes 8 mm ($\frac{5}{16}$ inch) in diameter and 9 mm ($\frac{3}{8}$ inch) deep[123].

Commercial queen rearing

On a horizontal stick or bar 12–20 cells are mounted at intervals, leaving a space 2 inches at each end. Staggering the cells rather than placing them in a straight line may reduce building of burr comb between cells, as does placing a piece of foundation at each end[86]. To save space, grooves or slots may be cut in the side pieces of a frame so that 3 sticks, 5 cm (2 inches) apart, can slide in and out easily. Alternatively, a nail through the frame into the bar will provide for tilting the bar and the frame can thus be laid flat[57], or a wedge-shaped centre portion can be made removable[61].

The wooden cell receptacles, each fitted with a wax cup, are pressed into a streak of wax placed along the bar. Adequate illumination is needed in front of the operator, who uses a transfer tool; this may be purchased, or fashioned from a matchstick, quill, toothpick, bent darning needle, copper wire, twisted horse-hair, a suitable hardwood twig or grass stem, short piece of watch mainspring attached to a wooden handle, etc. The chosen tool is inserted underneath a larva to lift it from the worker cell with as much brood food (royal jelly) as possible; the larva is placed in one of the cell cups on the frame bars. With experience and optimum conditions, up to 85% of the transplanted larvae will be accepted and reared by the bees as queens.

Various precautions are believed to influence acceptance by the bees, though some may not be critical[167,170]:

1.   Giving the wax cups on a frame to a colony a few hours before using ("acclimatizing") has been shown to be unnecessary[24,171].

2.   Priming cells with royal jelly before placing larvae in them results in stunted larvae.   The jelly is quickly removed by the bees[49,74,118], and if it gets on both sides of a larva, it will block the spiracles[136].   Small colonies prefer "wet" grafts (larvae on a drop of brood food)[24].

3.   A damp cloth or paper towelling kept over the frames from which the larvae are being taken, as well as the cell cups that will receive them, minimizes drying of the larvae.   Bees will have been brushed off the comb before use.

4.   A shed or room that can be kept at 25–30°C (80–93°F) and relative humidity of about 50%, or a portable shed or tent in out-apiaries, can prevent overheating or chilling larvae.   When manipulations must follow a schedule in spite of poor weather, the value of a beehouse for queen rearing is indisputable[142].

5.   The cells into which larvae have been transferred should be placed as quickly as possible into the hive prepared for them; (1) swarm-box; (2) starter colony; (3) combination starter-finishing colony; or (4) strong nucleus (if only a few cells are introduced).   However, larvae can survive outside the colony from 3 to 24 hours depending on their condition and age[167].

6.   A bar of 12–20 cups is usually given on three successive days, or all three bars might be given together to a very strong colony.   When a deep super is used for queen rearing, the cells can be mounted on the bottom-bar of a shallow or half frame with open honey and pollen in the comb.   Phillips recommended a frame without a bottom piece, so that the cells could be lowered into the mass of bees occupying the space, and the bees would then cluster on the cells immediately.   Rosser and Arthur pushed cells into each side of a brood comb between the brood and pollen areas, where bees usually build queen cells for swarming[135]. C. A. Greig fastened the cell cups at intervals over the surface of a comb containing fresh pollen and honey, dipping the base of the cells into hot wax before pressing them firmly into position[172a].

7.   Without a honey flow, sugar syrup must be fed at least 3 days prior to transplanting, and throughout the cell building period.   Phillips[122] preferred to rear queens during a light flow, or none at all, to avoid the mess of burr comb and honey around the cells, and this point is underscored by Roberts[130].   More royal jelly is produced during a poor nectar flow than during a good flow[30].

8.   Little or no smoke should be used during manipulations.

Zhdanova found optimal conditions for queen rearing during the main flow and recommends that young nurse bees be provided 25 days before transplanted larvae are offered.   She removed brood and other queens 10 days beforehand, and fed syrup until the cells were sealed[178].   The classical Zander method in Bavaria used a colony queenless for 9 days[136].

Double grafting

In "double grafting" a worker larva is transplanted into a queen cell, and 1–2 days later it is replaced with a new young larva.   The queens produced by this technique are slightly heavier than those from single transplanting[20,98,107]. Volosevich considered double-grafted queens almost as good as queens from swarm cells, but single transplants poorer than queens from other methods[160]. Weiss found no significant correlation between queen weight and number of ovarioles[172], although Hoopingarner and Farrar did[59a].

Cocoon transplants

Pridgen transferred the cocoon containing a larva to a cell cup, to avoid disturbing the young larva as in Atchley's method of fastening the cocoon on to a pointed stick[125]. Perret-Maisonneuve designed special equipment for this procedure and sharply rebutted criticisms that the method was difficult[120].

Egg transplants

The transfer of eggs into cell cups was practised by Gusev before 1860, and advocated by Reidenback in 1893. In 1952, Örösi-Pál developed a technique of punching out a cell base containing an egg for use instead of a grafted larva; his method required about as much time as double grafting with larvae. He found eggs just over 2 days old more satisfactory than those less than 1 day old or nearly hatching[5,117].

Jordon tried Örösi-Pál's method and obtained superior queens, but 50% of the transplants failed[75]. The various ways that Weiss tried for transplanting eggs resulted in poorer acceptance than the use of larvae, and he did not find the age of the egg critical (except that the colony would not accept eggs older than 3 days)[164,165]. He recommends attaching pieces of comb to cell cups[168]. Pieces of comb with eggs (*Eistück*) can be sent by post, and withstand a temperature as low as about 18 °C for not more than 2 days, but must be introduced into a colony when or before they are 2½ days old[166]. Such conditions might require personal transport on a plane. Taber devised forceps with which the eggs can be removed from comb and transferred to a container, and 75% hatched whether in a colony or an incubator[158].

Historical note

G. M. Doolittle is generally credited with the transplant or grafting method as used today. In a letter to C. C. Miller, now in the University of California Library, Davis, Doolittle indicated that he used cell cups in 1875–76 and dipped cells in 1880 or 1881, but not later than 1882. He remembers that in the bee papers "someone" had proposed making queen cells to order on a stick. A. I. Root also mentions that "somebody" spoke to him of making artificial queen cells by dipping a wet stick into melted wax[83].

In 1883, Doolittle met D. A. Jones of Canada, who since 1879 had been in partnership with F. Benton of the U.S.A. in a bee-breeding venture in Europe. It is not unlikely that they heard of the transfer of larvae by Weygandt in 1880, and the ingenious implements and methods for raising queens by transplant which W. Wankler devised and exhibited between 1881 and 1883. Benton purchased a set of Wankler's equipment at an exhibition in 1883[17]. German texts can fairly discuss queen rearing methods without reference to American work.

In 1878, W. L. Boyd suggested fastening just-started queen cells on a stick for transfer of worker larvae, and L. Heine reported some success with "artificial queen-cells" but was sceptical of their practical value.[63]. A. G. Beljavsky upset all claims for priority by revealing that in Russia E. Goosev [Gusev[5]] had received a prize for the transfer of eggs in 1860[15]. F. Mehring, the inventor of comb foundation, is said to have transferred larvae in 1866[99].

Pratt "locked" pressed cells into a frame like that printers use for type, and placed it in a queenless, broodless nucleus[124]. A laying queen introduced 6 hours later was expected to lay eggs in the cups, and thus eliminate the "troublesome task of transplanting larvae by hand". Örösi-Pál succeeded in getting queens to lay eggs in as many as 65 of 70 cups, but the larvae did not develop, and the bees eventually discarded almost all the eggs[116]. Queens whose front legs had been amputated have been observed to place eggs in artificial queen cells[147]. Bognoczky was successful in getting queens to lay in hexagonal plastic tubing 6 mm in diameter and 7 mm deep, coated with wax[23].

Swarm-box for starting queen cells

A colony preparing to swarm, or which has just swarmed, is excellent for rearing not more than ten maximum-weight queens[59]. For routine queen cell production on a large scale this arrangement is impractical, and a closed, screened box is commonly used, for instance by about 60% of the southern U.S.A. queen rearers[131].

Nolan's description of the Alley and Pratt swarm-box methods summarizes the procedures and theory:

"Alley advised smoking and drumming a sufficient quantity of young bees into an empty hive-body and keeping them there long enough to realize their queenless condition. It was his idea that they would then have a large amount of larval food on hand, since they had been deprived so suddenly of brood, and had filled up with honey on being smoked and drummed. The prepared cell-cups were next inserted between frames of honey and pollen in another hive-body, which was then set over the hive-body containing the queenless bees. At the end of 24 hours the cells were transferred to another colony, queenless but with brood, and were left there until sealed. Then they were given to a third queenless colony, each queen cell protected in a nursery cage. Doolittle, on the other hand, advocated the rearing of queens over an excluder in a queen-right colony. His success in this manipulation is attested by the fact that in a single season he reared 600 queens in the same colony over an excluder. [Of southern producers, 15% use queenless colonies, and 85% use a queenright cell finisher[131].]

"Pratt combined to some extent the two methods. In devising the Swarthmore swarm-box he followed Alley but instead of first confining queenless bees, shaken or drummed into an empty hive-box, he confined them in a specially constructed five-frame swarm-box containing only three frames of honey and pollen, with an empty frame-space on each side of the center comb. In slits in the cover over these vacant spaces were fitted slats for containing the cell-cups. The swarm-box, as soon as filled with bees, was given empty cell-cups. It was then well covered on top, and set in a cool place. When the empty cell-cups had remained in the swarm-box for about six hours, larvae were transferred to them and were left in the swarm-box about eighteen hours for acceptance. Pratt in this way could give his swarm-box a new lot of cell-cups every twenty-four hours, thus using the same bees for about three or four successive lots. Pratt considered the combination of a cool place and a warm covering for the top a most essential factor in the manipulation of swarm-boxes. It was his idea of this operation that the cool air outside would cause the bees to tend to cluster tightly, while the warm covering at the top of the swarm-box would cause the upper part to be so warm as to induce the bees to form and keep their cluster there. Thus the bees would remain clustered tightly around the cell-cups and the young larvae would at all times have sufficient heat and other conditions conducive to their proper acceptance. The cell-cups, after being started, were transferred to a cell-finishing colony either over an excluder or even in the lower story, provided an excluder nursery cage as devised by him was fitted over the bar of cells."[63]* The superiority of broodless, queenless colonies for acceptance of newly grafted larvae is borne out by analysis of beekeeper practices in England.[52].

Various modifications have brought us present practices; some are set out below.

(1) Jay Smith noted the new swarm-box Swarthmore recommended in the "Government bulletin on queen-rearing"[65] and gave it prominence in his later writings. He advised that its depth should be twice the depth of the standard frame to ensure that the bees would not suffocate. The wooden bottom had a 5-cm (2-inch) rim above it, making a container for food or water as needed. The sides below the frame space were screened for ventilation. Jay Smith used 6–8 lb (3–4 kg) of bees (spare bees from three or four colonies) for 50 cells, and 10 pounds for 100 cells[150].

(2) W. B. Bray published a "Modified Pratt [Swarthmore] system"[25] and noted the importance of light intensity in causing the cluster to break. R. A. Morse has since shown that bright light inhibits the onset of comb building by clustered bees[108].

(3) Instructions for making ventilated boxes with covered slots for introducing frames of cell cups can be found in books by Smith[149] and Sladen[148].

(4) Use of a funnel for filling boxes with bees during active flight will ensure that most are young nurse bees[148].

(5) If the bees are knocked to the bottom by jarring the box, relatively few escape when frames are removed or put into the box.

(6) Bees no longer needed are shaken out in front of the colony from which they were taken.

(7) Water must be available, and can be given in a comb or in feeders. Substitution of thin sugar syrup for honey prevents spread of disease organisms in honey.

---

* The practice by F. J. Wardell in 1899 of raising queens "a la Doolittle" in the brood nest, with the queen present and carrying out her normal activities[132], was also reported by Lensky and Darchen in 1962[89]. Nearly 100% acceptance of cells was obtained if the colonies were large (20–30 frames of bees), with a substantial proportion of nurse bees and a limited number of worker larvae[88].

After a misunderstanding of verbal directions, one of the authors (TSKJ, 1961) placed a frame of queen cell cups into the middle of a 10-frame brood nest of a queen-right colony. There had been no prior preparation, but the bees built queen cells in spite of the presence of the queen. Such observations undermine the rationale of methods which require the removal or isolation of the queen from the cell building portion of the hive in order that cell building may occur.

Cell-starter colony

Since bees in a swarm-box are confined and must be renewed frequently, commercial rearers in California commonly use a two-storey queenless colony to start queen cells; two-thirds of them use the same colony to finish the cells[131]. J. Smith used 15 lb (7 kg) of bees in a hive box to start 50 cells and added a further 6 lb and 50 more cells every third day throughout the season, removing completed cells on the next day. Three such colonies furnished 1000 mating hives with cells[149].

In the cell-starter colony, the queen and brood are moved away, whereas in the swarm-box it is the bees that are moved. One strong starter colony which can provide 45–90 cells daily requires 3–6 finishing colonies, into which bars of 15 cells each are placed. Queenless bees have the impetus to start more queen cells than they can properly feed[130].

Method A. The queen, and 2 or 3 combs of sealed brood and honey with the adhering bees, are placed in an empty hive body (nucleus) behind the parent colony with its entrance facing in the opposite direction. The remainder of the combs of unsealed brood and eggs are brushed free of bees and given to some other colony to care for, but the combs of honey, pollen and sealed brood remain with the parent colony. If the starter colony does not cover most of the combs, additional bees should be provided from other colonies.

Larvae in cell cups (or larvae from some other method) should be given to the starter colony 2–4 hours after the colony has been set up. Bees desert a queenless hive, and if queen cells are not given for 24 hours, the colony will be considerably weakened[145]. Accepted cells are removed 24 hours later and given to a finishing colony, and a new set of grafted cells given to the starter colony. After starting a few sets of cells, the starter colony and brood are reunited with the parent colony. If the starter colony is to be maintained on a continuing basis, combs of emerging brood must be added every 7 days or as required, since the number of cells started decreases with advancing age of nurse bees[126]. If stores of pollen are not also replaced, the number (and quality?) of queens produced will be affected[131].

Laidlaw and Eckert suggested leaving two combs of young larvae with a comb of pollen between them[83]. These combs of larvae are removed 1 hour prior to the time of grafting, and the frame of grafted cells put in their place to ensure a cluster of nurse bees on hand to accept the cells immediately. G. W. Phillips advised removal of the bottom bar of the grafting frame, to avoid breaking up the cluster as the frame is lowered into the hive[122].

Method B. L. Stachelhausen used a queenless colony established above a queen excluder on a strong colony, 8–9 days prior to grafting. The hive body was prepared with 4 or 5 combs of open brood from other colonies, and the rest of the box filled with empty combs. In 8–9 days this brood was capped. A frame was removed to provide a vacant space for a frame of grafted cells, and this upper storey moved to a new stand. A few hours later, cells were given to this colony to start, and the next morning it was returned to its original position over the parent colony[154].

Method C. The queen and capped brood are confined in the bottom brood chamber with a queen excluder. When the young brood in the upper box is capped, 8–9 days later, the lower box with the queen is placed on a new stand. The top box is placed in position on the bottom board and the grafted cells inserted.   The excluder is left under this top box to prevent any virgin queens entering and destroying the cells[105].   Gontarski recommended this as the best method to meet the requirements for queen rearing.   The queen is confined on a comb in a cage made of queen-excluder zinc for 9 days, and then removed for 1 day, when a comb of eggs is placed in the colony.   Larvae are punched out of the comb, and attached to bars from which the workers rear queen cells to be removed on the 14th day[53].

Method D.   "Go to a very good colony, take away the queen and use her as you like.   Leave the colony queenless six days, when queen-cells will have been started.   At the end of the six days take all the brood, queen-cells and all, away from the colony.   They will then want a queen so badly that they will be willing to give cells the best attention.   Then give back grafted cells to this colony containing larvae from the queen you wish to use as a breeder.   This colony will rear a nice lot of cells.   Try this if you do not believe me"[9].

Method E.   Any strong one-storey colony can serve as a starter colony if it is made temporarily queenless.   The queen and the frame she is on can be placed in a hive body above a queen excluder on another colony, or in a nucleus.   G. W. Phillips caged the queen amongst her own bees and released her when he removed the accepted queen cells the next day.   It would be best if the cage used were one which will contain a whole frame, so that the queen is not subjected to the stress of sudden cessation of egg laying.   She could also be put in a side compartment made of queen-excluder zinc, large enough to hold 2 or 3 frames, including emerging bees.

Doolittle recommended an upper storey over a queen excluder as the most desirable, since it created artificial "supersedure" conditions.   He placed a frame of unsealed brood on either side of the grafted frame, and 24 hours later the accepted cells were removed and placed in a finishing colony.   Nolan credits Fooshe with originating this method[63].   Queens reared with combs of open brood receive more royal jelly[19], as do queens reared in colonies about to supersede[146], resulting in heavier queens with more ovarioles[21].   Weiss found no significant correlation between weight and number of ovarioles[172].

Finishing colony

A queenless, broodless starter colony will accept a high percentage of cells.   These may be left to be "finished" in the colony if this is moved outside its original flight range, so that the field bees remain to bring in pollen and nectar; cells may, however, not get the best care in such a "stage of emergency".   The started cells are therefore commonly transferred to finishing colonies in which a supersedure impulse is created by confining the queen to a lower brood chamber.   However, recent evidence indicates that queens reared in queenless colonies are slightly heavier than those from queenright colonies[98].   Queenless colonies were found to feed all larvae three times as frequently as queenright colonies, to cap worker cells sooner, and to produce worker pupae with three times as many ovarioles and larger pharyngeal glands[81].   Of queens sold in the Southern United States, 85% are from queenright cell-finishing colonies[131].

In the Stachelhausen technique (B above) the starter colony is housed on the finishing colony (as it can also be in C), and moved to a separate stand when cells are to be started.

1.   The queen on the frame where she is found, and empty combs in which she can lay eggs, are confined to the lower brood chamber by a queen excluder.

A check for space should be made in one week.

    2.   Emerging and sealed brood is placed in an upper chamber.

    3.   Unsealed brood is removed and placed in other hives but can be returned after the queen cells are finished.

    4.   The colony has all stages of brood, except those requiring feeding, and will give full attention to the 15 queen cell cups introduced the next day, and every second day thereafter up to a total of 45 cells.

    5.   If the nectar flow is light, colonies are fed several days before they are given cells, and throughout the period when they contain cells.

Combination starting-finishing colony

A.   A strong colony with brood in most parts of two brood chambers can be used for both starting and finishing queen cells, and will be most likely to appeal to beginners because it does not require excessive manipulation, disruption of colonies in preparing starter colonies, precision of timing, nor additional equipment.   The hive is prepared essentially as in the "induced supersedure" method described above, except that it is used for a single frame of queen cell cups (or prepared comb) and can be kept in use continuously.   It was Doolittle's method of choice[43] and warmly seconded by E. Penna[119]. A. S. Ivanova recommended it after extensive trials[64], as have W. C. Roberts[130] and Z. M. Marshenkulov[97].

    1.   The colony should have brood in 2 lower hive bodies and honey in at least 1 super on top.

    2.   One queen excluder is placed between the honey and the brood, and a second excluder is placed above the box of honey on which another hive body is placed (cell building chamber).

    3.   The arrangement of combs in the upper cell-building chamber (starting at one side) is: honey, pollen, open brood, open brood (youngest larvae), space for cell cups, open brood (youngest larvae), open brood, pollen, honey.

    4.   Empty combs are used to replace the combs of open brood taken from the brood chamber.

    5.   When the open brood in the cell-building chamber is capped, the combs should be exchanged with uncapped combs from the brood chambers below that in which the queen is laying.   This will ensure the continuous presence of nurse bees in the upper cell-building chamber.

The colony can be used over a period of time, and requires only that unsealed brood be lifted up from the lower brood chamber when new cells are introduced.

    B.   A two-storey colony with at least 6 combs of brood is used.   The comb with the queen and adhering bees is placed into an empty hive body along with at least one comb each of honey and pollen.   After the box has been filled with empty combs and emerging brood, it is placed on the bottom board and covered with a queen excluder.   The remaining box of brood and stores is placed above the excluder, with a crown board (inner cover) and a feeder in an empty box above it.

After at least 3 days of feeding (unless there is a good nectar flow), rearrange the boxes, placing the bottom one with the queen on top, and a bottom board or other solid board under it.   A small entrance is provided towards the rear. The foragers will join the queenless bees below, and in a few hours be in ideal condition for starting queen cells. The feeder should be replenished if necessary.

Once started, the colony is rearranged again, the box with the queen being put back on the bottom board, and the queen excluder over it. The box with started queen cells is placed above the queen excluder, and the box with the feeder is again uppermost[34a].

Disposition of queen cells

If more cells are produced by starter and finishing colonies than can be handled, it is best to discard the smaller ones, since these are correlated with queens that weigh less and have fewer ovarioles[91]. But queens from small emergency cells may have as many ovarioles as the larger beekeeper-reared queens[152] (see Weiss[172]). Mitchell suggested "candling" queen cells by holding them up to a strong light (as done with eggs), to detect those with dead queens and avoid the loss of time and bees in providing them with a mating nucleus[105a].

The average number of cells produced by a finishing colony per day (6–10) requires some 100 mating colonies (50–200 per starting colony). Here the queen will emerge, take mating flights, and begin to lay eggs. If the cell is mounted on a wooden block or cup, it can be pressed into the face of a comb and held in place by pushing the neighbouring comb against it. C. C. Miller used a hive staple to hold the cell in place, but Wankler's wire holder bent over the top bar is less likely to slip, as are some of the alternatives devised by Perret-Maisonneuve[121].

The spiral coiled queen-cell protector devised by West can also serve as an introducing cage, but J. B. Free and Y. Spencer-Booth[52] found that the use of cell protectors did not increase the percentage of mated, laying queens produced. They also found that queen cells given to colonies dequeened for 3 hours or less were the least successful, those in colonies dequeened 3 days or more being the most successful.

Commercial queen rearers use "baby nuclei" to reduce costs, but a standard shallow or deep hive box can be divided into three compartments each holding three frames. Tiny colonies are more economical of bees when rearing 30 000 to 50 000 queens in a season, but they require close attention and experience for success[69]. Queens in the smallest nuclei were found to take longer to mate, and only 70 % (60 % in USA[131]) were successful. With three times as much comb area, the rate of success increased to 92 %[45]. On the other hand, the stress of sudden interruption of a queen's egg laying may be less when she is taken for shipment from a small nucleus than when she is removed from a larger colony.

Increasingly, commercial beekeepers in the northern United States move a portion of their bees south by truck in the fall, and return the next spring bringing 4–6 nuclei produced from each colony. Such nuclei build up better than packages, and fewer queens are lost from nosema disease and other causes[32].

Cells can also be placed in "nursery" cages for the queens to emerge, before they are introduced as virgins to mating nuclei. This was once done on a commercial scale, and one Canadian and most European supply houses still sell such equipment. Introducing virgins is hazardous, but for research purposes it might be desirable to have queens available in an incubator for selection of particular characteristics[71]. Settman suggested a "queen-tube" for incubation in the colony (where conditions are optimal) as part of an elegantly simple system of queen rearing[144].

A. W. Woodrow found that water was the critical factor in survival of queens in cages outside the colony, whether attendant bees were present or not. Survival is best at 25–30°C and 45–70% humidity[173,114]. The method of storing queens each under a plastic cup on the outside of a screen cage, with bees inside, has the attributes of simplicity, easy management, and demonstrated success[44]. M. Reid investigated the role of diet in determining length of life[128].

Hives for queen rearing

Special hives for queen rearing are not common. The most elaborate may be Beyleveld's double-compartment revolving hive[18]. J. F. Diemer used a double hive with three compartments, as did J. W. Bain[39,12]. Bain's hive also contained small frames for mating nuclei; it was described in bee journals between 1934 and 1949, but was never produced commercially[13]. Schmitz designed a hive with a compartment for rearing queens or housing a nucleus[140]. The long hive body of Goodacre extended behind the hive to provide a separate section for queen rearing[54]. E. R. Harp[58a] has reported the techniques developed by C. L. Farrar, using normal strong colonies in which the queen was confined in a two-frame compartment of queen-excluder zinc. Twice a week the two combs are removed to a brood-rearing colony (and left there until they are capped), and replaced in the compartment by empty combs.

A special bottom board with space for two hives can be used to switch flying bees from one hive to another; such a device was used by J. E. Hand and modified by L. H. Johnson[58,73]. Alternatively, shifting of bees can be done vertically by the use of a modified bee escape board (inner cover, crown board), for instance that designed by Snelgrove or Morris[151,27]. A combination hive-cover and nucleus-box can be used for feeding and queen rearing[38].

Swarthmore's box for holding shell cups for queen cells above the brood frames was the forerunner of Perret-Maisonneuve's *hausette d'élevage* and Stanley's Perspex cover for queen rearing[123,121,155]. The Eriksson model (*drottningodlingslåda*) is available in Sweden[22].

Swarthmore and Keyes attached small boxes (or larger ones to hold a frame) to the sides of the hive for producing queen cells[123,78]. Settman used a tinplate box in which to confine the old queen until the new queen was mated and laying[143]; a queen excluder covered a hole in the side, and one or two frames of emerging bees were placed with the queen. M. Ambrožič used a large cupboard with 60 compartments, each holding a six-frame nucleus and with passageways for uniting when laying queens were removed[29].

Most of the hives designed especially for queen rearing are concerned with providing small colonies (nuclei) in which the queen cells are placed to emerge and mate[35,71,82,110]. Partitions placed in hive bodies divide them into compartments of various sizes for regular or small frames[10]. If shallow hive boxes are used, there are more frames of brood (although not more brood) with which to make nuclei.

Critical factors in successful queen rearing

1. Schedules for queen rearing must arrange for the mating of queens to coincide with the availability of mature drones.
2. Optimal conditions prevail during the swarming season, or in the early part of a honey flow.

3. Bees must be fed if there is no nectar flow.

4. Colonies must have ample stores of honey and pollen.

5. Colonies should have an abundance of young bees.

6. Simple methods should be used while the operator learns more demanding techniques such as transplantation.

7. Methods which do not require the beekeeper to find the queen or eggs may be as successful as those which do.

------ ------------------

References

Reference numbers such as 332L/65, 473/66 indicate entries in *Apicultural Abstracts*. The list below does not include references cited complete in the text. References for names quoted in the text but not found in alphabetical sequence below should be sought under the reference number appearing next after the name in the text.

1. Anonymous (1931) Requeening. *Am. Bee J.* 71(8) : 373

2. A. (1965) Ett Samhälle har utbyggt 28 vaxkakor. *Bitidningen* 64(12) : 387

3. [ABUSHÂDY, A. Z.] (1920–1921) Late queen introduction. *Bee Wld* 2(5–11) : 57

4. AIKIN, R. C. (1898) Age of queen-cell larvae. *Glean. Bee Cult.* 26(24) : 921–923

5. ALBER, M. A. (1965) A study of queen-rearing methods. *Bee Wld* 46(1) : 25–31   [332L/65

6. ALEXANDER, E. W. (1905) How shall we make our increase? *Glean. Bee Cult.* 33 : 425–427, 606

7. ALFONSUS, E. C. (1931) The life of Anton Jansha. *Am. Bee J.* 71(11) : 508–509

8. ALLEN, M. D. (1965) The production of queen cups and queen cells in relation to the general development of honeybee colonies, and its connection with swarming and supersedure. *J. apic. Res.* 4(3) : 121–141   [473/66

9. ALSOBROOK, R. (1931) How to get a colony to rear good queens. *Am. Bee J.* 71(8) : 371

10. ANDERSON, E. J. (1955) A two-queen system in one hive body. *Am. Bee J.* 95(8) : 310–312

11. ATWATER, E. F. (1907) Queen-rearing. *Glean. Bee Cult.* 35(8) : 560–561

12. BAIN, J. W. (1937) Producing queens and honey. *Glean. Bee Cult.* 65(5) : 276–278

13. ———— (1949) Queen rearing. *Am. Bee J.* 89 : 338–339, 386–387

13a. BANSBACH, H. (1953) Imker-ABC. . . *Lahr (Baden): Moritz Schauenburg*

14. BARBEAU, E. (1919) The Barbeau system of queen rearing. *Am. Bee J.* 59 : 234–235, 308–309; *Bee Wld* 1(7) : 150

15. BELJAVSKY, A. G. (1933) On the history of artificial queen-rearing. *Bee Wld* 14(9) : 99–100

16. BENTLEY, R. (1960) Increase with queen rearing. *Am. Bee J.* 100(5) : 190–191

17. BETTS, A. D. (1924) Die Königin [The queen] by Wilhelm Wankler. *Bee Wld* 5(12) : 192

18. BEYLEVELD, G. P. (1934) An ingenious queen rearing method. *Glean. Bee Cult.* 62(8) : 467–471

19. BILASH, G. D. (1962) [Conditions of queen rearing and the inheritance of characters in bees.] *Pchelovodstvo* 39(4) : 9–11 *In Russian*   [326/64

20. ———— (1963) [Methods of queen rearing and the quality of queens produced.] *Pchelovodstvo* 40(6) : 8–12 *In Russian*   [160/65

21. ———— (1964) [Queen rearing methods.] *Trud. nauch.-issled. Inst. Pchelovodstva:* 24–42 *In Russian* [793/65

22. BIREDSKAPSFABRIKEN (1970) Catalogue No. 29 *Töreboda, Sweden.*

23. BOGNOCZKY, J. (1967) Queen rearing in plastic cells. *XXI Int. Beekeep. Congr. Paper* 116 : 346–348

24. BÖTTCHER, F. K. & WEISS, K. (1962) Zur Frage der Darbietung des Zuchtstoffes im Pflegevolk in Form von Maden. *Z. Bienenforsch.* 6(1) : 1–8 [351/63

25. BRAY, W. B. (1919) Modified Pratt system. *Glean. Bee Cult.* 47(8) : 494–496

26. BROWN, J. G. (1915) The Alexander method of increase. *Glean. Bee Cult.* 43(1) : 27–28

27. BROWNRIDGE, T. S. M. (1953) The Morris board way of rearing queens. *Br. Bee J.* 81 : 148, 165–166, 178, 194

28. BUCKISCH, W. (1861) Bee-culture. *Report of the commissioner of patents for the year 1860 Agriculture. Washington, D.C.* (p. 268–301)

29. BUKOVEC, A. (1953) Na obisku pri Mihaelu Ambrozicu. *Slov. Ceb.* 55(12) : 332–335 [150/55

30. BURMISTROVA, N. D. (1960) [The influence of the size and form of queen cups on queen quality.] *Pchelovodstvo* 37(6) : 22–24 *In Russian* [795/63

31. BUTLER, C. G. (1962) Bee Department. *Rep. Rothamsted exp. Stn for 1961* : 157–161

32. CARLILE, B. (1970) Timely chats about beekeeping. *Am. Bee J.* 110(9) : 358

33. CARY, W. T. (1915) Keep the queens apart. *Glean Bee Cult.* 43(18) : 770

34. CHAMBERS, J. E. (1906, 1909) Chambers' cell starting device. *Glean. Bee Cult.* 34(5) : 293–295, 1059–1060; 37(6) : 178

34a. COOK, V. A. (1963) Using a bee colony for queen cell raising without impairing honey production potential. *N.Z. Jl Agric.* 107(4) : 334–335, 340 [363/64

35. CORKINS, C. L. (1931, 1932) Rauchfuss system of queen rearing. *Am. Bee J.* 71 : 460–461, 471; 512–513; 550–552; 72(1) : 17, 37–39

36. ———— (1932) Queen-rearing for the commercial beekeeper. *Am. Bee J.* 72(1) : 17, 37–39

37. CRAWFORD, R. M. (1949) Queen rearing outfit. *Southern Beekeeper* 3(2) : 14

38. CROW, E. M. (1915) A new wrinkle in hive-covers. *Glean. Bee Cult.* 43(22) : 933

39. DALTON, J. (1931) Triple cell building hives. *Am. Bee J.* 71(7) : 335

40. DEMAREE, G. W. (1892) How to prevent swarming. *Am. Bee J.* 29(17) : 545–546

41. DOOLITTLE, G. M. (1882) How I rear my queens. *Am. Bee J.* 18(29) : 454–455

42. ———— (1889) Several criticisms answered on rearing queens. *Am. Bee J.* 25(51) : 812–813

43. ———— (1899) Mr. G. M. Doolittle's queen-rearing methods. *Am. Bee J.* 39(28) : 435–436

44. EDWARDS, J. F. & POOLE, H. K. (1971) A simplified method for storing honey-bee queens. *Am. Bee J.* 111(7) : 270

45. EICKMEYER, K.-A. (1958) Erfahrungen mit verschiedenen Begattungskästchen. *Nordwestdtsch. Imkerztg* 10(9) : 133–136 [122/60

46. ENGLERT, E. (1967) Zur Paarungsbiologie der Drohnen. *Allg. dt. Imkerztg* 1(4) : 113–117 [345/68

47. ERSHOV, N. M. (1969) [Methods of rearing honeybee queens artificially.] *Trudy vost.-kazakh. gos. sel'. khoz. opyt. Sta.* 2 : 268–277 *In Russian* [439/72

47a. EVANS, E. (1953) Queen rearing. The Badgerdell system. *Br. Bee J.* 81 : 72–73

48. FLOWERS, W. E. (1889) Raising cells above a queen-excluding honey-board; who has the priority of the idea now? *Glean. Bee Cult.* 17(18) : 743–744

49. FOOSHE, J. D. (1900) Queen cells from drone comb; why it is prefered; dispensing with royal jelly. *Glean. Bee Cult.* 28(18) : 733–734

50. FRADENBURG, A. A. (1883) How to get queen-cells, with the old queen in the hive. *Glean. Bee Cult.* 11(1) : 12–13

51. ——— (1889) Raising queens above queen-excluding honey-boards, again. *Glean. Bee Cult.* 17(18) : 742

52. FREE, J. B. & SPENCER-BOOTH, Y. (1961) Analysis of honey farmers' records on queen rearing and queen introduction. *J. agric. Sci.* 56 : 325–331 [614/63

53. GONTARSKI, H. (1952) Zuchtmethoden in Anpassung an die biologischen Vorgänge bei der Entstehung der Königin. *Dtsch. Bienenw.* 3(3) : 41–44
[157/52

54. GOODACRE, W. A. (1920) A combined productive and queen-raising hive. *Agric. Gaz. N.S.W.* 31 : 666–668

55. GRAY, J. (1916) Timely hints on queen-raising. *Glean. Bee Cult.* 44(14) : 601–603

56. GRIMMOND, D. (1952) The story of 92 queen cells. *Scott. Beekpr* 28(10) : 205 only   [217/53

57. HAINES, G. W. (1904) A tilting cell-bar. *Glean. Bee Cult.* 32(9) : 446

58. HAND, J. E. (1911) Bee-keeping by twentieth century methods. *Medina, Ohio: A.I. Root Co.*

58a. HARP, E. R. (1973) A specialized system for multiple rearing of quality honeybee queens. *Am. Bee J.* 113(7) : 256–258, 261

59. HEJTMÁNEK, J. (1956) Štúdie metódy chov včelich matiek z vajičok. *Pol'- nohospodárstvo* 3(4) : 520–535   [147/66

59a. HOOPINGARNER, R. & FARRAR, C. L. (1959) Genetic control of size in queen honey bees. *J. econ. Ent.* 52(4) : 547–548   [226/60

60. HOPKINS, I. (1919) Horizontal-comb method of queen rearing. *Bee Wld* 1(7) : 143–144

61. ILLINGWORTH, L. (1941–1943) Some hints on queen rearing. *Bee Wld* 22(1) : 3–5; (2) : 9–11; 23(11) : 86; 24(3) : 20

62. INOUE, A. (1962) Preliminary report on rearing of Japanese honeybee queens in colonies of the European honeybee. *Bee Science, Nagoya* 3(1) : 10 only; see also Tokuda (159a)

63. VII INTERNATIONAL BEEKEEPING CONGRESS, QUEBEC (1925) VII International Apicultural Congress. *VII Int. Beekeep. Congr.* : 500 pages

64. IVANOVA, A. S. (1962) [Queen rearing in queenright colonies.] *Pchelovodstvo* 39(5) : 17–19 *In Russian*

65. JAY (1907) Pointers from the rear end of the bee told by the Jay. *Glean. Bee Cult.* 35(8) : 547

66. JAY, S. C. (1964) Rearing honeybee brood outside the hive. *J. apic. Res.* 3(1) : 51–60   [874/64

67. JEAN-PROST, P. (1956) Quelques points de la biologie des abeilles en Provence. *Rev. franc. Apic.* 3(120) : 1558–1561   [344/57

68. ———(1958) Le séquestration naturelle des jeunes reines d'abeilles. *C.R. Acad. Sci., Paris* 247 : 2042–2044   [260/62

69. JOHANSSON, T. S. K. & JOHANSSON, M. P. (1970) Establishing and using nuclei. *Bee Wld* 51(1) : 23–35

70. ——— (1971) No-sweat queen rearing. *Glean. Bee Cult.* 99(7) : 250

71. ——— (1971) Queen introduction. *Am. Bee J.* 111 : 98–99, 146, 183–185, 226–227, 264–265, 306–307, 348–349, 384, 387

72. JOHNSON, A. P. (1939) Requeening. *Am. Bee J.* 79(3) : 133

73. JOHNSON, L. H. (1951) Improved methods of queen rearing. *N.Z. Jl Agric.* 82(2) : 140–142   [41/53

74. JONES, H. L. (1899) Queen-rearing. *Am. Bee J.* 39(47) : 747 [from Australasian Bee Kpr]

74a. JORDAN, R. [1953] Zwei Königinnen-Zuchtmethoden in Wort und Bild.

75. ———— (1960) Die Zucht Königin, ausgehend vom Ei. *Bienenvater* 81(1) : 3–7, 44   [113/62

76. ————(1961) Zuchthygienische Massnahmen zur Verhütung der Nosemaverbreitung durch Königinnen. *Bienenvater* 82(12) : 331–334   [610L/63

77. KASHKOVSKII, V. G. (1960) [The best method of requeening in the apiary.] *Kemerovo : Kemerovo Book Publishing House In Russian*   [849/63

78. KEYES, D. R. (1903, 1904) Rearing queens in full colonies. *Glean. Bee Cult.* 31(12) : 536–537; 32(1) : 75

79. KOTELKOV, N. Z. & BLASHKIN, V. I. (1957) [Experiment on rearing worker bees and queens in enlarged cells.] *Pchelovodstvo* 34(2) : 33–36 *In Russian*   [269/59

80. KURENNOI, N. M. (1953) [When are drones sexually mature?] *Pchelovodstvo* (11) : 28–32 *In Russian*   [89/54

81. KUWABARA, M. (1947) Ueber die Regulation im weisellosen Volke der Honigbiene, besonders die Bestimmung des neuen Weisels. *J. Fac. Sci. Hokkaido Univ. Ser.* 6, 9(4) : 359–381   [212/52

82. LAERE, O. VAN & BRANDE, J. VAN DEN (1958) Une méthode pour l'élevage de reines en grande nombre. *XVII Int. Beekeep. Congr.* p. 290–293 [422/58

83. LAIDLAW, H. H. Jr. & ECKERT, J. E. (1950) Queen rearing. *Hamilton, Ill.: Dadant & Sons, Inc.*   [50/51

84. LANGSTROTH, L. L. (1853) Langstroth on the hive and the honey-bee, a beekeeper's manual. *Northampton: Hopkins, Bridgman & Co.*

85. ———— (1872) Are artificial queens inferior to natural queens? *Am. Bee J.* 7(12) : 267–268

86. LATHAM, A. (1916) Easy queen-rearing. *Glean. Bee Cult.* 44(14) : 593–594

87. LAWING, S. S. (1920) Old letter by Demaree. *Glean. Bee Cult.* 48(6) : 340–341

88. LENSKY, Y. (1971) Rearing queen honeybee larvae in queenright colonies. *J. apic. Res.* 10(2) : 99–101   [157/72

89. LENSKY, J. & DARCHEN, R. (1962) Quelques observations sur la construction des cellules royales en présence de plusieurs reines d'abeilles. *C.R. Acad. Sci., Paris* 255 : 1778–1780   [117/65

90. LEVICHEVA, A. I. (1961) [Characteristics of queens reared artificially and under the swarming and emergency impulses.] *Dokl. TSKhA* 62 : 547–552 *In Russian*   [159/65

91. ———— (1964) [The size of queen cells and the quality of the queens.] *Pchelovodstvo* 41(6) : 28–29 *In Russian*   [81/66

92. LÖFFLER, A. (1961, 1963) Beeinträchtigen imkerliche Störungen und Entweiselung des Bienenvolkes die Sammeltätigkeit? *Z. Bienenforsch.* 5(5) : 131–144; 6(5) : 117–134   [256/62; 780/63

93. LUKOSCHUS, F. (1955) Stoffwechselvorgänge während der Entwicklung von Königin und Arbeiterin und ihre mögliche Bedeutung für die künstliche Aufzucht von Königinnen. *Z. Bienenforsch.* 3(2) : 40–45   [115/57

94. ————(1956) Stoffwechselstimulierende Hormone als Ursache des Verhaltens der Honigbiene bei der Aufzucht von Geschlechtstieren. *Insectes sociaux* 3(1) : 185–193   [82/58

95. MARTINEZ LOPEZ, J. F. (1955) Plastic cell cups for queen rearing and the production of royal jelly. *Bee Wld* 36(9) : 163–164

96. McKINLEY, W. (1963) Grafting—how it is done. *Glean. Bee Cult.* 91(7) : 404–409, 443

97. MARSHENKULOV, Z. M. (1964) [Problems concerning the possibility of rearing honeybee queens in colonies with queens, and the so-called "queen substance".] *Uchen. Zap. kabardino-balkars. gos. Univ.* (20) : 161–165 *In Russian* [767/69

98. MÂRZA, E. (1965) Calitatea mătcilor obţinute prin folosirea diferitelor metode de pregătire a materialului biologic. *Lucr. ştiinţ. Staţ. cent. Seri. Apic.* 6 : 15–21 [623/70

99. MEHRING, F. (1901) *Glean. Bee Cult.* 29(12) : 502 [Dorf-Zeitung 1866]

100. MILLER, C. C. (1901) Do queenless bees prefer too old larvae for queen-rearing? *Am. Bee J.* 41(50) : 798–799

101. ———— (1907) Stray straws. *Glean. Bee Cult.* 35(8) : 535

102. ———— (1911) Fifty years among the bees. *Medina, Ohio: A.I. Root Co.*

103. ———— (1914) Failure in rearing queens in upper stories. *Glean. Bee Cult.* 42(19) : 775; 43(3) : 95

104. MILLER, E. S. (1932) Mating queen from a top story. *Am. Bee J.* 72(10) : 403

105. ————(1939) A handy way to rear queens. *Glean. Bee Cult.* 67(8) : 496

105a. MITCHELL, K. E. (1948) in "Annual convention of the Ontario Beekeepers' Association" by H. H. Root. *Glean. Bee Cult.* 76(12) : 778–779, 786

106. MOE, M. W. (1910) A substitute for grafting cells. *Glean. Bee Cult.* 38(23) : 765–766

107. MONTAGNER, H. (1962) Influence de la technique de double greffage sur le développement des reines de *Apis mellifica*. *Insectes sociaux* 9(1) : 91–99 [612/63

108. MORSE, R. A. (1965) The effect of light on comb construction by honeybees. *J. apic. Res.* 4(1) : 23–29 [112/66

109. MORSE, R. A. & McDONALD, J. L. (1965) The treatment of capped queen cells by honeybees. *J. apic. Res.* 4(1) : 31–34 [110/66

110. MÜLLER, O. (1952) Dronningavl under nordiske forhold. *Nord. Bitidskr.* 4 : 65–71; 117–122 [see also A.A. 296/56] [53/55

111. NOLAN, W. J. (1924) Localization of queen-rearing. *Glean. Bee Cult.* 52(12) : 760–765

112. OBED. (1861) Raising queens. *Am. Bee J.* 1(6) : 143

113. OBSERVER (1931) A simple method of mating queens. *Am. Bee J.* 71(7) : 324

114. ÖRÖSI-PÁL, Z. (1952) Kísérletek az anyanevelés köréböl [I]. *Allattenyészt. Kutatóintéz. Évk.* 1950 : 203–226 [326/65

115. ———— (1956) Kis méhészkönyv. *Budapest: Mezógazdasági kiadó* [154/57

116. ———— (1959) A petés anyanevelés eredménye 1959-ben. *Méhészet* 7(11) : 205–207 [878/64

117. ———— (1960) A pete kora anyaneveléskor. *Méhészet* 8(9) : 163–165 [879/64

118. ———— (1960) Kísérletek az anyanevelés köréböl II. *Kisérletügyi Közlemények* (1) : 31–79 [327/65

119. PENNA, E. (1922) Some items in queen-rearing. I. *Bee Wld* 3(11) : 271–273

120. PERRET-MAISONNEUVE, A. (1924) Practical queen-rearing. *Bee Wld* 6(1) : 1–2

121. ———— (1933) L'apiculture intensive et l'élevage des reines. *Paris: Presses Universitaires de France*

122. PHILLIPS, G. W. (1903-1948) Queen rearing. *Glean. Bee Cult.* 31(24) : 1048–1050; 32(1) : 19–20, (2) : 79–81 [correction p. 120], (3) : 133–134, (18) : 890; 75(8) : 454–455; 76 : 273–276, 350–352, 426–427, 492–495; 77(9) : 548–551

123. [PRATT, E. L.] (1901) The Swarthmore system of queen-rearing. *Glean. Bee Cult.* 29(14) : 434–437, 504–507, 588–591, 634–635

124. PRATT, E. L. (1906) Forcing the breeding queen to lay eggs in artificial queen-cups. *Sixth in a series of papers on apiculture by Swarthmore*

125. Pridgen, W. H. (1900, 1902) Commercial queen-rearing in all of its details. *Am. Bee J.* 40(26) : 401–405; *Glean. Bee Cult.* 28(18) : 719–722; 30(13) : 564–566

126. [Pritchard, M.] (1938) Rearing a few queens. *Glean. Bee Cult.* 66(1) : 47

127. Rauchfuss, F. G. (1921) Swarm control. *Glean. Bee Cult.* 49(5) : 266–267, 275

128. Reid, M. (1972) Relation of diet and age to the physiology of longevity in caged honeybees (*Apis mellifera* L.). *Univ. Guelph: M.S. Thesis*

129. Roberts, D. (1958) Simplified queen bee rearing. *N.Z. Jl Agric.* 96 : 319, 321, 323–324, 486–487, 489

130. Roberts, W. C. (1965) Save-a-step queen rearing. *Am. Bee J.* 105(12) : 446–447   [518/66

131. Roberts, W. C. & Stanger, W. (1969) Survey of the package bee and queen industry. *Am. Bee J.* 109(1) : 8–11   [172/71

132. Root, E. R. (1899) Editorial. *Glean. Bee Cult.* 27(11) : 437

133. ———— (1900) Editorial. *Glean. Bee Cult.* 28(17) : 694–695; see also (11) : 430

134. Root, H. H. (1909) Alexander's writings on practical bee culture. *Medina: A.I. Root Company*

135. Rosser, J. H. (1934) Queen rearing. *Bee Wld* 15(10) : 111–112

136. Sauer, F. (1950) Königinnenzucht im weiselrichtigen Volk. *Imkerfreund* 5(3) : 37–38   [106/50

137. Savvin, J. (1956) Přirozený a "umělý" chov matek. *Včelařství* 9 : 22–23, 42–43   [294/57

140. Schmitz, W. (1962) Das Umschaltverfahren: ein neuer Weg in der Bienenzucht. *Wuppertal: published by the author*   [573/65

141. Scholl, L. (1908) When to requeen. *Glean. Bee Cult.* 36(7) : 629

142. Sechrist, E. L. (1947) Now I have seen it. *Glean. Bee Cult.* 75(5) : 268–271

143. Settman, T. (1936) Requeening, swarm control. *Glean. Bee Cult.* 64(2) : 93

144. ———— (1940) Simple queen rearing on a small scale. *Bee Wld* 21(2) : 15–16

145. Shcherbina, P. C. (1950) [How to make a queen-rearing colony.] *Pchelovodstvo* (3) : 175–176 *In Russian*   [129/51

146. Shiniaeva, V. A. (1953) [New data on queen rearing.] *Pchelovodstvo* (5) : 22–28 *In Russian*   [53/54

147. Simpson, J. (1960) Induction of queen rearing in honeybee colonies by amputation of their queens' front legs. *Bee Wld* 41(11/12) : 286–287 [448/62

147a. Simpson, J. & Riedel, I. B. M. (1963) The factor that causes swarming by honeybee colonies in small hives. *J. apic. Res.* 2(1) : 50–54

148. Sladen, F. W. L. (1913) Queen-rearing in England. *London: Madgwick, Houlston & Co.*

149. Smith, J. (1933) Rearing your own queens. *Am. Bee J.* 73(3) : 93–94

150. ————[1942] Supplement to "Queen rearing simplified". [typescript copy]

151. Snelgrove, L. E. (1949) Queen rearing. *Bleadon: I. Snelgrove*

152. Soczek, S. (1965) Wpływ niektórych metod sychowu matek pszczelich na liczbe ich rurek jajnikowych. *Pszczel. Zesz. nauk.* 9(1/2) : 63–76 [445/66

153. Southwick, A. M. (1942) Supercharger queens. *Glean. Bee Cult.* 70(5) : 270–271, 313

154. Stachelhausen, L. (1901) [Queen-rearing.] *Am. Bee J.* 41(20) ; 307

155. Stanley, P. W. (1949) The Stanley system of queen rearing. *Wilts. Beekprs' Gaz.* See also 47a.

156. Stricker, M. H. (1952) Improving stock. *Glean. Bee Cult.* 80(2) : 73–75, 119

157. Swahn, A. (1914) The Alexander method of increase. *Glean. Bee Cult.* 42(24) : 979–981

158. TABER, S. III (1961)   Forceps design for transferring honeybee eggs.   *J. econ. Ent.* 54(2) : 247–250   [231/62

159. TONTZ, C. (1947)   Early spring increase pays off.   *Glean. Bee Cult.* 75(2) : 65–67

159a. TOKUDA, Y. (1924)   Studies on the honeybee, with special reference to the Japanese honeybee.   *Bull. Imp. Zoo. exp. Stn Chiba Japan* 1(1) : 1–27

160. VOLOSEVICH, A. P. (1954)   [An evaluation of queen-rearing methods.]   *Pchelovodstvo* (8) : 28–31   *In Russian*   [55/55

161. [WAGNER, S.] (1861)   *Am. Bee J.* 1(6) : 136

162. ——— (1871)   Editorial.   *Am. Bee J.* 7(1) : 21–22

163. WEDMORE, E. B. (1952)   Researches on methods of management of bees. *London: Bee Research Association*   [37/53

164. WEISS, K. (1960)   Über die Lebensfähigkeit von Bieneneiern ausserhalb des Volkes.   *Z. Bienenforsch.* 5(2) : 42–48   [223/61

165. ——— (1962)   Versuche zur Methodik der Königinnenzucht aus dem Ei. *Z. Bienenforsch.* 6(2) : 37–47   [611/63

166. ——— (1962)   Vom "Eistück".   *Imkerfreund* 17(1) : 6–8   [613/63

167. ——— (1962)   Über die Lebensfähigkeit von offener und gedeckelter Brut ausserhalb des Bienenvolkes.   *Z. Bienenforsch.* 6(4) : 104–114   [608/63

168. ——— (1964)   Alte und neue Erfahrungen in der Zucht aus dem Ei.   *Imkerfreund* 19(5) : 154–159   [334L/65

169. ——— (1967) Über den Einfluss verschiedenartiger Weiselwiegen auf die Annahme und das Königinnengewicht in der künstlichen Nachschaffungszucht. *Z. Bienenforsch.* 9(3) : 121–134   [972/70

170. ——— (1967)   Einfluss der Darbietung auf die Annahme des Zuchtstoffs. *Imkerfreund* 22(5) : 144–148   [697/71

171. ——— (1967)   Müssen künstliche Weiselbecher aus Jungfernwachs geformt sein und ist die Eingewöhnung der Weiselwiegen ins Pflegevolk von Nutzen?   *Imkerfreund* 22(6) : 177–179   [324/69

172. ——— (1971)   Über Ausbildung und Leistung von Königinnen aus Eiern und jungen Arbeitermaden.   *Apidologie* 2(1) : 3–47   [746/72

172a. WINTER, T. S. (1948)   Beekeeping in New Zealand.   *Wellington: Dep. Agriculture* pp. 69–70

173. WOODROW, A. W. (1941)   Some effects of temperature, relative humidity, confinement, and type of food on queen bees in mailing cages.   *Washington: U.S. Dep. Agric.*

174. WOODS, E. F. (1959)   Electronic prediction of swarming in bees.   *Nature, Lond.* 184 : 842–844   [366/61

175. WORTHINGTON, J. C. (1871)   Primitive movable comb system.   *Am. Bee J.* 7(6) : 2 beyond 144

176. WOYKE, J. (1971)   Correlations between the age at which honeybee brood was grafted, characteristics of the resultant queens, and results of insemination. *J. apic. Res.* 10(1) : 45–55

177. ZECHA, H. (1961)   Die Zucht von Königinnen, insbesondere mit Hilfe der "Federleiste".   *Bienenvater* 81 : 109–111

178. ZHDANOVA, T. S. (1969)   [Optimal conditions for artificial queen rearing.] *Trudy tatar. respub. gos. sel'.-khoz. opyt. Sta.* (2) : 476–484   *In Russian* [698/72

CHAPTER 6

FEEDING SUGAR TO BEES

I. FEEDERS AND SYRUP FEEDING

Introduction

Feeding may have been one of the first manipulations of bees, as evidenced by directions for feeding found in the earliest writings (226/58).*   Bees do not need to be fed regularly as other livestock does, but there are occasions when supplementary or emergency feeding is required:

1.   A late spring or bad weather which prevents foraging during a nectar flow.
2.   Periods of dearth in the active season, or a generally poor season.
3.   Newly established natural swarms, divisions, nuclei, or package bees which need food for making comb and rearing brood.
4.   Manipulations such as inspecting bees, uniting, queen rearing.
5.   Insufficient winter stores in years when the bees cannot obtain enough nectar to provide enough honey stores for themselves.
6.   Colonies used for pollination on a crop that does not provide much nectar and/or pollen (alfalfa), or if the weather reduces the opportunity for flights.
7.   A price differential between sugar and honey which makes it profitable to remove most or all of the honey, and replace it with sugar.
8.   Stimulation of brood rearing in order to increase the population in anticipation of spring pollination (e.g. almonds in California), or of a nectar flow, or making divisions, or shaking packages in the spring.
9.   A counterbalance for pesticide damage.

General principles

1.   At best, feeding should be considered a necessary evil that is to be avoided whenever possible.   It is messy and expensive, and the inexperienced beekeeper is liable to initiate robbing.   When combs of sealed honey are not available, the best food is sugar syrup made from beet or cane sugar.
2.   Precautions against robbing by the fed colony, as well as by the unfed neighbouring colonies, must be carefully observed at all times:

(*a*) Feeding changes the guard behaviour of the fed colony, permitting unchallenged entry by robbers.

(*b*) Feeders must prevent bees from outside the hive getting to the feed.

(*c*) When the colony is fed a small quantity of syrup during the day, the bees take it all in a short period. They then search for more food and will "pry" into everything, including weak colonies and nuclei.

(*d*) A slow feeder that makes a small quantity of syrup last 24 hours, until the next feed, may prevent the problem in (*c*).

(*e*) Feeding at dusk, using a rapid feeder, enables the colony to clean up all the syrup in a short time, especially in warm or tropical climates.

(*f*) The odour of warm syrup is attractive to robber bees.

3. No matter what time of year bees are fed, the closer the feed is placed to the cluster in the hive, the better. Bees should be able to reach the food on cold days without breaking cluster. Young nurse bees do not leave the brood nest to feed on pollen supplements. A 1:1 syrup* fed daily at 17 h (5 p.m.) was taken by only a few bees 1-11 days old, but by 36 bees 12-21 days old and 56 bees 22-40 days old (118/64).

4. It is probably best to give, at a single feeding, all the food it is intended to provide.

5. A colony that needs feeding is often weak, and care should be taken to avoid chilling the brood. Avoid leaving openings through which warm air from the cluster can escape, or through which robbers can gain entrance.

6. Rather than feeding weak colonies, it is better to unite them until you have strong colonies.

7. Feed sugar syrup for winter stores as soon as it is obvious that this will need to be done. The bees will have time to "ripen" (invert) the sugar syrup and avoid the risk of fermentation, possibly followed by dysentery. It is better to feed early than too late.

8. While nectar is unavailable, bees will take any quantity of syrup, storing it as they do nectar, and eventually swarming—even if there is not sufficient nectar from natural sources to maintain the colony. If comb space is limited, there may not be enough empty cells left for the eggs, and the colony will be short of brood and young bees.

9. Large colonies can be fed to produce combs of sealed syrup for smaller, less able colonies.

Feeders for sugar syrup

1. *Using the hive itself*

(*a*) Place a brick under the front of the hive to tilt it backwards, then pour warm syrup (16°C, 60°F) over the tops of the frames at the back of the hive. Care should be taken not to cause robbing by giving so much syrup that it will run out at the entrance, or out between the hive and the bottom board if the two are not tightly propolized together.

(*b*) The bottom board of the hive can be modified as a feeder by nailing a strip of wood (2 cm × 2 cm × width of the hive), 10-12 cm back from the entrance. The bees will seal up the cracks with propolis but, if it is necessary to use the feeder immediately, the trough must be rendered watertight by sealing up all the cracks with melted beeswax or paraffin.

---

*x: y syrup means x parts sugar to y parts water, both by weight.

The hive is tipped backwards while approximately 5kg (11lb) of syrup are poured in. Pieces of cork or wood as floats will prevent bees from drowning in the syrup. When it is necessary to refill the feeder, push the brood chamber forward a few centimetres, and pour the sugar syrup in at the rear. The brood chamber can be left in this position and the opening closed with a board, making it easier to refill.

(c) The Cary "feeder bottom board" had a permanent feeder built into the back. Since J. L. Eyrich's drawer-like feeder in 1768, removable versions have been used. Alexander's feeder is placed along the back of the bottom board, and the hive pushed backward to cover it, but its use may be troublesome on uneven ground.

(d) The best method of feeding starving (quivering) bees during cold weather is to fill 3 or 4 combs with warm, heavy sugar syrup (2:1), and place these in the hive on each side of and in direct contact with the bees (first removing empty combs to provide space).

1. The combs are filled from a 5-litre (gallon) can fitted with a sprinkler, or from a 2-5 kg honey pail whose bottom is perforated with nail holes. The combs are held at an angle of 10-20 to the horizontal, over a large pan or tub; syrup is poured into the open cells, beginning at the high end. When both sides are filled, a comb will carry about $1\frac{1}{2}$ kg of syrup.
2. A vacuum chamber has also been used to fill the combs with syrup (160/63).
3. When the weather does not permit removal of combs, syrup can be sprayed in between them (120/67).

(e) Plastic bags are available which fit over a frame (with or without a comb), the top of the bag being secured by a rubber band. The bees crawl down into the bag to feed.

2. C. C. Miller "overall" or overhead type of box-feeder

This is the preferred method of feeding large quantities of syrup.

(a) The first modification of the Miller feeder to fit flush with the outside of the hive may have been made by D. E. Lyon in 1905. Miller feeders have been made by fastening aluminum pans in a comb honey super—leaving a slot between them for the bees to get to the syrup.

(b) The hive should be set level to ensure that the feeder will hold the maximum quantity of syrup, and that all of it will be available to the bees.

(c) Bees come up through a tunnel or "bee-way" in the centre, above the cluster, to reach the top of the syrup. A cover of wire screening (wire gauze) or metal over the tunnel prevents the bees floating away and drowning.

(d) The feeder can be left on the hive all year round, and can hold chaff or other insulating material in winter; N. Visser's "Dutch feeder" also provides a top entrance.

(e) Bee supply houses in Canada and Europe carry various modifications of the Miller feeder. A Finnish version made of plastic has a transparent cover over the tunnel, and the cover has slots situated above the tunnel to vent the water vapour rising from the cluster in the brood chamber. This should prevent water condensing and collecting in the feeder.

(f) European catalogues list a variety of feeders made of metal or plastic, with a "bee-way" tunnel in the centre, to be placed over the bee-escape hole of an inner cover (crown board). Such a feeder can be made at home from a tubular cake tin with a central hollow cone to give the bees acces to the syrup. A wire screen cone inserted over the tube will prevent bees drowning in the syrup (*Bee World* 23: 36 (1942)).

3. *G. M. Doolittle's "dummy" hollow division-board feeder*

This is an "internal" feeder which fits in the space of one frame (or two when 5 cm wide). It is excellent for feeding smaller amounts of syrup (2-4 kg), which is easily accessible to the bees (*Bee World* 1: 54, 56 (1919)).

(*a*) When used as a feeder, it should be placed at one side of the brood chamber, next to the first frame of brood. If it is left in the hive all year, against one wall when not in use, the bees may build comb in it.

(*b*) Wooden floats, straw, or preferably a V-shaped piece of wire screen in the feeder will help to ensure that bees will not drown in the syrup.

(*c*) A normal hive frame (without foundation) can be modified to make a feeder by nailing thin wooden panels to the sides, leaving a space at the top for the bees to enter (*Am. Bee J*. 99(3): 100 (1959)).

(*d*) Doolittle feeders can be purchased assembled or in the flat ("knocked down"), or moulded in plastic. Walter Kelly recommends the use of plastic roofing cement rather than paraffin wax for making the joints of wooden feeders watertight.

4. *Atmospheric pressure feeders*

Devices similar to those used for watering chickens are popular with beekeepers. The partial vacuum inside the container prevents the syrup from running out. If these feeders are placed on a block or platform, with wire screening to keep the bees off the feeder itself, this can be refilled without bees getting in the way.

(*a*) A jar placed upside down on a saucer (or several for fast feeding) suffices where only a few hives are involved. Three or four tooth picks should be put between the jar and the saucer to ensure that, as the bees take up the syrup, air will enter the jar and more syrup will flow out into the saucer.

(*b*) Large screw-top jars with 2 or 3 holes (more for faster feeding) punched in the lid are easier to use than jars and saucers which have to be flipped over, with the risk of making a mess if the operation is unsuccessful.

(*c*) Friction-top cans, tins or pails, or plastic pails, holding 2-3 kg (5 lb), are commonly used by beekeepers for feeding; a much larger can is more likely to leak.

Several small holes (about 1 mm) are punched in the lid, held inner side up on a block of wood; the holes should be evenly spread out round the centre of the lid, within a circle say 6-7 cm in diameter. The can is completely filled with syrup and then inverted over the bee-escape hole in an inner cover; the recessed flange in the lid provides space for the bees to reach the holes. An empty bee-tight super or brood box is placed around the feeder to raise the hive cover (lid, roof) clear of it.

When the tin is inverted some syrup will drip from the holes, until the air pressure is sufficiently reduced at the top of the container. These drips should be caught in a bucket and not allowed to spill on the ground. The feeder should not be used if the syrup continues to run out; a faulty lid can allow the syrup to escape too rapidly, wasting it and starting the bees robbing.

The rate at which the syrup can be taken is regulated by the number of holes in the lid—2 or 3 for stimulative feeding, 20-40 for rapid supplementary feeding in the autumn. A pail with holes over the entire lid must be kept level, or the last of the syrup will leak out when air can enter the can through the highest hole.

Instead of using an inner cover, tins can be placed directly over the frames, on some sticks to provide space for the bees to reach the holes. Newspaper or cloth (burlap, sacking) placed over the frames and around the pails will prevent loss of heat.

(*d*) An improvement over holes in the can lid is a single hole punched through the bottom of a can from the outside inward, so the burr is on the inside. A flat-headed nail is fitted into the hole with the head resting on the burr. Syrup will not leak out with the lid pushed in tightly, and the can may be refilled without inverting it or disturbing the bees.

(*e*) Bee equipment suppliers in Europe stock various types of glass and plastic feeders based on the principle of atmospheric pressure. Bee-escape boards are available with options of openings for feeding. The British "Moreton quilt" has panels of glass and wood that can be interchanged or removed, to provide openings for feeding over the cluster wherever it may be situated.

(*f*) The Boardman entrance feeder incorporates a block that can be inserted into the hive entrance; the block holds an inverted canning (preserving) jar, whose lid has several small holes that allow syrup to escape only as fast as the bees will take it. The feeder has some disadvantages: in direct sunlight the expansion of the air inside the jar may cause some of the syrup to overflow; in cold weather the bees do not go to the entrance to get the syrup, and the syrup may freeze; when placed on small new colonies (packages), stronger established colonies are likely to start robbing.

The Boardman feeder may be used at the top of the hive by drilling through the bottom of the block and placing the feeder over the hole in the inner cover.

5. *External feeders*

Feeders can be hung on the back (or front) of the hive, against a hole in the hive wall through which the bees can enter. The ease of refilling may be overbalanced by the lack of heat from the colony to keep the syrup warm; this is equally true for the Boardman entrance feeder (741/72).

6. *Miscellaneous feeders*

(*a*) Open pans of syrup can be placed on top of the frames. Floats or a piece of cheese-cloth dampened with water will prevent bees drowning and can be easily cleaned with boiling water.

(*b*) A large tin, jar, crock or other vessel, without a lid, can be placed upright in an empty hive box on the bottom board. A handful of straw pushed into the vessel before the boxes of bees are replaced will provide foothold for the bees between the frames and the syrup in the vessel. But even with a contracted entrance, this method is suitable only for large colonies that can protect themselves from robbers.

(*c*) Litre or quart plastic bags filled two-thirds full of syrup and sealed with ties or preferably zip-locks can be placed above the frames. One large access hole (on the upper surface) is better than several small holes, which may close up (950L/71, 784/75).

7. *Feeders for observation hives and cages*

Many commercially available observation hives do not have provision for feeding the colony. A simple method for providing this is to drill a hole in the top of the hive to fit the cover of a bottle, jar or vial. Wire screening on the inside will prevent bees escaping when the container is removed for refilling. Two such jars were provided by E. F. Bigelow for his Educational Bee-hive (1905). He also incorporated a removable glass trough feeder, with a lens that could be passed around, so that students could watch the bees feeding. Von Frisch's book (289/69) is helpful.

L. J. Nickels (1911) incorporated a Miller type feeder on top of his observation hive. Bees had access to it through a well or tunnel in the centre. Where pipes or tunnels are used as passage ways for the bees, a side-arm or extension can be provided with a screened opening that supports the jar of syrup. At least one supplier (Steele & Brodie, Scotland) stocks a feeder for observation hives with a sliding entrance and bee escape.

Other appliances that may be suitable include feeders made of glass tubing, with a trough extending into the hive (much like the small animal drinking tubes available with or without 1-ml interval graduations), and drinking bottles used for small animals.

For cages containing a few bees, or even a single bee, the use of a suitably calibrated burette or pipette makes it possible to measure accurately the small volumes of liquid ingested without waste or loss of fluid by evaporation. Vials covered with cheese cloth or wire mesh, turned upside down and set on the cage, can also be used.

8. *Observation feeders*
G. Mosolevsky suggested installing a feeder outside a window for experimental study or amusement (*Bee World* 13(6): 62-64 (1932)). The muslin he used required periodic adjustment. The perforated zinc plate used by W. C. Cotton (1842) in his observation feeder might be more practical. Bees have been found to prefer open dishes to "artificial flowers" made of plastic. Burning old honey comb at the feeder site and adding oil of anise to the syrup have been suggested as means of attracting bees to the feeder. Feeding can be recorded mechanically (49/61).

Filling feeders
For large-scale operations, a tank-trailer with a 50-metre hose, and a pump powered with a gasoline motor or a power take-off on the truck transmission, can be used to fill feeders. For smaller outfits, a tank on a truck bed, 250-litre steel drum with a faucet, or 25-kg cans can be used.
1. Avoid spilling honey or syrup, since this may start the bees robbing.
2. Feed at dusk, when few bees will be flying, or when the weather prevents the bees from flying.
3. Warm the syrup to at least 15 C (60 F), but do not feed it hot.

Outdoor (open air) feeding
After repeated admonitions to avoid exposing sweet materials in the open during the robbing season, it may appear contradictory that in some circumstances it is advisable to feed the entire apiary from exposed feeders. In Europe, some apiaries are routinely fed in outdoor feeders.

1. *Special circumstances*
  (a) A large number of colonies can be fed with a minimum of labour when bees are able to fly.
  (b) Individual hives do not have to be opened.
  (c) When robbers interfere with necessary manipulations of the colonies, sweetened water in outdoor feeders diverts the robbers by creating an artificial flow. As when bees are busy in the field during a natural nectar flow, hives can then be opened without robbing.
  (d) Outdoor feeders can be used to "call bees off" when they are robbing outdoor facilities such as candy and fruit stands.

(*e*)   If a whole apiary is on the verge of starvation, outside feeding can be used to tide the bees over until an expected nectar flow starts, or until feeders can be installed in the hives and filled.

(*f*)   It has been suggested that outdoor feeding after the final flow of the season is a hygienic measure, which keeps the bees flying and reduces the likelihood of diseases such as nosema.

2.   *Methods of open air feeding*

(*a*)   Troughs, tubs or pans with a large surface must be used, so that the bees are not crowded.   A roof or cover prevents dilution of the syrup by rain or heavy dew.

(*b*)   Provision of only as much syrup as will be used up by the bees in one day will avoid the likelihood of spoilage during warm weather.

(*c*)   Floats of sticks, straw, corks, etc should be used to prevent the bees drowning.

(*d*)   The strongest colonies will get the largest share; if necessary this can be corrected by taking filled combs from strong (disease-free) colonies and giving them to the weakest ones.

(*e*)   A dilute solution of sugar in water (1: 3 by weight) is not very attractive to colonies already having large stores, and likely to be safe.   The syrup usually fed in feeders on a hive (2: 1) will create an uproar in the apiary.

II. WHEN AND HOW TO FEED

Supplementary feeding

1. If colonies are short of honey stores, the deficiency can be provided in the form of sugar syrup. J. L. Eyrich may have been the first (1768) to advocate feeding the then expensive cane sugar rather than mixtures of fruit juices, honey, beer, etc., that had been in use earlier.

2. The best time to feed is as soon as it is known that colonies will need feeding for winter (August-October).

   (a) In the autumn it is a seasonal task to make certain that all hives have enough honey for winter, preferably by weighing. The beekeeper who does not know how to determine whether he has left sufficient stores in his hives, or who is too greedy, may leave insufficient stores in years when the next spring nectar flow is extremely late, or bad weather prevents foraging by the bees.

   (b) In the United States, the confusion as to what is "sufficient" is at least partly due to deliberate understatement by E. F. Phillips and G. S. Demuth of the quantity of honey required for wintering. For whatever motives, they recommended just half (45 lb, 20kg) of the quantity (90 lb, 40kg) they knew to be necessary to ensure survival of a colony in the northern tier of states [*Bee Wld* 13 : 98-100 (1932)].

3. Feed while the weather is warm enough to allow colonies to process the syrup into stores, but not so early that they use the feed for rearing brood instead (951L/71) .

   (a) Small portions (0·75 litres on 14 days) enabled colonies to seal their stores completely, whereas 3 portions (3 litres on 3 days) or 6 portions (1·5 litres on 7 days) did not (244/52).

   (b) Colonies fed early in the autumn, especially where there was no late nectar flow, developed more rapidly in the spring (530/68).

   (c) Syrup fed in early September gave stores with 12% more invert sugar than syrup fed in mid-August, i.e. more sucrose had been converted into glucose + fructose (361/64).

   (d) Concentrated syrup (67% w/w) fed in mid-September instead of in August produced 10% more stores (109/52).

   (e) Syrup provided in feeders large enough, so that bees can take 4-6 lb (2-3 kg) per day, will only slightly stimulate egg laying. If more than one can of syrup is required, all should be put on at once, to reduce the likelihood of stimulating brood rearing.

   (f) It was once the practice in the north to feed about 5 kg of sugar syrup after brood rearing ceased, with the idea that the sugar stores would be used first during the period of confinement, and reduce the imagined dangers of dysentery from eating honeydew honey high in dextrins (38/50).

4. Concentrated syrup (67% w/w) produced one-third more stores than 33% syrup, but encouraged more brood rearing, especially when fed in early autumn (109/52).

   (a) Syrup made of 20 lb sugar in 9 British pints of water (i.e. 64% w/w) [or 60% (789/65)] is recommended for autumn feeding as it is the highest concentration without risk of granulation in the feeder (109/52).

   (b) When syrup contained 50% sucrose, granulation of stores was minimal (244/53).

   (c) A 1 : 2 syrup was "riper" (i.e. more sucrose was inverted to fructose and glucose) than a 2 : 1 syrup (740/72).

Emergency feeding

This is one operation that is most successfully practised by avoidance. Feeding in the spring should be considered strictly as an emergency measure and not regarded as a substitute for provisions the bees should have stored before the end of the previous season. Bees carrying larvae and pupae out of the entrance, or driving drones from the hive (except in autumn), are signs that the colony is approaching starvation.

1. A colony should have 14-18 kg (30-40 lb) of sealed stores of honey (equivalent to 6-8 solid combs in Langstroth deep frames) at all times, to ensure it will not cut back its brood rearing; 23 kg or 50 lb of honey are required to produce a colony of 50 000 bees. Even a very small colony should probably have at least 7 kg (15 lb). If a colony is desperately short of stores in the spring, some method of feeding might prevent starvation, but the likelihood of obtaining surplus honey that same season is slight.

2. Taking frames of honey from disease-free colonies with excessive stores is the best, easiest, and usually the cheapest method of feeding colonies.

(a) Break open some of the cappings to give quick access to the honey, if the bees have no sealed honey of their own.

(b) Remove empty combs from the outside (none with pollen) and replace them with combs of honey, late in the day when there is no risk of inciting robbing.

(c) Put 2 or 3 combs of honey in the centre of a super of empty combs, and place the super on top of the colony. This also provides additional space for brood rearing and for storage of early surplus honey.

(d) Lay a frame of sealed honey over the frames, and cover with cloth (burlap, sacking to keep it warm.

(e) A frame of emerging brood and adhering bees, with a frame of honey, can be given from a stronger colony at the beginning of April. Feeding can then be put off until May. Nurse bees will emerge at the end of April, and the colony will rear three extra frames of brood in May. Such doubling will not occur if May is chilly, but fed colonies will develop faster than unfed ones.

3. Extracted (liquid) honey should not ordinarily be fed to colonies, because the odour is so attractive to robber bees. There is risk of spreading disease even with one's own honey, but a greater risk if honey of any sort is purchased to use as feed. Although it is possible to sterilize honey, this requires careful processing, and surveillance of the colonies must continue for more than one year. If a large steam-jacketed pressure cooker is available, the process can be done efficiently (125/55).

(a) If honey must be fed, feed it at dusk, so that the colony can clean it up before bees are flying next day.

(b) Add 10 % sugar syrup to liquid honey to prevent crystallization.

4. Granulated honey can be fed to bees, as they can ingest the fine crystals along with the liquid, but they cannot break up hard masses of glucose, and these are thrown out by the bees after they consume the surrounding solution of glucose and fructose (233/53).

(a) A jar of granulated honey placed upside down over the feed-hole in the inner cover of a hive has been used to save a starving colony in early spring.

(b) Colonies supplied with granulated honey as their only winter food supply have wintered normally, indicating that losses sometimes attributed to granulation may be due to other causes.

(c) Granulated honey is suitable as a food if the bees can obtain sufficient water to dissolve the honey, or if the humidity is unusually high. When bees were wintered in cellars, the high humidity provided the necessary water through condensation. Where the temperature is unlikely to fall below freezing, a bottle of water could be kept in the hive (1035L/71). Otherwise, the bees need to be able to fly to get water.

5.   If honey is not available, and the weather permits checking early enough in the spring to discover any colony desperately short of stores, the following options are open :

(a) Artificial combs filled with sugar solution and sealed by spraying wax over the surface have been found satisfactory (717/67).

(b) Sugar can be fed in the form of candy or as dry sugar (see Part III).

(c) A feeder jar (see Part I " Feeders for sugar syrup ") of warm syrup can be placed on top of the frames in direct contact with the cluster. Whatever is not taken down promptly should be removed and replaced by more warm syrup. A large colony may be able to take 5 litres in 24 hours.

(d) The hive can be brought into a shed or cellar for feeding.

(e) Ideally, the feeding should start during a mild spell when the weather permits flights to collect pollen for inclusion in the sealed food.

Spring stimulation

The rationale in beekeeping manuals, from the earliest to the present day, for feeding colonies in the spring has been that it will stimulate brood rearing, and thereby secure a significantly greater surplus of honey (151/65, 135/66, 149/72). But, as early as 1885, Jan Joder concluded that a colony cannot rear more larvae than there are nurses to feed them, and recent investigations appear to support this view.

1.   Feeding sugar syrup had an effect on brood rearing only in a bad year.

(a) It may be difficult to determine a time to begin feeding for stimulation, since the first nectar flow can be 2-3 weeks earlier or later than average in any given year.

If delayed, the hives would be boiling with bees requiring costly feeding to prevent starvation, and they might eventually swarm. If earlier, the bees would emerge too late to return the investment in sugar with an increased harvest from the nectar flow.

(b) Bees do not collect syrup when they can forage for nectar.

(c) Colonies collected more pollen while being fed syrup, and this may be a useful technique to increase pollination of field peas and red clover (603/63).

2.   Earlier colony development resulted in no better (or even a poorer) honey yield, especially when pollen was not plentiful (107/54).

3.   Activities associated with increased brood rearing shortened the life span of the winter bees and resulted in a shortage of foragers (55/54).

4.   So long as a colony has 5 kg (10 lb) of capped honey, feeding will not accelerate the primary natural proclivity of the colony to expand its brood nest, as climatic and seasonal factors permit.

5.   A constant dribble of sugar syrup alone is apparently not a stimulus. It is the presence of ample stores of capped honey and pollen that encourages the colony to expand its brood rearing.   Hence the admonition by Doolittle, Miller, etc., that spring feeding is best done in the *autumn*.

6.   A colony which is well stocked with honey may be fed if the colony is to be divided later for establishing a new colony, or for pollination.
   (*a*) Feeding may help the population to reach its peak sooner, with the associated possibility of swarming.
   (*b*) Feeding a small quantity (250 g) of syrup every or every other evening reduced the chance of robbing. Use a friction-top can or a Boardman entrance feeder with 1-4 holes made in the lid, just large enough to fit a common pin. The number of holes depends on the size of the colony.
   (*c*) Very large colonies fed syrup in spring showed no extra development, but small colonies (8 frames or less) showed a 36% increase in bees and 55% increase in brood over their unfed control twins (68/52).
   (*d*) Whether fed or not in spring, all colonies had the same amounts of brood in the spring of the following year (148/72).

Autumn stimulation

1.   Colonies substandard in early August can become substantial by mid-September when pollen is plentiful, and the generations of bees accumulate. Sugar is turned into bees, thus fulfilling the skeppist's axiom: " A pound of September bees is worth five pounds of July bees".

2.   Autumn stimulation is justified when the queen was mated very late, as in a new colony built up from a nucleus, or a small late swarm.

3.   Small colonies tend to rear more brood longer than large colonies, but even newly mated queens are " reluctant " to lay eggs late in the season. Both small and large colonies will probably have the same amount of brood in the spring.

4.   " Equalizing " brood frames in the autumn may cause colonies that lose bees to be short of nurse bees early in the spring. Colonies from which bees are taken should be fed to stimulate brood rearing, or—preferably—the smaller colonies fed.

5.   Stimulative feeding with 1 : 1 syrup in autumn resulted in stronger colonies with more brood the following May, in years when the flow had finished in July, but there was little difference in years when the flow continued well into August (775/75).

6.   Of 750 marked bees which emerged after feeding, only 13 lived until the main flow next spring, 249 days (414/74).

Replacement feeding

1.   Where the price of honey is higher than that of sugar, it is sometimes the practice to remove all the honey above the brood chamber, and to feed sugar syrup for winter stores.   The economics of this practice warrant close attention except where the cost of labour is not a factor, or where there is, say, a three-fold difference between the prices of honey and sugar.

(a) 23% of the sugar is used by the bees in processing the syrup (789/65). More energy is required to process dilute solutions than concentrated ones (145/72).

(b) In the absence of early spring flows, the substitution of sugar reduces the colony yields so much that replacement feeding is uneconomic (313/69).

2. Sugar alone may be not altogether equal to honey as a food for bees.

(a) Colonies wintered entirely on stores derived from syrup had less brood in spring than those wintered with some honey (244/53). Colonies fed dilute rather than concentrated syrup produced less brood the following spring (145/72).

(b) Colonies not fed sugar syrup in the autumn wintered better, used less food, were more populous, and produced more brood in the spring than those fed sugar (351/64, 290/66).

(c) Bees fed sugar syrup had less invertase than normal, and their lives were 24·6% shorter (290/66, 485/69). But tests with caged bees showed longer average survival when fed sucrose syrup than when fed honey diluted to the same sugar concentration (58/75).

Feeding to force honey into the supers

Some beekeepers believe that feeding bees prior to the honey flow will cause the bees to fill the cells in the brood nest with sugar syrup, and that the nectar will then be stored in the honey supers. Bees place *all* incoming nectar into recently vacated cells inside the brood nest. It is not moved up into the supers until the water content has been reduced to a certain concentration (188/53). Cells outside the brood nest are kept vacant while the queen is laying. Beekeepers using syrup made from dyed tax-free sugar discovered this to their discomfort and financial loss.

For personal use " sugar-honey " is acceptable (174/67). If it is sold, the high sucrose content and colouring will cause it to be considered adulterated. A taste test conducted at Rothamsted Experimental Station demonstrated a difficulty in detecting as much as 25% sugar-syrup honey added to natural honey. Sugar syrup not fed to bees could be detected, suggesting that some flavour ingredient is altered during processing by the bees (888/74).

The use of syrup produced from corn starch by an enzymatic process presents a more difficult detection problem, because the proportions of fructose and glucose are similar to those of honey.

Experimental feeding of biologically active substances in syrup

1. Plant growth hormone (Belvitan) produced a 41·7% larger brood nest than in control colonies (104/62).

2. Folliculin (oestrone) and vitamin E helped to build up colonies for the honey flow (385/73).

3. Sugar syrup (alone or with penicillin), beaten egg, or milk, resulted in increased yields of honey and wax (382/73).

4. Growth stimulants derived from petroleum, Filatov tissue preparation, or gibberellic acid, stimulated brood rearing and production of honey and wax only when sufficient fresh pollen was available (838/74).

Making sugar syrup*

1. Grade of sugar

(a) The older literature specified sugar from cane rather than beet, but with present techniques of manufacture there are no impurities in beet sugar, and no differences between them. Unrefined beet sugar, brown sugar, molasses, etc., will cause the bee rectum to fill with residue, and so is not suitable for wintering (99/60, 951L/71).

(b) In the UK sugar syrup marked with green dye has been sold at concessionary prices for winter feeding; but it may be moved up into supers added in spring, and thereby mixed with honey offered for sale (210L/71). In the US, " exquota " sugar has been sold at the world market price since January 1976, for use as livestock feed, free of excise tax. In Germany, denatured sugar is sold in 50-kg bags labelled *Bienen-futterzucker*; it is dyed with iron oxide which gives " honey " made from it a reddish colour (739L/72).

2. " Easiest method "

(a) Fill a tin or other container 7/8 with sugar.

(b) Stir continuously while pouring in boiling water (in which sugar dissolves more rapidly than in cold water) until the tin is full.

(c) Continue stirring until all the sugar is dissolved.

3. Professor L. Armbruster's method

(a) Pour sugar into a container.

(b) Mark the surface of the sugar with a pencil or tape, or measure it with a metre rule or strip of paper.

(c) Add boiling water and stir. Continue adding water until the level of the mixture is again at the mark or just above it (more water avoids granulation).

(d) The result is approximately 56% sugar syrup (w/w).

(e) For spring feeding add an extra $\frac{1}{2}$ pint water to each 2 lb sugar.

4. Usual method

(a) Bring a measured volume of water to boiling.

(b) Remove from source of heat and add the same volume of sugar, stirring until it is dissolved.

(c) *Or*, leave it on the heat and add the sugar slowly; stir vigorously until dissolved.

(d) Add one 5-lb bag of granulated sugar to 1 US quart of hot water and stir until the crystals disappear.

---

*Editor's note

1. *Volumes*. The authors quote volumes in USA imperial units. British imperial units (pint, quart, gallon) are 25% larger; if these are used, corresponding weights of sugar must be increased by 25%.

2. *Crystal size*. The crystals of " granulated " sugar vary from country to country, and have commonly become finer in recent years. The weight of a given volume of sugar may vary by 40% or more according to when and where it was manu-factured. Unless metric units are used, the safest way to determine the concen-tration of syrup is by weight: for winter feed use 5 parts of sugar to 4 parts of water, for spring feed 1 to 1, all *by weight*.

5. *Steam*

This can be applied to the mixture from a hose; this has the added advantage of agitating the mixture while it heats the water.

6. *Direct heating*

It may be necessary to heat the more concentrated mixtures to get the sugar to dissolve readily, but great care may be required to avoid scorching the syrup, particularly if undissolved sugar settles on the bottom. Any seams or joints in pans used for heating should be resoldered to remove any cracks where sugar can collect and burn.

(*a*) Mix the sugar and water.

(*b*) Heat the mixture, while stirring, until it is a clear solution with every particle of sugar dissolved; the syrup must not be allowed to boil. Solutions made by methods 2, 3 and 4 may be heated in the same manner.

(*c*) The syrup will caramelize slightly.

(*d*) If the syrup does scorch, it can be fed to bees in the spring, when they are rearing brood, provided they are able to fly and void their faeces.

7. Boiling the syrup hinders fermentation, and does not induce granulation if the temperature does not exceed 112°C (234°F) (134/66).

8. If cold water is used, add the measured quantity of sugar a little at a time to a measured quantity of water, stirring continuously.

9. *Mixing*

(*a*) An extractor or honey tank should not be used because of the possible danger of spreading American foul brood.

(*b*) A large food mixer is advantageous. The sugar is poured in, and the water added with a hose while the mixture is agitated.

10. Disinfecting the containers and the syrup (Chinosol 0·5g to 8 litres (839/63)) will avoid the formation of slime resulting from the growth of *Leuconostoc mesenterioides* (226/53, 698L/70, 164/71, 165/71).

11. Sugar syrup can be purchased in 5 gallon cans, or in larger containers from some suppliers (e.g. in California).

Inverted bee feeds

Older recipes for sugar syrup call for the addition of an organic acid such as tartaric, and heating " to prevent the formation of crystals which the bees cannot use without waste " (E. F. Phillips, 1927). Sucrose is readily inverted by dilute acids into glucose and fructose.

1. In 1925, L. E. Dills reported that uninverted sugar syrup was taken from feeders faster (100%) than syrup inverted by the enzyme invertase (86%), or than acid-inverted syrup (30%), or even than honey (36%). The colonies fed uninverted sugar syrup lost fewest bees and least weight during the winter. Colonies fed acid-inverted syrup lost most bees; those fed invertase-inverted syrup lost more bees than colonies fed either uninverted syrup or honey, and lost twice as much weight as those fed uninverted syrup. Dills' conclusion has been confirmed, that inverted feed is un-

satisfactory for wintering because "it is possible that some of the side reaction products [still unknown] acted as repellents", some colonies developed dysentery, and considerable amounts of the feed granulated (503/67).

2.   The addition of acid *arrests* inversion, and *accelerates* crystallization, which argues against the long-established rationale for inverting sugar syrup in the first instance (995/72).

3.   Control colonies capped their food sooner (and during the feeding period reared 37% more brood) than did experimental colonies fed acidified syrup (360/64).

4.   Bees ripened 50% sucrose solution more completely and more quickly than other concentrations. The basic process of ripening syrup lasted 3-5 days; concentration of the syrup ended on the 5th day, and inversion on the 10th-12th day (361/64). Sucrose constitutes 0 to 100% of the sugars in nectar (mean 50%).   Contrary to early views, inversion of honey or sugar syrup does not continue during the winter. Since the addition of acids appears to be repellent, the use of acetic, lactic, oxalic, or tartaric acid is counter-indicated (244/53).

5.   Glucose manufactured from starch is an inexpensive source of sugar first developed by the French during the continental blockade in 1806-1814. Even 25% glucose has not been found good for winter stores (950/70), although as spring feed it might be ideal. The addition of 15% glucose (termed the "doctor") in syrup and candy prevents or retards the crystallization of the sucrose.

Some beekeepers are using Drivert or other partially inverted cane and/or beet sugar, and believe the bees take them better than sucrose. Less expensive corn syrup solids are available under various trade names, and the new, high-fructose enzymatic process (US patent 3,616,221) should be free of the adverse effects of methods using the older acid hydrolysis.

III. DRY SUGAR AND CANDY

Candy

1. White sugar candy was first advocated in 1766 as feed for bees, because in its preparation the harmful ingredients of unrefined beet sugar were eliminated (226/58). Feeding in mid-winter is not advisable, but if absolutely necessary (to avoid loss of a colony) and if temperatures are so low that syrup might freeze, candy can be fed.
2. Candy also can be used to feed a colony during shipment or travel (22 days in one instance).
3. Candy is taken more slowly than syrup and does not excite the bees so much.
4. Bees need water to enable them to use candy :
    A. There may be sufficient condensation of water vapour from clustered bees in the hive in winter.
    B. When temperatures are above freezing, water can be fed within the hive or in outside feeders.

Soft candy (fondant)

1. Add sugar to hot (or cold) water (4:1 or 3:1) slowly. Stir until every grain of sugar is wet (undissolved sugar may burn). Do not leave any isolated crystals on the sides of the container.
2. Add 1 tablespoon of glucose per $1\frac{1}{2}$ kg (3 lb) of sugar, to prevent the sugar from granulating during boiling. Candy makers use 15% glucose for " excellent " fondant. Decreasing the proportion of glucose (3-10%) produces a crumbly texture; increasing it (to 30%) produces a tougher, chewy candy. K. Weiss recommends 5% (849L/74).
3. Hang a candy thermometer with the bulb 2-3 cm below the surface in the container and slowly bring the mixture to a simmering boil (110°C, 230°F) over low heat. Stir continuously and do not permit the mixture to scorch. Rinse and dry the spoon or stirrer after use.
4. Wipe down the inside of the container to the syrup edge with a small brush dipped in water, or with a fork wrapped in a damp cloth.
5. Heat the syrup to 112-115°C (234-240°F) as rapidly as possible (2-3 minutes) *without* stirring or scraping the sides. A stiffer candy will result at higher temperatures. K. Weiss recommends 113°C. E. B. Wedmore suggests 243°F (117°C) to prevent the candy softening over a strong cluster of bees. The only sure way to determine when the candy is done is to use a candy thermometer. An imprecise alternative is the cold water test : drop $\frac{1}{2}$ teaspoon of the candy into a cup of cold water and let it stand 1 minute; a " soft ball " that flattens on removal from the water indicates that the fondant has boiled sufficiently.
6. Allow the syrup to cool to 40-50°C (100-125°F). Moving or jarring the container may induce crystal formation and produce grainy candy.
7. Stir until the candy stiffens. Allow it to " cure " for 1 hour, then knead until smooth. Alternatively, pour the candy on to a marble slab to a depth of 3-4 cm. When cool enough, beat it with a wooden spoon or paddle and then knead it.
8. Cover the fondant with a damp cloth and store in an airtight container to avoid hardening.

Hard candy

1. Dissolve sugar (nearly $\frac{1}{2}$ by volume) in water, and boil to 150-154°C (300-310°F). A test drop in cold water will be hard and brittle in the water but softens in the mouth.

86

2. Pour on to waxed paper placed on a level table, using sticks a few mm high to confine the syrup to the area desired.
3. When nearly hard, score the candy so that it can be broken up into squares for feeding.
4. Invert sugar for feeding to bees is available in 7-pound blocks from at least one supplier in England (E. H. Thorne).

Methods of feeding candy

1. Slabs of candy can be placed on top of the frames using sticks (e.g. top bars) as spacers.
   A. A layer of candy 2-3 cm deep poured into greased dishes or pans can be removed when cool and hard, for placing on the frames.
   B. Paper picnic plates with hardened candy can be inverted over the frames.
2. A raised wire-screen platform can be used to support the candy and to provide access by the bees from below.
3. Pour candy on to an inner cover, first covering the bee-escape hole with paper.
4. Feeders of various designs are available from European suppliers with a bee escape and closure, so that the feeder can be closed during prolonged cold, or wet weather when condensation of water would spoil the candy and make it unattractive to the bees.
5. A hive frame can be modified by planing off " self-spacing " edges of the end bars and replacing the bottom-bar with one as wide as top and end pieces.
   A. $\frac{1}{2}$-inch (1-1$\frac{1}{2}$cm) wire mesh (hardware cloth) is cut into 12 cm (5 inch) strips to fit inside the frame, leaving a 6 mm ($\frac{1}{4}$ inch) space at the ends.
   B. Two wire box nails are driven down through the centre of the top-bar, long enough for the ends to be made into a hook on which to hang the wire mesh. One nail in each end is bent into an L to hook on the wire mesh, and then turned down to tighten the mesh.
   C. A false bottom-bar can be inserted into the frame to reduce the space for the cake of candy; a full-depth Langstroth frame would carry 3$\frac{1}{2}$-4 kg (8-9 lb) of candy.
   D. One of these frames placed in the hive, three frames in from the wall, will help brood rearing in seasons when winter stores are scarce.
   E. If a frame of candy is placed next to the wall, the bees will feed from the inner side only, and pieces are liable to fall off the opposite side.

Dry sugar

There are occasions when it is very useful to feed with dry sugar, although collection and storage of solid sugar (even granulated honey or candy of the same sugar composition as honey) gives the bees more rather than less work to do than collecting and storing syrup (829/64).
1. S. Simmins promoted his percolating or self-acting feeders in 1887, whereby it was possible to mix the sugar and water directly into the feeder without heating. A revival uses friction-top pails (lever-lid cans) (839/63). Like R. Lunder, Simmins used the percolation technique with large quantities (100 kg, 200 pounds) (294/58, 738L/72).

2.   C. C. Miller poured the sugar required by the colony into a Miller feeder, made a depression in the sugar, and added a pint ($\frac{1}{2}$ litre) of water.   Shortly after, he added as much water (by volume or weight) as sugar. Additional water was added daily until the sugar was all taken.

3.   When the weather is warm and bees are flying freely, dry sugar can be fed without moistening, in emergencies or during migration. There is some wastage by bees carrying crystals out of the hive (125/57, 829/64). Large colonies take dry sugar best.

   A. The sugar is dissolved in salivary secretion, and diluted more than honey or concentrated syrup (256/58, 16/61, 525/65). Such a quantity of water is added that during storage the bees may need to evaporate as much or more than from the usual feeding syrup (55-65 % w/w sucrose). They must then collect water to maintain their supply of saliva; 20 % comes from the breakdown of the sugar consumed during collection (829/64).

   B. If there is no water in the hive as a result of condensation, the bees must be able to fly every day to get water.

   C. Below 20°C the water economy of bees is not the same as at higher temperatures, and they can maintain their water level with food containing 20 % water (honey) and continue longer on dry food without additional water (256/58).

   D. In June, dry sugar moistened with water was consumed more slowly than syrup, creating less excitement and therefore less danger of robbing (101/55).

   E. Dry sugar was used in large amounts only in times of insufficient nectar flow (322/65).

   F. Most of the dry sugar was taken by bees 18-20 days old—even while older bees were foraging for nectar (357L/63, 329/64).

   G. In autumn, 1 kg of dry sugar was taken up by a colony in 6-7 days (297/55).

   H. " Honey " produced from dry sugar had 2-3 times the enzyme content of normal honey, so its production may have an adverse effect on the bees producing it (192/59).

   I. Dry sugar dyed with methylene blue, etc., was found as sealed "honey" in the brood nest and the honey chamber (super) (329/64, 322/65).

Methods of feeding dry sugar

1.   If the colony is starving, pour up to 2 kg (5 lb) of sugar between the outside combs and the hive wall.   Block the front of the bottom board to prevent waste. P. F. Thurber places a strip of aluminium foil 12 cm (5 inch) wide between the upper and lower hive bodies, and at the back of the hive, to keep the sugar in the upper hive body.

2.   Pour the sugar along the sides and back to avoid getting the sugar on the brood, which will kill it.

3.   Some beekeepers tilt the hive, pour dry sugar into the entrance, and then reduce the entrance.

4.   Spread a sheet of newspaper over the frames and punch a hole or two in the paper. Pour 1-2 kg (3-5 lb) of dry granulated sugar on to the newspaper, and spread it evenly. Place a wooden rim or empty shallow hive body under the cover if this does not fit down tightly over the sugar.

5.   The sugar can be poured on to an inner cover which has a hole in the centre, or on a square of tar paper placed over the frames and covered by a queen excluder.

6.   If quilts are used, a small stick under the quilt will provide sufficient space for the bees to work the sugar placed on a paper over the frames.

7.   A "feed rim" can be made of masonite or hardboard; it has the same cross-section as the hive, a rim 3-4 cm high, and an entrance at the rear. Behlows used 200 lb sugar, 30 lb honey and $2\frac{1}{2}$ gallons of water heated in a double-jacketed cooker at 240° F for 2 hours. When partially cool, the feed is poured inside a supply of feed rims and stacked until the feed solidifies in them. The rims are then inverted over the hives. The surface of the sugar is like a thin icing, and underneath it has the consistency of caramel. The $6\frac{1}{2}$ pounds of sugar in each rim will last 2-3 weeks and is not wasted as granulated sugar may be.

CHAPTER 7

FEEDING HONEYBEES POLLEN AND POLLEN SUBSTITUTES

" All life is one·continuous search after that most valuable element, nitrogen; and this is especially true of the *Apidae*."—(T. Rayment, 1915)

Contents

POLLEN

Nutritional value of pollen

The effectiveness of pollen as a food for the honeybee is due in part to its greater attractiveness to bees than other protein foods[124]. The protein content of pollen ranges from 7% to 30%, and the amino acids constituting the protein are also very variable[4]; Weaver[127] has set out the basic principles of protein chemistry.

Feeding amino acids activates the bees' hypopharyngeal glands[40]. Dandelion (*Taraxacum officinalis*) protein at a concentration of 0·625% was found equal to a 7·5% concentration of proteins of other pollens tested[101], in activating the glands. A mixture of different pollens is much richer in manganese and zinc than most single pollens[85].

Bee bread (pollen stored in the comb) results from the action of yeasts in producing lactic acid (as in grass silage), and can also be produced outside the hive in vitro[46, 87]. Although bee bread has greater food value than fresh pollen[110], fresh pollen or an extract in water is more effective in stimulating egg production[86]. The food value of bee bread deteriorates upon storage. For instance 1000 bees on a diet of fresh bee bread were able to feed 142-306 larvae, but if the bee bread had been stored at 0-16°C for one year, the same number of bees could feed only 49-75 larvae[111]. Bee bread (or pollen) stored at 18-26°C for a year has been found worthless[110].

At the start of the active season, pollen is usually available even before temperatures permit bees to fly to collect it. Where a shortage does exist, however, the beekeeper can collect pollen at other times and store it for feeding in the spring.

The total annual pollen consumption of a colony has been calculated as 20-30 kg (45-65 lb), but it may be as high as Å. Hansson's estimate of 50 kg[100, 115].

Effect of pollen and/or bee bread deficiency

Effects on the colony include the following:

1. In winter experiments in USSR, the colony consumed less honey, and fewer bees died, but there was less brood in spring[75].

2. When bees were confined to a flight room at 11°C in Belgium, the amount of brood was not related to pollen stores until after early April. Prior to this, brood development was closely correlated with total flight activity, and possibly also with external humidity[61].

3. Colonies deficient in pollen, overwintered in a cellar in USSR, had 57·2% less brood, and 76·8% fewer dead bees, than normal colonies[74]. When provided with pollen at the end of March, the colonies caught up and had even slightly more sealed brood than normal colonies[38].

4. Colonies will collect other substances with a protein content, such as fungal spores, embryo cheese mites, and humus[33,100]. There have been reports of bees collecting sawdust and coal dust, but these do not indicate what, if any, the source of protein was; sawdust would have various fermentation organisms and metabolic products, and coal dust could be contaminated with organic matter.

5. Many of the perennial troubles referred to as ' bee consumption ', ' disappearing diseases ', and so on, can be attributed to seasons of drought and/or pollen shortage[7. 8]. W. T. Wilson believes that the syndrome of disappearing disease in the USA is correlated with the hybridization of European bees with the African bee *A. m. adansonii* imported before 1900, and more recently in 1960 as semen for artificial fertilization[34].

Effects on individual bees include the following :

1. Drones are usually quickly eliminated from the hive, and those tolerated have a reduced sperm production.

2. Any queen produced is stunted and will be superseded[100].

3. Protein content in the bodies of bees was found to diminish during autumn feeding when bee bread was not available[134]. Deficient bees chewed cocoons, licked dried larval food and excreta, and tore apart dead bee bodies and sucked the interior[17].

Harvesting pollen

Many methods are available for collecting pollen for feeding to bees:

1. Place pollen-bearing flowers in a warm room, and collect the pollen fallen from the flowers on paper or in trays[100].

2. Pollen trapped from a single strong colony can be used to feed fifty other colonies with pollen supplement the following spring[11, 43, 65]. Trapping is recommended on days when bees collect at least 100 g of pollen per day[18]. It is unprofitable during a major nectar flow, because the grid slows down bee traffic and reduces honey production[116]. There has been dispute about any detrimental effect, but 30% of experimental trap colonies died compared to 13% of the controls[71]. A combined pollen collector and entrance restrictor has been patented[92].

3. Give surplus pollen-filled combs to colonies that need them. Combs containing pollen only, stored away from the hive during winter, are likely to mildew unless ' preserved ' with honey and capped by the bees[100].

4. Extract and preserve the pollen from combs to be discarded[94]:
  (a) steam combs in a steam-chest for 10-15 minutes;
  (b) dump the hot mass into cold water, where the pollen pellets will sink;
  (c) skim off the empty cells or cocoons;
  (d) allow the pollen to drain and then grind in a meat grinder;
  (e) tamp ground pollen into a drum, crock or can;
  (f) cover with heavy syrup (3 sugar : 2 water).

5. A warning is necessary that bee-collected pollen can be a source of bee diseases[50]. Pollen purchased from others is subject to a similar risk, especially if preventive chemotherapy with antibiotics is practised, which masks the signs of any residual disease.

Storing pollen

1. Mix 2 parts fresh pollen with 1 part granulated sugar (w/w). Cover the top with 5 cm of sugar, to guard against surface mould. This will keep for two years at room temperature, but feeding it will not enable colonies to produce as much brood as feeding fresh or frozen pollen pellets will do[118].

2. Knead pollen into a solution of disease-free honey (15%, and boiled, cooled water 25%, of the weight of the pollen). Tamp the mixture into a crock, cover with a weighted wooden disc, hold at 97°F (36°C) for about 5 days, tamp very tightly, seal from air with layer of wax (3 paraffin : 1 beeswax), store in a cool place. The preserved pollen can be used as equivalent to egg yolk in formulations requiring this[46].

3. Air drying:
  (a) Spread a layer of pollen, 1-2 cm thick, on a flat, porous surface in a warm, ventilated room such as a glass-enclosed porch or greenhouse[18].
  (b) Apply mild artificial heat (35-36°C, 95-97°F) for 24 hours, using a fruit or vegetable drier, a cabinet heated with four 40-watt electric bulbs, or an oven vented for moist air to escape. Raising the temperature to 49°C (120°F) for the first hour will retard fermentation[126].
  (c) When sufficiently dry (10-12% moisture content) seal the pollen in airtight glass or metal containers and store in a cool dry place (1-2°C, 34-36°F, 25% RH)[126]. Properly dried pollen pellets should not crush when pressed between the fingers, nor adhere to each other when squeezed together[118].
  (d) Air-dried pollen deteriorates, and will have lost considerable nutritional value after two years[118, 126].
  (e) Freezing pollen for a period of 24-48 hours before storing at room temperature will destroy eggs and larvae of any insects and mites in the pollen, that might otherwise damage it[118, 126].

5. Freeze-drying under vacuum (lyophilization) produces a superior product (1/3 more brood).

6. Freezing[18, 118]:

    (a) Fresh pollen placed in paper or plastic bags can be frozen and stored in a deep-freeze at $-18°C$ (0°F). It is equal to fresh pollen in nutritional value, and will keep for several years.

    (b) When removed from the freezer, frozen pollen must be used immediately, or dried.

Feeding pollen to bees

1. Place pollen-bearing plants near the colonies (in screened cages, flight rooms, or greenhouses)[100].

2. Feed small pieces of comb containing bee bread in the hive[12].

3. Place a shallow dish of fresh or thawed frozen pollen over the hole in the inner cover.

4. Use a pollen-feeding frame with the cavity against the outermost brood comb[60].

5. Suspend pollen in water, sugar syrup, or candy[12,81].

6. Mix fresh pollen with an equal volume of expeller-type soya-bean flour to absorb moisture and prevent moulding. Use of a modified food colander ensures thorough mixing. Store in a cool dry room until ready to mix with sugar syrup for feeding as ' cakes '[130]. If used alone, pollen must be stored dry or in a frozen state.

7. Add pollen to a pollen substitute, the product then being known as a pollen supplement. More brood is produced by feeding such a mixture than by feeding substitutes without added pollen.

    (a) A dry mixture fed outside the hive is convenient but wasteful[45].

    (b) A mixture in candy or syrup fed within the hive is the most economical method[45].

8. Pollen placed in the hive within 4-6 cm of unsealed brood is consumed most rapidly[23, 69, 95, 115].

POLLEN SUBSTITUTES

Historical note

In 1655 Samuel Hartlib recommended that dry meal or bean flour be added to ' tostes of bread sopped in strong ale ' as a cheap winter feed for bees, and wondered whether it would be better if first ' maulted '[44]. By 1900 beekeepers in Europe, especially Germany and Austria, routinely used feeds composed of sugar, pea flour and egg white, to stimulate breeding in the spring. In the United States a mixture recommended in 1888 was sugar, milk, fresh eggs, rye flour, salt and bone ash[70]. Previous suggestions for feeding bees had included hen-eggs in 1869[1], ' flour candy ' in 1877[117], asses milk in 1879,[64] and meat of chickens in 1922 (in Ireland)[3]. Johannes Mehring (1815-1878), the inventor of wax foundation, fed his bees by-products from a malt factory—one of the many ways in which he was ahead of his time[73].

In America some beekeepers believed that pollen was detrimental to successful wintering, and arguments appeared in 1904 bee journals for and against pollen[48,76]. As late as 1934, there were beekeepers in the United States who considered it abnormal for colonies to begin brood rearing in January. In fact, the brood-rearing cycle of the colony reflects the total quantity of protein it has obtained during that season, and the colony that collects the most pollen has the most brood[66, 96].

As human occupancy of land increases, there is less space for the spring flora whose pollen is so essential to bees for rearing brood. In 1977, the American Beekeeping Federation Research Committee considered it imperative that a satisfactory pollen substitute, available at a reasonable cost, should be developed.

Rationale for feeding substitutes

The need for pollen substitutes is clear-cut in areas where plants that yield nectar produce little or no pollen (for instance some *Eucalyptus* in Australia, alfalfa in California), or when bees are being produced for divisions and packages, or for pollination[100]. The following conclusion by I. W. Forster of New Zealand sets out the problem clearly:

It is difficult to make general recommendations as to when and where to feed pollen supplements. In most areas it is not easy to foresee just when pollen short-ages will occur. The effect of deficiencies in quality would be still more difficult to anticipate. To feed pollen supplement throughout the build-up period as an insurance against pollen deficiency may be worthwhile but would involve con-siderable labour and expense.

Beekeepers will learn to recognize a seasonal pattern that could result in pollen deficiencies only by studying conditions in their own districts. Undesirable colony symptoms that have no obvious explanation could well be suspected as due to pollen deficiencies (e.g. absence of essential amino acid), and trials should be made to see if they respond to the feeding of supplements. The effective use of pollen supplement must be treated as another skill in the art of beekeeping which requires considerable study if worthwhile practical results are to be obtained[35].

A pollen substitute is not likely to be necessary, in North America at any rate, if bees are wintered in three brood chambers to provide adequate space for pollen stored as bee bread[94]. A box of empty dark brood combs next to the bottom board appears to increase the quantity of pollen accumulated[30]. Feeding a substitute is not recommended, or of any value, where natural supplies of pollen are abundant[41, 80]. Bees prefer pollen to any substitute, but the total amount of pollen collected by the colony is reduced proportionately to the quantity of pollen, but not pollen substitute, fed to (and accepted by) the colony[37,123].

A colony should have the equivalent of 4-6 combs of stored pollen (bee bread) to begin brood rearing in January[10]. When pollen or bee bread is not available, or in short supply, it is possible to supplement the shortfall of protein in a variety of ways. In Australia average two-storey colonies consume about $\frac{1}{2}$ pound of supplement per week, and an average of 11 pounds over the whole year[27].

Ingredients used in substitute diets

There has been less success in finding artificial diets for honeybees than for some other insects. This may be due to the low degree of variability amongst honeybees, which makes it difficult to find genetic combinations able to survive on the diet. The diets have not been successful in averting the instinct of honeybees to contract their brood nest when winter is approaching[82].

Rye flour as a substitute for pollen was rated by Langstroth in 1861 as not equal to the " genuine article "; pea flour was another recommended substitute at that time[59]. But experience and research have shown that neither supports brood rearing.

Brewer's yeast is now considered the best of the substitutes, using brood rearing as a criterion of quality[100, 121]. Seven times as much soya-bean flour cake was consumed when 25% brewer's yeast was added, and the mixture was regarded as about equivalent to average pollen in brood-rearing potential[77, 100, 121]. A *Torula* yeast proved better than pollen of a *Pirus* species[39]. Foods containing 30% protein (egg yolk) were reported to be eaten better than those with less[85].

When natural pollen was lacking, dried skimmed milk protein produced 23·9% more brood than soya-bean protein (17·8%), and was as good as the less effective pollens[57,89,121]. There is a slight caramelization of the milk sugars and a change in the proteins during the drying process. The average number of micro-organisms in drum-dried skimmed milk is 2000/g; in the best spray product it is 200 000/g[53]. Whether the presence of bacteria lead to dysentery during such time as the bees cannot fly is not documented, but the milk sugars lactose and galactose are toxic to bees[6]. Since lactose exerts only about half the osmotic pressure that glucose does, the problem may be one of water regulation[72]. In the infant mammal, decrease with age of lactase (enzyme) activity is correlated with structural and histochemical changes, in which cells of the digestive tract lose their ability for membrane pinocytotic digestion[133].

The toxic effects of sugars in substitute feeds and/or diluted honey contrast with the advantages of honey itself as a feed for bees. The results were obtained in studies on caged bees without the benefit of cleansing flights, and the critical factor may be the absence of the bacteriostatic factor in honey which prevents or controls the deleterious growth of bacteria in the gut of the bees. The USDA Bee Research Laboratory at Tucson, Arizona, is at present testing pollen substitutes with free-flying colonies[102, 104].

Commercial caseins and yeast are effective replacements for pollen, but many investigations have shown that mixtures of foodstuffs are better than any one substance alone[57, 86, 112, 124].

Meal from germinating grain or beans, enriched with diastase, was found equal to, or superior to, some pollens[119]. Wheast (yeast and whey) is reported to give good results as an added ingredient to pollen in a ratio of 6 wheast : 2¼ pollen, with type-50 sugar (1 fructose : 1 glucose : 2 sucrose) added to form a dough. The lactose and mineral content may be harmful to the bees.

Amino acids[49,99] and enzymatic casein hydrolysate[128,131] have been discussed. Finally, salt mixtures with concentrations of zinc and manganese higher than in pollen may be preferable to Wessan or other mixtures with large amounts of calcium, that are potentially toxic to insects[84].

Methods of feeding substitutes

1. Dry materials (which can be mixed with dry sugar) may be fed outside the hive, in containers:
   - (*a*) shallow trays cut from cardboard boxes say 20-30 m from the hive, protected from rain, and strewn with some short pieces of straw for the bees to alight on[95];
   - (*b*) solar wax extractor[42];
   - (*c*) crocus blooms or other early cup-shaped flowers[13];
   - (*d*) ' stout shavings from new yellow deal ' sprinkled with feed; this 1875 suggestion indicates that balsam odour was believed to be attractive[13];
   - (*e*) rack of 8 trays that fit inside two hive bodies[29].

2. Feeding inside the hive is less wasteful:

   (a) Smear a paste of feed in honey or syrup, on the peripheral combs in the brood nest or on the arch of honey just above it[68].

   (b) Use a pollen feeding frame[2, 60].

   (c) Mix dry feed with syrup and place on top of the frames as a cake. Cover with waxed paper to prevent drying. If it is wrapped completely as a package, the bees will tear away the paper as they eat the food. It is important that the material remains soft, or the bees will not be able to eat it[27].

   (d) Pour uncooked fondant, made of $\frac{1}{2}$ kg (1 lb) of confectioner's or icing sugar with the stiff beaten whites of two eggs, into frames as for wired foundation, laid on waxed paper. When the fondant is hard, hang the frame next to the brood nest[90]. Pollen or other feed may be mixed with the fondant. Dried egg white is convenient, but the uncoagulated albumen without the yolk has a toxic effect on small animals. The gas-producing bacteria (10^6/g) might constitute a problem when bees cannot fly to defaecate[53].

3. Put out soya-bean flour in shallow dishes in early spring, to keep bees out of cattle feeding troughs. Bees have been known to neglect orchard blooms to collect soya-bean dust from the ventilators of a factory $\frac{1}{2}$ mile (0·8 km) away.

4. Rev. Scholz[95] recommended feeding meal to bees in the evening or at night only, or ' they will be impelled to fly however' unfavorable the weather may be '. The habit of the African hybrids of flying during inclement weather may make this advice of a century ago worth serious consideration, in localities such as California where extended feeding of sugar and pollen substitutes is now routine, but is accompanied by the death of some colonies (disappearing disease)[34].

Attractants

An attractant fraction extracted from pollen makes feed more attractive to bees[22, 24, 51, 91]. A Canadian Patent[52] covers the composition of the attractant, octadeca-*trans*-2, *cis*-9, *trans*-12-trienoic acid[52]. The present authors found that bees were attracted to fresh pollen in preference to a variety of extracts of pollen offered on glass microscope slides on the inner hive cover[51]. A record of the results was made on ciné film, as suggested by Doull and Standifer[22].

    Essential oils have been added to feed to attract bees: anise, camomile, fennel, dark rum, artificial honey essence[125]. Syrup and/or burning old comb may attract bees to a feeding site[9].

Effect of feeding substitutes as a total replacement for pollen

None of the substitutes are as good as the best pollen, but some are as good as medium quality pollens, and better than conifer pollens[123].

Brood rearing and colony population

These effects can be measured only if: the queen can lay eggs to her maximum ability; there is maximum brood rearing; food resources can be exploited fully[25]. If pollen substitute is stored in the brood nest, this may restrict space for egg laying[21]. In 1926 Parker found that although egg laying was stimulated, larvae died after the second day, i.e. in the period when pollen is normally included in their diet[88]. Dietz was also unsuccessful in rearing newly hatched larvae on artificial diets beyond 48 hours[19]. When pollen ash or inositol was added to the diet, brood was reared to the adult

96

stage[83]. When bees have access to even a slight quantity of natural pollen, substitutes have a negligible effect on brood[13, 35, 80, 95, 96, 103].

In the USSR larvae were found to develop faster in colonies fed with yeast than in colonies not so fed, and the average honey yield was 26 kg instead of 13 kg[121, 122].

In Germany, brood production was not increased in nuclei (small colonies), more field bees being lost than in unfed control nuclei[28, 32], but this would not necessarily be true of large colonies. In Californian experiments, colonies not receiving supplementary feeds, and/or being used for trapping pollen, showed population increases equal to or better than fed colonies[108]. In Norway, feeding soya-bean flour, with or without pollen, was found to result in 25-50% more pollen being collected, and an average of 11·5 kg more honey produced[120].

Pollen substitutes affect the physiology of adult bees as much as pollen does, or even more[40].

Honey production
Colonies fed N. Weaver's pollen substitute (enzymatic casein hydrolysate) produced 43% more honey (29 May—16 June) and 73% more honey (16 June—11 July) than unfed colonies; other colonies fed equivalent amounts of syrup produced only 3% and 10% more honey. There were no such differences in late summer, nor in the spring of the following year[131].

In New Zealand, colonies fed sugar *equal in cost* to pollen supplement increased their brood area by 2·2 combs, whereas in colonies fed the pollen supplement the increase was 1·2, 0·7 and 0·5 combs[36]. Substitutes are economical only during a pollen shortage, to build up colonies so that they can take full advantage of the major nectar flow[103].

Pollen collection
Data must be collected in areas where no natural pollen is available, since—as L. L. Langstroth observed in 1861—bees neglect substitutes as soon as natural pollen is available[51, 59, 95]. In the spring, however, bees fed substitutes in the evening have been found to continue to take them, even when natural pollen is available[100].

In England, feeding substitutes did not reduce the total pollen collection by the colony, contrary to the effect of feeding pollen[37]. In Austria, 30% skimmed-milk powder and 25% yeast were taken in an observation hive when pollen could not be collected outside[58].

Effects of feeding supplements (substitutes with some pollen added)
In Rumania, addition of 10% pollen (and yeast) ensured brood development in the spring[98]. The following are some results obtained in the USA. Addition of 1% pollen produced a significant increase in brood production and honey production[102, 105]. But Doull suggests that at least 10% of pollen is necessary, and that there is no evidence that 1-5% is of any value; even 20% of some pollens has little nutritional value[27]. Colonies fed 1% pollen in dry Drivert sugar had 32% more brood, but when moved to lucerne (alfalfa) the feeding did not improve pollination performance; 17% of pollen trapped was lucerne[96]. In other experiments addition of at least 5% pollen produced a significant increase in feeding (perhaps due to feeding-stimulants contained in the pollen?) and in brood rearing[105]. Colonies consumed 10 times as

much soya-bean flour cake if 25% pollen was added, and 7 times as much if 25% brewer's yeast was added[63, 77].

Supplements are taken for longer periods than substitutes alone. Dry mixtures are not utilized by bees when offered within the hive, unless pollen is added to them. Soya-bean flour or dried milk was found to be eaten better if 25% pollen was added[67].

In the USA, the average number of bees produced per colony was estimated as follows, for different foods[93]:

honey alone	575
pollen alone	8600
honey + soya-bean flour	2600
+ 12·5% pollen	4900
+ 25% pollen	5500
+ 50% pollen	7300

Pollen cakes fed inside the hive can reduce poisoning from insecticides, to the extent that foraging for pollen by the bees is reduced[78].

Colonies brought into a flight room where light intensity and temperature are controlled will produce brood all winter if they are supplied with cakes of pollen and honey or syrup.

FACTORS IN SUCCESSFUL FEEDING

The following points refer to pollen, pollen substitutes and pollen supplements.

1. Success is dependent upon the weather and the type of season: poor in cold weather; good in a normal spring[129].

2. Feeding is effective in stimulating brood rearing only when there is not enough natural pollen available, or it is of poor quality; when the colony has brood to feed; and when there is some stored pollen in the combs[20, 62, 79, 89]. The minimum area of pollen depends on locality and conditions for wintering. Two suggestions are: 4000 cm^2 (600 sq in), or the equivalent of 4 brood combs, in England[100]; 2000-6500 cm^2 (300-1000 sq in) in USA[31]. But unless the substitute or pollen to be fed is placed within 4-6 cm of unsealed brood, it be will used only slowly or not at all[69, 95, 115].

3. Failure of bees to consume non-pollen feeds may have several causes. In particular: the pollen may lack specific feeding stimulants[22]; the substitute may not be near enough to the brood nest; or the bees may be collecting fresh pollen, even if only in small quantities.

4. The addition of pollen collected the previous season, and stored carefully, increases palatability and nutrition of substitutes.

5. Bees ignore substitutes when pollen becomes available, but pollen substitutes, unlike pollen fed to a colony, do not reduce the total amount of pollen collected by foragers[37]. It is therefore suggested that the pollen should be fed separately (1 part pollen + 1 part yeast, with sugar and water to form a cake) along with a cake of pollen substitute. The bees will eat both, but the pollen-yeast feeding can be discontinued when the bees begin to collect pollen[27].

6. Feeding a pollen substitute is useful only if nurse bees consume it after it has been collected by the colony[25].

7. If honey stores are inadequate, the colony must be given combs of honey, or fed syrup, to avoid a suppression of brood rearing[5].

8. The availability of water to the colony is a necessary adjunct to feeding pollen or

substitutes[67]. Unless a natural source is available, water must be provided inside the hive, or in a watering device in the apiary. In the dry climate of Arizona, sponges in split plastic bags are being placed in experimental hives to maintain the humidity at a high enough level[27].

FORMULATIONS

Basic recommendations[14]

1.   Mix 1 part air-dried pollen (P) with 4 parts of hot water (H_2O) by weight.
2.   When the pollen is thoroughly softened, add 8 parts of granulated sugar (S) and stir until dissolved.
3.   Add 3 parts of expeller or screw-press processed, low-fat (5-7%) soya-bean flour (SBF). Soya-bean meal is too coarse for bees to eat.
4.   Knead until the dough is putty-like and can be formed into cakes.
5.   Allow to stand overnight and add additional fluid (or flour) to attain a consistency such that the cakes will stay on the top-bars without running down the sides.
6.   Form flat cakes of 0·5-0·75 kg, about 1 cm thick (1-1½ lb, ¼-½ inch), and press them down on squares of waxed paper. If prepared in advance, the cakes can be wrapped in waxed paper and frozen until used.
7.   Invert the cakes and place them directly over the frames of the brood chamber; the waxed paper cover prevents drying of the feed.
8.   Invert the hive inner-cover, or in some other way provide space for the cake, and push down on the cake to force some of the feed between the frame top-bars.
9.   If it is desired to use sugar syrup instead of dry sugar, use a small quantity of water to moisten the pollen into a paste first, then mix it with the syrup before adding the flour.
10.   If dried *Torula* or other yeast (Y) is used instead of pollen, it can be mixed with the floor before adding the sugar syrup. *Torula* is spray-dryed brewer's yeast containing 43% protein.
11.   Feeding should begin in early spring, several weeks before fresh pollen will be collected. Repeat it at 10-day intervals, or oftener if necessary, to keep a continuous supply of feed until natural pollen becomes available.
12.   A strong colony may consume up to 5 kg (10 lb) of pollen supplement, which will stimulate heavy brood rearing earlier in the season than usual. Colonies should be checked subsequently, to ensure they do not run short of pollen substitute and/or honey stores, and thus have to decrease brood rearing.
13.   Some colonies will take very little feed or none at all; similarly there is considerable variation amongst colonies in the consumption of sugar syrup.

Alternatives

Alternative 1.   M. H. Haydak

(*a*)   One part by weight of a dry mixture (4 SBF : 1 Y : 1 SM) is mixed with 2 parts of disease-free honey by weight, plus enough H_2O to produce a stiff paste. Syrup (2 S : 1 H_2O w/w) can be used in place of the honey. [SM = skimmed milk]
(*b*)   Three parts of dry ingredients (3 SBF : 1 Y : 1 SM) are mixed with 5 parts by weight of sugar syrup (1 S : 1 H_2O v/v)[6].

(c)   Mix 1 litre (quart) of cold sugar syrup (2 S : 1 hot H_2O v/v) with $\frac{1}{2}$ kg (1 lb) of the dry substitute in (b) above.   Adjust fluid until a cake can be formed that will stay on the top-bars.

(d)   The addition of 10% dried egg yolk (EY), and/or 10% finely ground commercial casein (C) manufactured from milk, will improve the food value of the substitute considerably , as in the following formulae[45]:

   (1) $2\frac{1}{2}$ SBF : 1 Y : 1 SM : $\frac{1}{2}$ EY was equal in protein content (12%) to the fresh pollen being collected by the bees, but the bees consumed twice as much of the pollen and produced 50% more brood.

   (2)   1 SBF : 1 Y : 1 SM : $\frac{1}{2}$ EY : $1\frac{1}{2}$ C (w/w) was superior to the pollen in protein content (21%) and equal to pollen in supporting brood production.

   (3)   To use fresh egg yolks, beat 7-9 yolks per kg (3-4 per lb) of dry substitute into a little sugar solution first.   Mix this into the dry feed.   The addition of 10% air-dried pollen is equal to the egg yolk[47].

Alternative 2.   USDA

3 SBF : 1 P : $2\frac{2}{3}$ hot H_2O : $5\frac{1}{2}$ S (w/w). If an equal quantity of yeast is substituted for the SBF, use 1 H_2O : 7 S[18].

Alternative 3.   H. Schaefer

16 SBF : 4 ground P (see Harvesting pollen, 4) : 12-13 hot H_2O : 28 S (w/w) makes 50-60 patties if above formula is in pounds, 120-140 if in kg.   Schaefer's substitute produced 1757 sealed cells compared to 1747 with trapped pollen, 1941 with fresh skimmed milk + fresh egg yolk, and 2880 with dried egg yolk substitute[47].

Alternative 4.   Sojapyl (Czechoslovak Patent No. 88456)

9 SBF : 1 Y with additional riboflavin, aromatic oil, and indole-3-acetic acid.   The substitute is fed dry, or 10 kg of feed is mixed with 1 kg of honey and formed into a stiff paste with the addition of powdered sugar[15, 114].

Alternative 5.   Krawaite

4 Krayest : 1 SM : 2 honey : 1 H_2O. Krawaite is manufactured by Kraft Food Limited (Melbourne, Australia), and is available in $\frac{1}{2}$-pound plastic trays, with invert sugar and an attractant to replace the honey[15].

Alternative 6.   D. Langridge

3 Krayest : 1 dried P : 1 dry icing S (w/w)[15].

Alternative 7.   California [27, 107, 132]

(a) $37\frac{1}{2}$% SBF : $37\frac{1}{2}$% food wheat : 25% P : Type-50 liquid sugar sufficient to make a semi-solid cake. The sugar is half sucrose and half simple sugars (1 fructose : 1 dextrose), with 23% H_2O.

(b)   C. Wenner. 50 Y (Torula) : 50 Y (Noobrew) : 5 P : 140 Type-50 liquid sugar.

(c)   Dry mixture. 5% SBF : 10% wheat : 85% Drivert sugar (91% sucrose, 9% simple sugars). The last item is intended to make the feed more attractive to the bees. The mixture tends to get lumpy and produces about the same results as sucrose alone[125].

100

Alternative 8. Tucson Laboratory (USDA) first series[27]

(a) 'H' 100 Y (brewer's or *Torula*) : 160 honey : 2 H_2O.
(b) 'S' 100 Y : 100 S : 50 H_2O.
(c) 'C/S' 100 Y : 100 corn syrup (Isosweet-100, 58% glucose, 42% fructose): 50 H_2O. The high percentage of glucose may cause hardening of the mixture, and wastage, since the bees cannot eat it. Adding water, and wrapping the cakes in waxed paper (or other waterproof paper), may be helpful. The problem will be eliminated when isomerized syrup with fructose contents of 60%, 75% and 90% is available on the market.

Alternative 9. Diets presently being tested at Tucson[106]

(a) 6 Y (Yeaco-20) : 6 corn syrup (Isosweet-100) : 3 H_2O (wrapped in heavy waxed paper and frozen until used).
(b) As above plus $\frac{1}{4}$ P.
(c) As above plus chloroform extract of $\frac{1}{4}$ part P adsorbed on Alphacel (cellulose powder) carrier.
(d) 2 P : $\frac{1}{2}$ Drivert sugar : $\frac{1}{2}$ sucrose sugar : H_2O sufficient to form a cake.
(e) 1 P : 1 Y : 1 ? sugar : ? H_2O to form a cake which is fed simultaneously with a cake of substitute, but the pollen feeding is discontinued when the bees begin to collect pollen.

Alternative 10. Herbert and Shimanuki*

Of various groups of 400-g colonies, those fed wheast produced the most brood (146 cm^2/week), and those fed Amber brewer's yeast (45% protein that receives a cold-water wash before spray-drying) were a close second (124). Yeaco colonies were a poor third (72). The consumption of Amber and Yeaco was increased rather more by the addition of sucrose than by the addition of other sugars or honey. Weights (g/week) consumed with different additives were:

sucrose	79
2 sucrose + 1 fructose	74
1 sucrose + 1 fructose	67
1 sucrose + 2 fructose	65
honey	64
invert sugar	59
fructose	55
isomerose	53

*Herbert, E. W.; Shimanuki, H. (1978). Consumption and brood rearing by caged honeybees fed five pollen substitutes fortified with various sugars. *J. apic. Res.* 17(1): in press.

Relative costs

Analysis of the protein content, and cost per unit weight of that protein, in pollen substitutes[97]: SBF 51% ($0·23); Y 38% ($0·27); SM 37% ($0·31); Haydak's formula (4:1:1) 48% ($0·24); Sojapyl 49% ($0·51); Krawaite 13% ($1·83); beekeeper-trapped pollen 20% (cost of collection).

All-liquid pollen substitutes

1. 600g S, 400 ml H_2O, 15g enzymatic C hydrolysate, 100 mg cholesteryl hydrogen succinate, 1g crude phospholipid, 0·5g sodium carbonate, 12 ml vitamin mixtures

(or 5g yeast extract), and 100 mg Wesson's salt mixture [not Wessan's Ingredients Section]. One colony fed from January reared brood, but by late March brood rearing had declined and the colony became disorganized. When given combs of pollen, the brood production quickly increased[128, 131].

2. Johansson and Johansson (1970, unpublished) fed an elemental diet designed for astronauts on space trips. The powdered bulk-free diet (Codelid 52H, Schwarz Research) contained 5% fat and was mixed with water for use. The small colonies confined in a bee house in July took the diet, but the queens ceased laying eggs until the bees were given freedom to resume flying to collect pollen.

Medication

Published formulations often include suggestions for incorporating various antibiotics into substitute pollen feeds, to prevent the onset of disease in the colonies. It is, however, now widely accepted that this measure defeats its own ends, for continuous use of antibiotics will in time select out resistant strains of the organisms they are designed to control; or, alternatively, other organisms will occupy the vacated niche[56].

References

Titles are given in the original language if this is English, French or German; otherwise the title is given in English and the language of the original is named.

Almost all publications listed are in the IBRA Library. Numbers at the end of the entry such as 37/50 give the reference to the journal *Apicultural Abstracts*; 37/50 is item 37 in the 1950 volume.

1. ADAIR, D. L. (ed.) (1869) Annals of bee culture for 1869. *Louisville, Ky : Hull & Bro.*
2. ——(1872) Progressive bee culture. *Cincinnati : Robert Clarke & Co.*
3. ADAMS, G. W. (1922) More beekeeping history. *Am. Bee J.* 62(3) : 104-105; *reprinted* 114(6) : 216-217 (1974)
4. AUCLAIR, J. L.; JAMIESON, C. A. (1948) Qualitative analysis of amino-acids in pollen collected by bees. *Science, N.Y.* 108(2805) : 357-358   37/50
5. BARKER, R. J. (1971) The influence of food inside the hive on pollen collection by a honeybee colony. *J. apic. Res.* 10(1) : 23-26   907/71
6. BARKER, R. J.; LEHNER, Y. (1976) Milk sugar poisons honey bees. *Am. Bee J.* 116(7) : 322, 332
7. Bee World (1921) Bee consumption. *Bee Wld* 3(1) : 18-19
8. ——(1933) Research notes. *Bee Wld* 14(8) : 95
9. ——(1942) Miscellany. *Bee Wld.* 23(3) : 23
10. ——(1970) Feeding bees for winter. *Bee Wld* 51(3) : 119-120   951L/71
11. ——(1976) Harvesting pollen from hives. *Bee Wld* 57(1) : 20-25   588L/76
12. BEUTLER, R.; OPFINGER, E. (1949) Pollenernährung und Nosemabefall der Honigbiene. *Z. vergl. Physiol.* 32(5) : 383-421   90/51
13. British Bee Journal (1875) Artificial pollen. *Br. Bee J.* 2 : 204
14. BURKE, P. W. (1970) Feeding bees. *Publ. Ont. Dep. Agric. No.* 131   383L/73
15. CHAMBERS, S. R. (1965) Substitutes for pollen in practice. *Apic. W. Aust.* 1(8) : 114-115   138L/66
16. CARR, E. G. (1937) Pollen substitutes. *Am. Bee J.* 77(4) : 181-182
17. COGITATOR (1899) " Boiler's " bagged bees. *Am. Bee J.* 39(6) : 82

18.   DETROY, B. F.; HARP, E. R. (1976) Trapping pollen from honey bee colonies. *Prod.*
      Res. Rep. USDA ARS No. 163   314L/77
19.   DIETZ, A. (1973) Longevity and survival of honey bee larvae on artificial diets. *J.*
      Georgia ent. Soc. 8(1) : 59-63   214/76
20.   DOULL, K. M.; PURDIE, J. D. (1966) Field tests with Krawaite pollen supplement.
      Preliminary results. *Aust. Bee J.* 47(4) : 13-15   691/66
21.   DOULL, K. M. (1968) Recent developments in pollen supplement research. *Am. Bee J.*
      108(4) : 139-140   140/69
22.   DOULL, K. M.; STANDIFER, L. N. (1970) Feeding responses of honeybees in the hive.
      J. apic. Res. 9(3) : 129-132   146/72
23.   DOULL, K. M. (1974) Effect of distance on the attraction of pollen to honeybees in the
      hive. *J. apic. Res.* 13(1) : 27-32   131/75
24.   ———(1974) Effects of attractants and phagostimulants in pollen and pollen supple-
      ment on the feeding behaviour of honeybees in the hive. *J. apic. Res.* 13(1) :
      47-54   152/75
25.   ———(1974) Recent research on the use of pollen supplements. *Bee Wld* 55 *Suppl.* :
      145-147
26.   ———(1975) Pollen supplements. *Am. Bee J.* 115 : 14-15; 54-55; 88-89, 99   820L/76
27.   ———(1977) Tucson pollen supplements. *Am. Bee J.* 117(5) : 296-297
28.   DREHER, K.; PERKIEWICZ, E. (1955) Reizfütterungsversuche mit Pollenersatzmitteln.
      Biene 91(1) : 11-12   298/55
29.   DUNHAM, W. E. (1945) Feeding a dry pollen substitute to bees. *Glean. Bee Cult.*
      73(5) : 192-193, 241
30.   FARRAR, C. L. (1934) Bees must have pollen. *Glean. Bee Cult.* 62(5) : 276-278
31.   ———(1936) Influence of pollen reserves on the surviving populations of over-wintered
      colonies. *Am. Bee J.* 76(9) : 452-456
32.   FEDERL, F. (1951) Höselhefe als Pollenersatz, praktische Erprobung im Frühjahr 1950.
      Imkerfreund 6(6) : 192-194   155/52
33.   FOOTE, H. L. (1957) Possible use of microorganisms in synthetic bee bread production.
      Am. Bee J. 97(12) : 476-478
34.   FORE, T. (1977) Disappearing disease link to African bees seen. *Speedy Bee* 5(12) : 2, 5
35.   FORSTER, I. W. (1966) Pollen supplements for honey bee colonies. *N.Z. Beekpr* 28(3) :
      14-21   748/68
36.   ———(1968) Pollen supplements for honey bee colonies. Trials during 1967. *N.Z.*
      Beekpr 30(3) : 16-17   167/71
37.   FREE, J. B.; WILLIAMS, I. H. (1971) The effect of giving pollen and pollen supplement
      to honeybee colonies on the amount of pollen collected. *J. apic. Res.* 10(2) :
      87-90   997/72
38.   GANAEV, A. I. (1959) [Do bees need pollen during wintering?] *Pchelovodstvo* 36(8) :
      33-34 *In Russian*   374/61
39.   GIORDANI, G. (1957) [Yeast in the feeding of honeybees.] *Apicoltore d'Ital.* 24(5/6) :
      125-160 *In Italian*   292/58
40.   GONTARSKI, H. (1954) Untersuchungen über die Verwertung von Pollen und Hefe zur
      Brutpflege der Honigbiene. *Z. Bienenforsch.* 2(6) : 161-180   296/55
41.   GOODERHAM, C. B. (1950) Pollen substitutes. *Prog. Rep. Dominion Apiarist Canad.*
      Dep. Agric. 1937-1948 : 8-10   138/50
42.   H. (1950) Pollenersatz. *Imkerfreund* 5(2) : 17-18   105/50

43. HARP, E. R. (1966) A simplified pollen trap for use on colonies of honey bees. *U.S. Dep. Agric. ARS* 33-111   787/68

44. HARTLIB, S. (1655) The reformed common-wealth of bees. *London: Giles Calvert*

45. HAYDAK, M. H. (1957) Is there a pollen substitute equal to pollen? *Am. Bee J.* 97(3) : 90-91   327/58

46. ———(1958) Pollen—pollen substitutes—beebread. *Am. Bee J.* 98(4) : 145-146 332/58

47. ———(1959) Pollen substitutes—still a controversy ? *Am. Bee J.* 99(4) : 131-132

48. HEDDON, J. (1881) Pollen detrimental to wintering. *Am. Bee J.* 17(36) : 283

49. HILLIARD, D. E. (1955) Feeding amino acids to bees. *Bee Wld* 36(11) : 207

50. HITCHCOCK, J. D.; REVELL, I. L. (1963) The spread of American foulbrood by pollen trapped from bees' legs. *Am. Bee J.* 103(6) : 220-221   385/64

51. HOHMANN, H. (1969) Concerning the effect of scent substances and pollen extracts on the collecting and courting [recruiting] behaviour of pollinating bees (*Apis mellifica* L.) *XXII Int. Beekeep. Congr. Summ.* : 132   376/70

52. HOPKINS, C. Y.; BOCH, R.; JEVANS, A. W. (1975) Honeybee attractant compositions. *Canad. Pat.* 970, 209

53. JENSEN, H. R. (1931) The chemistry, flavouring and manufacture of chocolate confectionery and cocoa. *Philadelphia : P. Blakiston's Son & Co. Inc.*

54. JOHANSSON, T. S. K.; JOHANSSON, M. P. (1964) Unpublished data (film)

55. ———(1970) Unpublished data

56. ———(1971) Antibiotic resistance. *Am. Bee J.* 111(2) : 56-57, 60   394L/73

57. JORDAN, R. (1957) Untersuchungen mit Trockenmagermilch als Pollenersatz. *Bienenvater* 78(7/8) : 200-207   326/58

58. ———(1963) Lassen sich Flugbienen durch Verwendung an Pollenersatz reichhaltigem Teig von der Aufnahme eines solchen abhalten? *Bienenvater* 84(5): 131-136 612/64

59. KIRKPATRICK, J. (1861) First American Beekeepers' Convention *Am. Bee J.* 1(2) : 67-70

60. KORNELY, R. (1970) A way to feed pollen substitutes. *Glean. Bee Cult.* 98(3) : 137-140

61. LAERE, O. van (1965) L'effet de quelques facteurs sur le développement du nid à couvain de l'abeille (*Apis mellifera* L.) *Ann. Abeille* 8(4) : 285-297   472/66

62. LANGRIDGE, D. F.; RUFFORD-SHARPE, J. (1966) A successful protein supplement for honey bees. *J. Agric. Vict. Dep. Agric.* 64(1) : 27-31   693/66

63. LANGRIDGE, D. F. (1967) Preparation of protein supplement for bees. *J. Dep. Agric. Vict.* 65(2) : 3-7   373/68

64. LANGSTROTH, L. L. (1879) Stimulating bees to promote early breeding. *Glean. Bee Cult.* 7(4) : 131-132

65. LOUVEAUX, J. (1958) Recherches sur la récolte du pollen par les abeilles (*Apis mellifica* L.) *Ann. Abeille* 1 : 113-188, 197-221   330/61

66. ———(1963) Le rôle du pollen dans l'alimentation de la ruche. *Ann. Nutr., Paris* 17(1) : A313-A318   348/64

67. LUNDER, R. (1950) [Can bees be stimulated early in spring ?] *Nord. Bitidskr.* 2(2) : 33-39 *In Norwegian*   55/54

68. McCORD, D. A. (1880) Pea flour for pollen. *Glean. Bee Cult.* 8(3) : 110

69. McGREGOR, S. E. (1952) Collection and utilization of propolis and pollen by caged honey bee colonies. *Am. Bee J.* 92(1) : 20-21   161/53

70. McLAIN, N. W. (1888) A report of some experiments in apiculture. *Am. Bee J.* 24(30) : 487-489

71. McLELLAN, A. R. (1974). Some effects of pollen traps on colonies of honeybees. *J. apic. Res.* 13(2) : 143-148   894/74

72. MESSER, M.; KERRY, K. R. (1973) Milk carbohydrates of the echidna and the platypus. *Science, N.Y.* 180(4082) : 201-203

73. MICHELS, J. (1958/1959) Johannes Mehring. *Südwestdtsch. Imker* 10 : 230-234, 294-295   319/60

74. MIKHAILOV, K. I. (1960) [Investigation on wintering bees without pollen.] *Pchelovodstvo* 37(3) : 8-12 *In Russian*   123/63

75. ———(1964) [The nutrition of bees in winter.] *Trud. nauch.-issled. Inst. Pchelovodstva* : 73-85 *In Russian*   777/65

76. MILLER, C. C. (1904) Stray straws. *Glean. Bee Cult.* 32(15) : 739

77. MOELLER, F. E. (1967) Honey bee preference for pollen supplements or substitutes and their use in colony management. *Am. Bee J.* 107(2) : 48-50   372/68

78. ———(1972) Honey bee collection of corn pollen reduced by feeding pollen in the hive. *Am. Bee J.* 112(6) : 210-212   412/73

79. MØLBY, T. (1949) [Feeding bees—aims and means.] *Tidsskr. Biavl* 83(3) : 28-33 *In Danish*   107/54

80. MOMMERS, J. (1968) [Pollen substitutes.] *Bijenteelt* 70 : 129-131, 140-141 *In Dutch*   691/71

81. NACHBAUR, A. J., Jr. (1968) Feeding liquid pollen. *Am. Bee J.* 108(5) : 187   142/69

82. NATION, J. L.; ROBINSON, F. A. (1966) Gibberellic acid: effects of feeding in an artificial diet for honeybees. *Science, N.Y.* 152(3730) : 1765-1766   698/66

83. ———(1968) Brood rearing by caged honey bees in response to inositol and certain pollen fractions in their diet. *Ann. ent. Soc. Am.* 61(2) : 514-517   546/68

84. ———(1971) Concentration of some major and trace elements in honeybees, royal jelly and pollens, determined by atomic absorption spectrophotometry. *J. apic. Res.* 10(1) : 35-43   86/72

85. NATION, J. L. (1974) Nutrition of honey bees. *20th A. E. apic. Soc. Conf., Guelph, Ont.*

86. PAIN, J. (1963) L'alimentation de la jeune abeille. *Ann. Nutr., Paris* 17(1) : A307-A312   312/64

87. PAIN, J.; MAUGENET, J. (1966) Recherches biochimiques et physiologiques sur le pollen emmagasiné par les abeilles. *Ann. Abeille* 9(3) : 206-236   110/67

88. PARKER, R. L. (1926) The collection and utilization of pollen by the honey bee. *Mem. N.Y. Agric. Exp. Stn No.* 98

89. PEREL'SON, I. E. (1961) [The value of protein feeding.] *Pchelovodstvo* 38(11) : 16-19 *In Russian*   152/64

90. RAYMENT, T. (1915) Brood-rearing successful with albumenized candy. *Glean. Bee Cult.* 43(2) : 151-152

91. ROBINSON, F. A.; NATION, J. L. (1968) Substances that attract caged honeybee colonies to consume pollen supplements and substitutes. *J. agric. Res.* 7(2) : 83-88   962/70

92. ROOT, V. E. (1967) Combined pollen collector and entrance restriction for bee hives. *U.S. Pat.* 3,350,728   503/70

93. SCHAEFER, C. W.; FARRAR, C. L. (1941) The use of pollen traps and pollen supplements in developing honey bee colonies. *Publ. U.S.D.A.* E-531, rev. 1946

94. SCHAEFFER, H. A. (1947) One way to salvage pollen in the comb. *Am. Bee J.* 87(1) : 12-13

95. SCHOLZ, Rev. (1861) Meal feeding. *Am. Bee J.* 1(4) : 78-79

96. SHEESLEY, B.; PODUSKA, B. (1969) What happens to honey bees in alfalfa seed pollination . . . feeding results. *Am. Bee J.* 109(3) : 90-93   692/71

97. SMITH, F. G. (1966) The cost of protein in pollen substitutes. *Apic. W. Aust.* 1(9) : 132-133   695/66

98. SPĂTURA, C. L.; LAZĂR, S.; CZEISLER, G. (1967) [Investigations on the effect and effic- iency of supplementary feeding of honeybees with brewer's yeast as a substitute for pollen.] *Lucr. științ. Inst. agron. Timișoara Seri. Mednă vet.* 10 : 525-534 *In Rumanian*   744/72

99. SPĂTARU, C. L. (1970) [Stimulating effedt and productive efficiency of proteins and amino acids fed to bees as pollen substitutes.] *Tezei de Doctor in Agronomie, Institutul Agronomic "N. Bălcescu" București, Rumania. In Rumanian*   509/76

100. SPENCER-BOOTH, Y. (1960) Feeding pollen, pollen substitutes and pollen supplements to honeybees. *Bee Wld* 41(10) : 253-263   108/62

101. STANDIFER, L. N. (1967) A comparison of the protein quality of pollens for growth- stimulation of the hypopharyngeal glands and longevity of honey bees, *Apis mellifera* L. (Hymenoptera : Apidae). *Insectes soc.* 14(4) : 415-425   502/68

102. STANDIFER, L. N.; WALLER, G. D.; HAYDAK, M. H.; LEVIN, M. D.; MILLS, J. P. (1971) Stimulative feeding of honeybee colonies in Arizona. *J. apic. Res.* 10(1) : 27-34   149/72

103. STANDIFER, L. N.; OWENS, C. D.; HAYDAK, M. H.; MILLS, J. P.; LEVIN, M. D. (1973) Supplementary feeding of honeybee colonies in Arizona. *Am. Bee. J.* 113(8) : 298-301   183/74

104. STANDIFER, L. N.; HAYDAK, M. H.; MILLS, J. P.; LEVIN, M. D. (1973) Value of three protein rations in maintaining honeybee colonies in outdoor flight cages. *J. apic. Res.* 12(3) : 137-143   184/74

105. ———(1973) Influence of pollen in artificial diets on food consumption and brood production in honey bee colonies. *Am. Bee J.* 113(3) : 94-95   185/74

106. STANDIFER, L. N. (1976). The elusive pollen substitute and other projects (Part 1). *E. apic. Soc. Convention, Blacksburg, VA*

107. STANGER, W.; GRIPP, R. H. (1972) Commercial feeding. *Am. Bee J.* 112(11) : 417, 419   742L/72

108. STANGER, W.; LAIDLAW, H. H. (1974) Supplementary feeding of honeybees (*Apis mellifera* Linnaeus). *Am. Bee J.* 114(4) : 138-141   151/75

109. STANLEY, R. G.; LINSKENS, H. F. (1974) Pollen : biology—biochemistry—manage- ment. *Berlin : Springer-Verlag*   585/76

110. STROIKOV, S. A. (1963) [Food value to bees of bee bread and pollen.] *Pchelovodstvo* 40(6): 23-25 *In Russian*   131/65

111. ———(1967a) [Protein : the basis of colony yields.] *Pchelovodstvo* 87(5) : 27-28 *In Russian*   392/70

112. ———(1967b) [Ability of bees to digest nutrient material from pollen substitutes.] *Trudy nauchno-issled. Inst. Pchel.* : 89-106 *In Russian*   425/70

113. STURTEANT, J. H. (1937) Substitute pollens badly needed. *Am. Bee J.* 77(2) : 79

114. SVOBODA, J.; SIPEK, A. (1961) [Bee food preparation.] *Czech. Pat.* 101,415 *In Czech.*   840/63

115. TABER, S., III (1973) Influence of pollen location in the hive on its utilization by the honeybee colony. *J. apic. Res.* 12(1) : 17-20   647/73

116. THOMPSON, V. C. (1960) Nectar flow and pollen yield in south-western Arkansas 1945-1951. *Rep. Ser. Ark. agric. Exp. Sta. No. 94*   371/61

117. TODD, F. D. (1910) Artificial substitutes for pollen. *Glean. Bee Cult.* 38(4) : 122-123

118. TOWNSEND, G. F.; SMITH, M. V. (1969) Pollen storage for bee feed. *Am. Bee J.* 109(1) : 14-15　169/71

119. TURTUREANU, G. (1961) [Flour from various grains enriched with diastase as a new pollen substitute.] *Apicultura, Bucureşti* 14(11) : 18-21 *In Rumanian*　323/65

120. VILLUMSTAD, E. (1964) [Investigations on feeding soya-bean flour and pollen to bees in 1963.] *Birøkteren* 80(1) : 9-13 *In Norwegian*　151/65

121. VINOGRADOVA, T. V. (1951) [Experiments in changing bees (by feeding with vitamin extracts).] *Moscow: Lenizdat In Russian*　10/53

122. ———(1951) [The effect of feeding colonies with yeast.] *Pchelovodstvo* (12) : 17-18 *In Russian*　11/53

123. WAHL, O. (1954) Untersuchungen über den Nährwert von Pollenersatzmitteln für die Honigbiene. *Insectes soc.* 1(3) : 285-292　55/56

124. ———(1963/1964) Vergleichende Untersuchungen über den Nährwert von Pollen, Hefe, Sojamehl und Trockenmilch für Honigbiene (*Apis mellifica*). *Z. Bienenforsch.* 6(8) : 209-280; 7(1) : 22　873/64

125. WALLER, G. D.; HAYDAK, M. H.; LEVIN, M. D. (1970) Increasing the palatability of pollen substitutes. *Am. Bee J.* 110(8) : 302-304　150/72

126. WALSH, R. S. The preparation of pollen for the market. Typescript.

127. WEAVER, N. (1964) A pollen substitute for honeybee colonies. *Glean. Bee Cult.* 92(9): 550-553　136/66

128. WEAVER, N.; CHAUTHANI, A. R. (1967) An all-liquid pollen substitute for honey bee colonies. *Am. Bee J.* 107(4) : 134-135　344/67

129. WEISS, K. (1961) Neue Versuche zur Frühjahrsreizfütterung. *Imkerfreund* 16(3) : 74-76　670/62

130. WHITEFOOT, L. O.; DETROY, B. F. (1968) Pollen—milling and storing. *Am. Bee J.* 108(4) : 138, 140　622/68

131. WILLE, H.; SCHÄFER, H. (1970) Fütterungsversuche mit einem flüssigen Pollenersatzmittel. *Schweiz. Bienenztg* 93(10) : 483-494　148/72

132. WYNDHAM, R. J. (1973) Interest in bee feeding soaring in California. *Am. Bee J.* 113(2) : 52

133. YEH, K.; MOOG, F. (1974) Intestinal lactase activity in the suckling rat : influence of hypophysectomy and thyroidectomy. *Science, N.Y.* 182 (4120) : 77-79

134. ZHEREBKIN, M. V. (1963) [The amounts of protein and fat in the body of the honeybee.] *Pchelovodstvo* 40(11) : 34-36 *In Russian*　90/65

CHAPTER 8

PROVIDING HONEYBEES WITH WATER

This is the first comprehensive publication on bees' requirements for water and on its provision in the beekeeper's management programme through the year. This is a most important part of the beekeeping practice.

Contents

Introduction

The limited space devoted in most beekeeping manuals to the subject of water contrasts with its importance to bees. Although bees' critical need for water might be considered too obvious to mention, a beekeeper was recently fined $200 for failure to take responsibility for his thirsty bees, which had made a nuisance of themselves searching for water and finding it in swimming pools, dripping faucets, livestock watering troughs, bird baths, washed clothes hung out to dry, etc. The failure to provide water, and subsequent complaints about bees constituting a nuisance, have resulted in municipal bans against keeping bees altogether.

In 1930, the county supervisors in California made it an offence punishable by a fine of $25 or 25 days in jail, or both, not to provide water for bees when the nearest source of running water was more than $\frac{1}{4}$ mile away[105]. It is essential that each beekeeper should provide water for his bees before they frighten neighbours; bees have even entered houses and shared water with the family at the dinner table[3, 145, 157].

During an Australian heat wave, an apiary of 150 hives emptied a 20-gallon tub of water (100 litres) in less than three hours, sucked perspiration from bare arms, and alighted on a cup of water before the pourer could raise it to his lips[139].

The provision of water for bees should be given as much, if not more, attention than any other phase of successful bee management[2, 65, 109, 150]. Bees collect some water every day. Since it is often not possible to anticipate when they will need large quantities of water, it is best to have it available continuously, more especially early in the flying season. The bees' lack of activity at a water source is a convenient measure of nectar secretion, because as the collection of nectar increases, the collection of water decreases, and vice versa[16]. Bowen used the activity at the water trough as a harbinger of rain[39]. A. W. Woodrow warns that bees must be provided with a source of water as they are moved to a new site, because they may not find a local source soon enough to prevent a set-back in brood rearing, or even the death of the colony[144].

This compilation includes the available basic information on water collection, so that alternatives can be devised for unique situations or circumstances that do not fit the simplistic obvious recommendations.

Behaviour of honeybees in collecting water

It has been considered for some time that certain bees might undertake the activity of carrying water only[100], and this has indeed proved to be true[132]. A Swedish experimental apiary has counted the number of bees collecting water for 1 minute, at noon, every day since 1946[106].

Scout bees can find water by the higher relative water-vapour content of the air above the surface of the water[132], and they can detect a relative humidity difference of 5%, using hygroreceptors located on the 8 distal segments of the antennae[94].

Water-collecting bees regurgitate 70% of the water they have collected to hive bees, who then function as "reservoirs" for the water until it is needed. The remaining 30% of the water is ingested, a negligible quantity being absorbed by the lining of the digestive tract. Nearly all of the ingested water passes through the gut, to be ejected from the anus with undigested food material, excretory material from the Malpighian tubules, and incidental inclusions such as *Nosema* spores[118].

In German experiments water collectors averaged 56 trips a day, and could make as many as 100. A round trip was made in 3 minutes or less by 67% of the carriers, and in 10 minutes or less by 92%. The time spent in the hive was usually 2 to 3 minutes, rarely as long as 5 minutes. In the hive the water carriers performed a dance before transferring their load to 2 or 3 individuals, or to as many as 18. Preparations for the next trip included a small sip of food from a house bee, or from a cell of honey. It required 5 water carriers to supply the water necessary to feed 100 larvae[99].

A one-frame observation hive had 1300 bees (half the colony) serving as reservoir-bees by the end of the day. Their honey sacs shrank during periods when water could not be collected. A majority of them had a little honey mixed with the water. During the spring when nectar is not yet available, the reservoir-bees may deposit some of this diluted honey into cells within or near the brood nest[76].

Water is essential to maintain a constant temperature in the brood nest during hot dry weather[49,50]. Water may be deposited in: (*a*) small cell-like enclosures made of wax and propolis on the top bars of the frames in hives; (*b*) indentations in the cappings of honey cells, until these look as if they had been sprinkled with water; (*c*) cells of combs, especially those containing eggs and larvae. When such water evaporates, it has a cooling effect and keeps the larvae and eggs from drying. Evaporation is also effected by bees spreading a film of water or nectar between their mouth parts[76]. Whereas nectar collection is affected by the external temperature, water foraging is not. Reducing the hive temperature had no effect in the spring, but in August it led to a higher honey yield[98]. Although a colony of bees usually stores water in only a few cells, there is one record of a colony in California with approximately 1½ gallon of water (7½ litres) contained in two large combs. The bees' nearest source of water was one mile away, and they may have taken advantage of unusual rain to store water[149].

Effect of lack of water on the colony

The requirements of adult bees for water are not known precisely[12], but observations on bees in confinement give some indication of how long bees can live without water, for instance queens crossing the Atlantic Ocean on board ship. When sent without water, some of the bees accompanying the queen were usually dead on arrival[117]. Maurizio found that bees will live 3-4 times as long if they have access to water[34]. Workers and queens caged on candy take a great deal of water if it is offered, and live much longer than those not given water. Only 10% of queens fed candy alone survived more than 5 days; whereas all queens fed candy and water lived more than 5 days[152]. Water consumption increased rapidly between 45° and 50°C, and bees provided with a liquid diet lost more weight during exposure to high temperatures than those fed candy[98a].

In areas of high temperatures a colony uses as much as a gallon (5 litres*) of water on a hot day. Some water is obtained from nectar, but a colony unable to collect water will die within a day or so[121]. It is interesting to note that such a colony can appear to have been killed by an insecticide, although none was used[144]. Colonies confined in anticipation of an application of insecticide spray suffered considerably less mortality when provided with water than when left without water[148].

Need for water by bees

The main use that bees have for water is to dilute any honey or syrup which contains 50% or more sugar, including honey to be used for feeding young brood[140]. This is more essential than is usually appreciated[23, 24, 69, 142]. R. Jordan considered the sudden spurt in brood rearing in the spring to be caused by access to water rather than pollen, which is stored in plenty in the hive[23]. In Israel, trickling water into the brood nest increased the queen's laying in summer, with the most pronounced differences at the higher temperatures. In August, the brood areas were 5700 and 3900 cm^2 respectively in watered and unwatered colonies[98].

Since bees do not normally store water in the hive, except in the honey sacs of reservoir bees, bees confined for any length of time must be provided with water[69, 76].

Outdoor-wintered bees in the cold north can utilize the water vapour that condenses on the interior surface of the hive[5, 23, 125] (as much as 5 litres a month[80]); they require water since the air is drier in winter at lower temperatures[112]. When bees uncap

---

* In the USA a gallon is 3·79 litres; in the British Commonwealth a gallon is 4·55 litres. But in this paper the term gallon rarely indicates a precise measurement.

cells of honey, the honey can absorb its own weight of water in 24 hours at 15°C, and thus become diluted without the bees having to collect water outside the hive[6].

In the early spring when there is brood to feed, the lack of water, or lack of opportunity to collect it due to inclement weather, may mean the difference between strong and weak colonies when the main honey flow arrives[151]. Bees can produce some brood without pollen, using the nitrogenous sources within their own bodies, but none can be produced without water[1, 66].

Beekeepers who practice stimulative syrup feeding in the early spring should provide water in the hive when bees cannot fly to collect it[69]. The metabolic water resulting from the digestion of sugar will provide not more than one-eighth of the needed water[140].

Bees need water to maintain a moisture content within the hive that is high enough for eggs to hatch, and to prevent larvae from drying[27, 66a, 69, 130]. It is required when they ingest solid sugars, including granulated honey[69, 107, 155].

In Norway, more pollen substitute was eaten when water was provided in the hive, and the substitute dried out less rapidly[102].

Bees cool the hive by evaporation of water when there is brood to care for. Lindauer reported the temperature just above the floor board in a partly shaded hive to be only 33°C when the outside temperature was 53°[99]. Bees have survived 128°F (53°C) in Death Valley, California[28].

Some of the "spring dwindling" blamed on nosema disease may in fact be due to a shortage of water, and its occurrence under adverse conditions, especially lack of water when bees cannot fly during bad weather, can produce significant losses[36, 101]. The practice of feeding sugar syrup in the spring is perhaps more important for the water it provides than for the sugar[57].

Factors in water collection

Quantity used

Beekeepers do not always realize how much water is used by their colonies, since the bees find it on their own. Chauvin and Pawletta recorded isolated periods of flight by bees at night, and it would be interesting to attempt to correlate these with conditions of water dearth, since dew may be available at night—for instance in deserts[51, 123]. In Sweden Hansson calculated that a colony used approximately 31 litres during the season, the daily collection being as follows[86]:

March 1	42 g	July 1	230 g
March 15	47 g	July 15	184 g
April 1	55 g	August 1	134 g
April 15	76 g	August 15	118 g
May 1	151 g	September 1	101 g
May 15	249 g	September 15	49 g
June 1	294 g	October 1	26 g
June 15	294 g		

The greatest quantity consumed was between May and August, when there is most brood rearing[19, 69]. There can also be an increase during autumn if stimulative feeding is practised[106].

Records of water collection from feeders are not easy to come by, but those located are reported below. The number of pounds (0·45 kg) of water collected per day during the brood-rearing season ranges from $0 \cdot 022$[109] to $0 \cdot 73$, with intermediate values of $0 \cdot 22$[142] and $0 \cdot 6$[111]. But it is the spectacular quantities collected during brief periods of extreme temperature and drought that receive most attention; examples are $1 \cdot 15$[115], $1 \cdot 77$[96a] and (by extrapolation) $4 \cdot 27$[139] pounds/colony/day. The authors remember the active water collection by bees at a rain barrel during six years of drought, and the comparative absence of bees during years when rainfall was normal or above normal. These records are consistent with Stanger's conclusions that an average colony of bees under average conditions may use $\frac{1}{3}$ pint of water per day during spring brood rearing, but that under hot drought conditions a strong colony may require one pint or several, or as much as one gallon per day [121, 144]; in litres the amounts are $0 \cdot 2$ in spring, or $0 \cdot 5$ up to 4 in heat.

Water preference

Bees prefer water warmer than April air temperatures[77, 110], and the fermentation activity around a compost heap[67, 125] can provide this warmth. Twelve colonies collected $16 \cdot 3$ lb of cold water, but $96 \cdot 3$ lb of warm water—six times as much[142]. Bees prefer water at temperatures above $65°F$ ($18°C$) and below $90°F$ ($32°C$), and they will not accept water much above $100°F$ ($38°C$)[71].

Water-foraging bees desert water-collection sites when nectar becomes available and provides the water required by the colony[48, 106]. Water containing green algae, and water to which anise had been added, has been found more attractive to bees than water without. Apparently detection is by the olfactory sense organs.

Bees have been observed collecting brine from the surface of a block of salt (NaCl) 15-25 rods (75-125 m) from the hive[104], and it was once a Cornish custom to hang out a salt pilchard fish for the bees[87]. Bees have been found to prefer salt water to fresh water (5 to 1)[55, 60, 136] when the concentration was less than 1%[111], and Butler determined that they perceived and preferred N/20 NaCl[46] ($0 \cdot 3\%$). Even 30-50% sucrose solution is refused when the salt content exceeds 1%[153]. Observations at a water-collecting site since 1946 have shown that a $0 \cdot 5\%$ salt solution attracted half as many bees as fresh water did[106].

Honeybees are attracted to urine for its salt content[94], but collect it only when very much diluted. If the volatile substances are removed with animal charcoal, the urine is no more attractive than distilled water. This is also true of cow-dung water, for which bees have been noted to show a marked preference[46].

There has been much controversy as to whether the preference of bees for salt reflects nutritional requirements[20]. The rectal glands of bees reabsorb sodium chloride and store it; as in other animals, salt together with proteins maintain fluid or osmotic pressure in the blood. The secretions bees use for food ingestion are nearly ion-free, so no reduction of salts in the blood is involved[1]. Piscutelli observed a preference for solutions containing minerals when colonies had unsealed brood[126]. Micro-radiographs showed increasing amounts of P^{32} from egg to pupa. Bees have reared brood successfully in a greenhouse on well water, without access to salts[99] (but they might then use salts from their body tissues). There is no apparent necessity to provide bees with salt, but it has been used to keep water from becoming sour[42], and also to lure bees away from watering sites where they were creating a nuisance[138]. Bees collected more distilled water when it contained $0 \cdot 1\%$ NaCl w/w[153]. Salt is increasingly toxic to bees in quantities exceeding $0 \cdot 5\%$, if they are unable to fly[64].

Energy expended in water collection over different distances

To collect one pint (1¼ lb, 0·6 litre) of water from a feeder 25 ft (7·5 m) from the hive, it has been calculated, requires 17 000 trips by the bees, covering a total flying distance of 16 miles (25 km)[22]. Stimulative feeding with concentrated solutions of sugar syrup may be counter-productive[9]. Jean-Lobstedt calculated the number of water-collecting trips saved (assuming the bees carry a full honey-sac load, 14-16 ml of water) by providing water in Doolittle-type feeders inside the hive during April, May and June as 30-35, 80-90 and 130-150 thousand respectively[142]. J. H. Dustin reasoned that drawing water up the mountain with his horse saved his bees the equivalent muscular energy which they could then use instead to produce honey[134].

If a considerable number of bees are involved in carrying water during a heat wave, the loss of honey production will not be as great if water is close by as if it is farther away. There is one report that colonies ¾ mile (1 km) from an irrigation canal secured only one-third the crop of those alongside the canal[9]. If the source of water is more than a mile (1·6 km) away, the colonies should be moved closer to it, or water should be provided near the apiary. In principle, full efficiency is possible only if water is closer to the apiary[121, 122], well within 100 metres (yards). When bees must fly against a strong wind, the maximum distance from which a colony can collect water, and still develop normally, is correspondingly less. A wind of 15 mph (24 km/h) reduces flights, and one of 20 mph (32 km/h) stops flight altogether[111].

Colonies with water at an average distance of 130 m showed a positive advantage from being fed sugar syrup in the spring, over colonies with water only 15 m away; the greater distance the former colonies would have to travel to collect water would otherwise be a handicap in developing the full potential for colony growth. The colony stores the sugar, but not the water[57], and thus benefits from a supply in or near the hive.

Air temperatures during water collection

Honeybees fly at lower temperatures when searching for water than for nectar[52, 69]. During the months of March, April and May, when the brood nest is expanding rapidly, there is an increasing need for water to dilute the honey in store. But upon occasion the weather can be so unfavourable that the opportunity to collect water is limited. After cold, rainy days bees come to water feeders by the hundreds and thousands at temperatures of 45-50°F (7-10°C). Like the bumble bee, the honeybee warms up before flying by contracting the thoracic flight muscles rapidly (shivering), and the heat generated during flight will maintain the minimum temperature necessary for the trip to the water collection site[88]. A passing cloud may reduce temperatures slightly, and the bees then become so chilled when they settle at the watering place that they are not able to return to the colony[60, 65, 66].

Whereas bees fly for water at minimal temperatures, they do not fly at such low temperatures to collect nectar, since nectar is not then being secreted. This fact is often ignored in discussions about breeding bees to fly at low temperatures. It would be a serious disadvantage to work with bees selected to fly to flowers in search of nectar at temperatures below which flowers will secrete it.

Apiary water supplies from natural sources

Bee-hunters know that feral colonies of bees in bee-trees are usually located near a stream or other source of water[52]. Swarms that escaped from the first apiaries that were established along the Fraser River in British Columbia, for instance, spread rapidly along the river and tributary streams, where they occupied the hollow trees killed in the fires made by loggers to clear the land[146].

When an apiary is located near a reliable natural source of water such as a small brook, shallow ditches or puddles, considerable trouble is avoided. But a large surface of water—such as a lake, bay or wide river—in the immediate vicinity of hives may cause the death of many bees during storms[69]. Pollen for spring brood rearing is more easily obtained in a region where water is plentiful.

If the nearest natural source is farther away than a source on a farm or around a dwelling, the bees will go to the latter; it is then necessary to place a water supply between the hives and the place where they are creating a nuisance.

During dry summers or unusual drought conditions, small creeks or ponds may dry up, forcing the bees to seek elsewhere for water. In an urban area with houses close together, one hive may be as bad for public relations as 6000 hives in a remote rural region[157]. Bees using irrigation ditches become a nuisance when the water is turned off, and it is wise to have other water available for the bees beforehand, to avoid disputes with neighbours.

Apiary water supplies in the absence of natural sources

The importance of water for bees is most obvious in warm regions, and where surface water is lacking altogether. Beekeepers cannot then leave it to the bees to find water wherever they can, but must provide it or their bees will perish. Water can be hauled in a large metal or wooden tank placed on a truck bed or on a trailer. Smaller containers such as steel drums, or 5-gallon (20/25-litre) honey or kerosene cans can be used. If a square piece is cut out of the top of each can, they can be filled and emptied rapidly[12]. Barrels or cans previously used for honey from diseased colonies should be avoided.

Large corrugated sheets of galvanized iron, placed so that they slope into a trough of cement or an earthenware sink, will collect rain water[29]; alternatively, sheets of plastic might be used. If there is a building at the apiary, metal or wooden gutters can be used to collect rain water from the roof, and the water stored in a tank, barrel, or dug cistern. A screened box or pan can serve as a funnel and also prevent animals and debris falling into the water[129].

Digging or drilling a well will provide a reliable supply of water, but may be too expensive where water is far below the surface. In 1930 Andrews[13] foresaw present shortages, where fossil water is pumped out in the summer and water dammed up during the winter when it should be replacing what was pumped out. In the western USA and elsewhere the water table falls appreciably each year[12].

A less expensive alternative to making a well may be bulldozing a small earth dam to hold rainwater or irrigation run-off in a pond, whose level can be regulated with a control gate.

In hot, dry regions, a solar moisture extractor would be a useful source of water when these become technically feasible. C. D. Owens (Arizona, 1963) found it most effective to use a covering of Mylar plastic film over the soil and the collector, but the quantity collected was insufficient to maintain bees[62].

Whatever the source of water, it must be dependable so that the supply is not suddenly cut off. The bees could then be worse off, since they would not previously have located their own sources, and in all likelihood they would be seeking water at a time when local sources had dried up[52].

Feeders for water

General characteristics[84]

Water feeders need not be expensive, but they must provide bees with continuous access to clean, fresh water in such a manner they can take it without risk of drowning. Containers left upright to fill with rain water can cause the death of many bees[52]. The natural inclination of bees is to suck up moisture from wet surfaces (e.g. wet soil, sand, brick, cement), rather than to draw water up from an open surface.

Water placed on top of the frames in the hive may be neglected, or if it is placed close to the brood the bees may carry it out, since it is not their inclination to store water in the nest[13]. Ratz avoided the problem by using a feeder in the side wall[19].

Feeders should make the water easily available to the bees, with more landing area than water surface, and with the water level close to the top of the container. It is only the margins of most feeders that are useful to bees. During peak use, in the spring and after the nectar flow, a watering area of 10-15 sq in (60-90 cm^2) per colony is required[13].

An arrangement to keep the water at about 70-80°F (21-27°C) is beneficial; bees will then collect 5-6 times as much water as at lower temperatures[110]. Place the feeder where the sun can warm it up on cold days.

Use some salt or sugar in the water initially in the spring, to get the bees to start using the feeding site provided, before they become accustomed to going somewhere else where they may become a nuisance later on. Provide a low cover to prevent contamination from rectal fluid from bees as they fly away, or from bird droppings and other debris. The cover will also keep the water cooler on hot days, and reduce evaporation. In order to prevent a potentially toxic concentration of minerals as a result of evaporation, and to reduce the spread of disease from contamination, change the water once a week. Dishes of drinking water in bee flight rooms are changed daily[115]. Milum considered that the danger of nosema infection made standing water a hazard, and preferred running-water feeders[111].

The capacity of the water feeder must be great enough to last until the beekeeper's next regular visit. Devices which provide dripping water waste the water when it is not used (as at night), and feeders which provide for automatic refilling by a siphon or float valve are preferable[115]. If livestock have access to the apiary, the watering equipment must itself be protected by wire or some other means, or a fence must be built to exclude the animals. In Australia, kangaroos can present a major problem. Any risk that vandals might shoot holes in the tanks, etc., must also be considered in locating the feeder.

Materials to absorb water and provide a landing surface for bees

Placing twigs, wood chips, or other materials into the water container will provide a greater surface on which the bees can land, as well as increasing the margins from which they can suck water. Such objects also reduce the chance that bees will misjudge the position of the water, splash into it, and possibly drown[68].

Easily renewed materials include bark, wood chips, cork (chips or bottle corks), firewood or sticks placed endwise into the container[110], reeds, straw or twigs, sphagnum moss, spent tea leaves[52], coarse gravel or pebbles, or sand. Some permanent materials are easily cleaned by boiling every week or two to control moulds and fungi[26]: burlap (sacking), flannel, or cheese cloth or other cloth, with a piece of thin wood across the feeder opening to keep the cloth near the surface. Synthetic sponge material can be sterilized by squeezing it free of excess water and submerging in water at 160-180°F (70-80°C) for 30 minutes[71]. Other permanent materials that should be cleaned every week or two to prevent the spread of disease include broken bricks, a concrete trough or slab (on which a spray or dripping water provides a wet surface) an earthenware ridge tile in a pan, which accommodates a double row of drinking bees[32], laths held together with a wire or cloth binding[9,11], and a wooden float covered with several layers of sacking or sphagnum moss[156].

Feeders for use inside the hive

Nine alternatives are given below.

1. A comb or two are filled with water by holding a sprinkling can or water hose about a metre (yard) above the combs, and these are placed at the side of the hive: (a) when bees are confined as during queen rearing[127]; (b) while the colony is being stimulated to rear brood by feeding sugar syrup, and poor weather prevents their flying to collect water[69,95] (bees require water even when fed 1:1 syrup[74]); and (c) while nuclei or colonies are being transported[72].

2. Boardman entrance feeders or other atmospheric-pressure feeders avoid disturbing the colony; this is important in early spring during inclement weather when great numbers of bees may fly out and become too chilled to return[83,143].

3. In a simpler version of the Boardman feeder, the hive is pushed forward 10 cm, and a board placed over the exposed part of the bottom board. One or more jars or cans of water are then placed over one or more holes in the board[124].

4. The cork of a vacuum flask is bored to receive a narrow glass tube whose end is slightly bevelled to permit water to flow out slowly as the bees suck at the tube. The flask is filled with warm water, and inverted over the hive[21].

5. The Miller overall or overhead type of syrup feeder has also been used to feed water. Brother Adam's variation (with the feeder block in the corner) is easier to fill, and there is no need to level the hive[141]. The Wardecker modification is along the lines of Visson's Dutch feeder, except that it has an additional compartment to hold a sponge, in addition to the vestibule, and a cover over the water tank[114,147]. Another feeder like Visson's, used in West Virginia, has just been described[40], as were others earlier[41a,89a]. All these feeders are basically on the same lines as the No. 231 feeder introduced by Mountain Grey Apiaries Ltd (Brough, Yorks, England) in 1947.

Feeders made of plywood may not withstand the constant moisture in the hive atmosphere[35], but the plastic feeders available in European catalogues would seem to be ideal where the feeder is to remain in the hive for long periods. The 14-pint No. 230 Mountain Grey feeder consists of a rust-proof tray of welded sheet steel, fitted into a wooden rim.

6. The Doolittle division-board feeder (placed along one side of the hive) has been used for water. As with the side-wall feeder used by Ratz, the bees apparently did not treat the water as a foreign material to be ejected from the hive, as they do when a feeder is used on top of the frames[19]. Feeders may also be mounted externally with a passageway for the bees through the wall[40a,93a,148a].

7. Sponges were used by Cheshire when he succeeded in shipping colonies of bees from England to India in the last century. A pouch holding a large sponge was placed beneath a 2-inch hole covered with queen-excluder zinc[52]. Sponges in plastic bags have been used to maintain humidity in experimental hives in Arizona, and (in a modified Miller feeder) to provide water for confined colonies[114]. R. Jordan tied a string to the sponge in his hives, so that he could remove it at intervals to sterilize it[23]. McLain fed brackish water in a sponge fitted into a wooden block[108].

8. Bottles have been used in various ways. McCord, a neighbour of L. L. Langstroth, devised a frame with both sugar candy and a bottle feeder for water[107]. But feeding syrup (without separate water) was a more successful method for shipping bees[73]. For queen cages, vials holding a dram (a few ml) have been used, with a groove cut in one side of the cork large enough for a bee to insert her tongue. A dozen bees consumed a dram of water in about 10 days, and queens were kept 4 or 5 weeks in this way. In shipping, two vials were used with the corks in opposite directions, in case the cage should be stood on edge, but the tin bottles in Peet cages were more successful[135]. The current practice is to ship queens and workers in cages with candy only.

9. For hives wintered in cellars, methods of providing water include the following. A saturated sponge or cloth is placed in the entrance so that it touches the cluster[61], or over a hole in the inner cover[8]. A shallow pan, saucer, or flat bottle is used, with a cloth or other wick[47,56]. A piece of comb, whose cells have been filled with water, is pushed into the entrance[69]; a syringe can be used to fill the cells if only a few hives are involved[52].

Insulated drinking cups of foam plastic, filled with water, have recently been used at the hive entrance; a cup would be emptied in as little as $1\frac{1}{2}$ hours, and some colonies took as many as 5 cups. The bees became less restless, and the room temperature dropped by several degrees[18].

Usually there is too much moisture in cellars, but if it becomes too dry the bees may become restless, especially at temperatures above 45°F (7°C)[63,93,96]. Water can then be sprinkled on the floor[4,19,79,97]. Recent experiments with wintering bees in air-conditioned buildings have been made, but unfortunately the relative humidity was not reported[17].

External feeders : standing water

Open containers, which can be filled with absorbent material that also provides a landing surface for bees (see previous list) include: automobile tyres split in half[70]; barrels cut in half, cleaned if necessary; pans, basins, crocks, earthenware sinks; buckets, pails and cans; a hollow tree stump; a sand bed[120]; a concrete slab with fine mist spray[120]; a cement-lined hole in the ground, with one end lower for flowing water (if it is large enough to accommodate plants and fish, wire screening is needed to keep out small children and animals); a solar wax extractor (which keeps water warm in the spring). Metal feeders can be coated with a cellulose enamel paint developed for the interior of livestock water tanks.

A feeding-stage is a commonly preferred alternative. This can be a board with grooves say 5 mm deep in the central area, on which an inverted water container stands in a fitting frame. A jar or bottle containing 1-20 litres is suitable. As the water is used up by the bees, air rises in the jar to replace it[60]. (The Mariotte-bottle principle incorporates a tube to the bottom of the container and prevents water being forced out by increased pressure when the sun heats the air in the container[116].) A dish or pan filled with sand can be substituted for the feeding-stage if the mouth of the bottle is bedded into the sand[82].

Alternatively a lever-lid tin (capacity 14 lb (6 kg) honey) or more is provided with two holes $\frac{1}{4}$ inch (6 mm) about 1 inch from the top. After filling with water, the lid is put on lightly, and the tin inverted in a bowl, pan or glazed flowerpot saucer[25].

A lamp to warm water for bees in the chilly days of early spring has been suggested[7]. Betts devised a 'warm-water drinking place' heated with a small wick kerosene lamp[38]. The *Warmwassertranke* of Th. Godden (Preisbuch Nr. 24, 1910?) was a manufactured version.

For out-apiaries where it is not possible to check frequently, a hose or pipe from a barrel or tank can be fitted to a feeder, so that water is provided automatically to replace what is used by the bees[33,52,119]. Morehouse used a 54-gallon (250-litre) steel drum made airtight with a rubber gasket and a plug in the upper end. A pipe $\frac{1}{2}$ inch in diameter and about 5 inches long (12 mm, 13 cm) was fitted near the rim at the bottom of the drum. This pipe was submerged near the bottom of a wooden trough, and air entered the pipe as water came down from the drum to replace that used by the bees. In this system there are no moving parts that might get stuck or fail to close tightly. The trough was V-shaped, made of two boards (one 2×6 in $\times$ 12ft, the other 2×8 in $\times$ 12 ft) nailed together with twenty 5-inch spikes [1 in = 2·5 cm; 1 ft = 30 cm]. A cross tie was nailed on about 14 inches from each end, to keep the trough from spreading apart from the weight of the filled reservoir which rests upon the end pieces[115]. Plastic cement in the joints of the board will prevent leaking[43]; alternatively a metal trough which will not warp may be preferable[103]. Other systems have been devised that use the float chamber from an automobile carburettor[41,45], a low-pressure water-level float control in a metal gutter with end-caps sealed tight, and a perforated tube placed in the bottom under a layer of gravel[121]. Galvanized feed pans are an alternative[90].

External feeders : running water[22]

A barrel or tank of water can be set on a foundation or stand with a hole punched in the bottom, or fitted with a tap or slotted plug, so that water drops slowly upon a slightly sloping board (10-12 in wide $\times$ 10 ft long, 25-30 cm $\times$ 3 m), with V cleats screwed to the board to prevent the water running off too rapidly. Waxing the board and adding cleats underneath will prevent warping. The board can be covered with sacking, flannel, or other cloth instead of cleats[22, 42, 154]. A manufactured feeder of this sort, with an optional heater for cold spring days, appeared in the 1931 Heinr. Thie catalogue.

A line of small water-pipes can be laid from a source of water to a shady and sheltered spot near the apiary, preferably the edge of a grove of trees, and connected to a small faucet set 8 in (20 cm) above the ground. Under this is placed a shallow trough, made simply of a piece of wood $2 \times 12 \times 24$ in ($5 \times 30 \times 60$ cm) with several longitudinal grooves $\frac{1}{2}$ in deep and $1\frac{1}{2}$ in wide (say 12×18 mm), running the length of the board, but 2 inches shorter at each end. These grooves are connected by several transverse grooves to allow water to run into all of them. A piece of burlap (sacking) is tacked over the whole surface close down in the grooves, and the faucet turned on so that just enough water will drip out to keep the cloth wet but not allow the water to run over. The bees take readily to such a watering-place, and there is no danger of bees drowning[137].

Luring bees away from an unauthorized watering site

The need of bees for water probably first receives the attention by the beekeeper that it deserves, when his charges create a nuisance by collecting their water at an 'unauthorized' source such as a swimming pool[44]. Where such a large surface is involved, the only solution may be to move the colonies to another location at least a mile away. Leave them there as long as possible, but at least two weeks, and have a waterer established at the original location when they are returned[90]. Adding a visual marker to the waterer[16], or an attractant such as honey or sugar[69], salt[23], or anise, may help to induce the bees to use it. Cotton balls soaked in anise can be placed in the corners of a trough[11].

If the unauthorized source can be covered (a livestock water trough, for instance), then a feeder can be placed alongside it and moved away a little each day. After a while it can be moved a few yards (metres) each day, in the meantime keeping the undesirable site covered. When it is established at the new site, keep the old place covered up for a few days. Water must be kept available without interruption, or the bees will return to the former site[110].

Repelling the bees from a trough they are using, by sprinkling a little dilute carbolic acid along it, may keep them away, and one can hope that they will begin collecting from a source of water provided in the apiary. This water might be sweetened when first offered, and then slightly salted[78].

If only a few bees are involved, a dish of water containing a little honey can be placed at the nuisance site, and removed to the water feeder with the bees drinking on the dish. Continue this process until no bees use the unauthorized supply[31].

For those who are bothered by bees around their dwellings and can find no bee-keeper in the vicinity, the use of a trap might be useful[151a]. If the unauthorized water source can be covered, a pan of water can be placed in a cage or box with screen sides and cones leading into it, with an opening just large enough to permit a bee to enter. All the water carriers will be trapped in due course, and it may be hoped that the colony will shift to some other source of water. If there is none, then the colonies will eventually die[92]. If the beekeeper can be located, and will co-operate, it might be interesting to attempt conditioning the trapped bees to shift their collecting site to one he provides near the apiary, by feeding them water to which flavouring has been added[75a,76]. Bees mark a collecting site by exposing their Nasonov glands, particularly if the water has no odour of its own[59,75].

Training bees to use a new water source can be exasperating as well as interesting, and an experience not soon forgotten by the beekeeper or the complainant. Prevention is far easier than allowing the problem to arise and then solving it. Water should be provided before the bees make their first flights in the spring. It may be advantageous to fill the feeder with sugar syrup first, to accustom the bees to using it; bees may ignore a water supply in the apiary unless they are confined in the hive for a day or two[111]. Woodrow baited feeders by using honey in an old comb, and then sugar syrup, first in the comb and then in an open dish which was later replaced by a feeder[153].

Where bees present a danger to persons hypersensitive to bee venom, more direct methods of trapping may be necessary:

(a) a hand-operated collector which will trap small numbers of bees rapidly and safely[15];

(b) a mouth aspirator fabricated from rubber stoppers, and glass and rubber tubing[85], or purchased from a scientific supply house (Micro Bio Gun, Magna Vision Corporation, Division of Ainsworth, 2151 Lawrence, Denver, CO 80205, USA);

(c) an electric vacuum cleaner, used to collect the bees which are then immobilized by freezing or with ether, and finally burned or drowned[37];

(d) a portable automobile vacuum cleaner powered from the battery, which has been modified to collect bees into food cartons or jars[53,54,91].

A harmless repellent that could be spread on the surface of the water offers a new approach to the problem of unwanted bees at water sources[113].

Provision of water during insecticide application

When colonies are confined in their hives to reduce mortality of bees during insecticide application, they are likely to need water. Covering hives with burlap (sacking) and wetting it with water may be a useful way to keep the colony cool and provide the bees with water to drink as well. Recent experiments in Arizona have used a waterer in the hive and a burlap (sacking) cover outside, during spraying[114]. Colonies supplied with water in a Boardman entrance feeder were not poisoned by arsenical sprays, even during a drought[143].

Since the need for water induces bees to collect droplets of spray containing poison, unshaded colonies in a hot arid region suffer more from poisoning than shaded ones. But bees are likely to carry out water provided within the hive, so it is best to provide the water as a dilute sugar syrup (5%)[30].

Research continues in an effort to find repellants that would prevent bees from foraging on a crop sprayed with insecticides[14]. Where the colonies are foraging on cotton, alfalfa, etc. next to other fields of the same crops (which are likely to be sprayed at the same time), or surrounded by desert, the critical factor may be the reduction of water available, which had been provided in large part by the nectar. Bees might not be able to find any water within an efficient flight range that was not contaminated by the repellant. The provision of a waterer on the hive would thus seem to be essential, whether the colonies are literally confined or whether they are suddenly repelled from their source of water (in nectar) essential for their survival.

120

References

Titles are given in the original language if this is English, French or German; otherwise the title is given in English and the language of the original is named. Almost all publications listed are in the IBRA Library. Numbers at the end of the entry such as 89/65 give the reference to the journal *Apicultural Abstracts*; 89/65 is item 89 in the 1965 volume.

1. ALTMANN, G.; GONTARSKI, H. (1961) Über den Wasserhaushalt der Winterbienen. *Symp. Genet. Biol. Ital.* 12 : 308-328   89/65
2. AMERICAN BEE JOURNAL (1866) [No title]. *Am. Bee J.* 2(4) : 67
3. ———(1879) From southern California. *Am. Bee J.* 15(9) : 403-404
4. ———(1887) Effect of water in bee-cellars, Query No. 372. *Am. Bee J.* 23(6) : 84
5. ———(1887) Water for the bees in winter quarters. *Am. Bee J.* 24(8) : 118
6. ———(1895) Water for bees in winter. *Am. Bee J.* 35(28) : 443
7. ———(1906) Editorial notes and comments. *Am. Bee J.* 46(14) : 291, 408, 509
8. ———(1908) Reports and experiences. *Am. Bee J.* 48(1) : 27
9. ———(1922) A practical watering device. *Am. Bee J.* 62(8) : 367
10. ———(1940) Watering devices. *Am. Bee J.* 80(4) : 160-161
11. ———(1946) Water for bees. *Am. Bee J.* 86(2) : 63
12. ———(1967) Scarcity of water by 1980. *Am. Bee J.* 107(6) : 205
13. ANDREWS, L. L. (1930) Water supply for Southern California. *Glean. Bee Cult.* 58(1): 36
14. ATKINS, E. L.; KELLUM, D.; NEUMAN, K. J. (1977) Repellent additives to reduce pesticide hazards to honey bees. *Am. Bee J.* 117(7) : 438-439, 457
15. BAILEY, L. (1956) A device for collecting samples of bees. *Bee Wld* 37(4) : 70-71 356/57
16. BALER, K. (1963) Marked drinkers for bees. *XIX Int. Beekeep. Congr. Suppl.*
17. BARKER, R. G. (1974) Wintering trip. *Glean. Bee Cult.* 102(10) : 307, 323
18. BARKER, R. G. (1975) Personal communication.
19. BEE WORLD (1929) Press mirror. *Bee Wld* 10(5) : 75
20. ———(1932) Editorial. *Bee Wld* 13(2) : 13-14
21. ———(1933) Press mirror. *Bee Wld* 14(5) : 55
22. ———(1933) Miscellany. *Bee Wld* 14(12) : 144
23. ———(1934) Press mirror. *Bee Wld* 15(5) : 55
24. ———(1937) Press mirror. *Bee Wld* 18(9) : 106
25. ———(1940) Press Mirror. *Bee Wld* 21(6) : 64
26. ———(1941) Press mirror. *Bee Wld* 22(12) : 93
27. ———(1942) Press mirror. *Bee Wld* 23(1) : 5
28. ———(1942) Press mirror. *Bee Wld* 23(3) : 21
29. ———(1942) Miscellany. *Bee Wld* 23(5) : 39
30. ———(1942) Editorial. *Bee Wld* 23(6) : 42
31. ———(1943) Press mirror. *Bee Wld* 24(6) : 43
32. ———(1944) Arena. *Bee Wld* 25(6) : 45
33. ———(1944) Press mirror. *Bee Wld* 25(10) : 76
34. ———(1947) Press mirror. *Bee Wld* 28(8) : 63
35. ———(1947) Press mirror. *Bee Wld* 28(11) : 78
36. ———(1947) Press mirror. *Bee Wld* 28(11) : 79
37. ———(1958) Notices and news. *Bee Wld* 39(1) : 18
38. BETTS, A. D. (1932) A warm-water drinking-place. *Bee Wld* 13(5) : 54
39. BOWEN, A. H. (1956) Water trough as weather indicator. *Am. Bee J.* 96(5) : 194
40. BRIMHALL, J. (1977) The Collins feeder. *Am. Bee J.* 117(9) : 552-553
40a. BRUHN, A. (1908) A feeder for the back of a hive. *Glean. Bee Cult.* 36(23) : 1438

41. BUMSTEAD, R. P. (1940) A simple drinking fountain. *Bee Wld* 21(12) : 113-114

41a. BURGESS, G. (1973) [A. Fox feeder] *Glean. Bee Cult.* 101(2) : 51, 63

42. BURGHARDT, J. (1936) Watering bees. *Glean. Bee Cult.* 64(8) : 476

43. BURNHAM, A. W. (1946) Watering bees. *Am. Bee J.* 86(4) : 153

44. BURR, J. (1890) Can we keep bees away from neighbouring water-troughs. *Glean. Bee Cult.* 18(19) : 713

45. BUTLER, C. G. (1939) An automatic drinking-fountain for the apiary. *Bee Wld* 20(10) : 119-120

46. ———(1940) The choice of drinking water by the honeybee. *J. exp. Biol.* 17(3) : 253-261

47. CARPENTER, I. C.; WARSTLER, H. L. (1882) Water for bees, and how to give it. *Glean. Bee Cult.* 10(8) : 399

48. CHADWICK, P. C. (1912) Beekeeping in California. *Glean. Bee Cult.* 40(14) : 435, 540

49. ———(1922) Ventilation. *Am. Bee J.* 62(4) : 158-159

50. ———(1931) Ventilation of the hive. *Glean. Bee Cult.* 59(6) : 356-358

51. CHAUVIN, R. (1963) Essais d'enregistrement simutané des principaux phénomènes de la vie d'une ruche. *Annls Abeille* 6(3) : 167-183   823/64

52. CHESHIRE, F. R. (1888) Bees and bee-keeping. *London: L. Upcott Gill*

53. CLINCH, P. G. (1970) A battery operated vacuum bee collector. *N.Z. Beekpr* 32(3) : 24-26   365L/72

54. CLINCH, P. G.; ROSS, J. G. M. (1970) Laboratory assessment of the speed of action on honey bees of orally dosed insecticides. *N.Z. J. agric. Res.* 13(3) : 717-725   782/72

55. CONGDON, H. W. (1897) Watering bees — wintering, etc. *Am. Bee J.* 37(11) : 172

56. COOK, H. C. (1912) Watering bees in a cellar. *Glean. Bee Cult.* 40(3) : 90

57. CRANE, E. E. (1950) The effect of spring feeding on the development of honeybee colonies. *Bee Wld* 31(9) : 65-72   68/52

58. CROWTHER, H. E. (1910) The best place for bait sections. *Glean. Bee Cult.* 38(1) : 22-23

59. DACY, G. H. (1932) How Uncle Sam ferrets our new facts. *Am. Bee J.* 72(8) : 322-323, 335

60. DAY, F. L. (1906) Watering-place for bees. *Am. Bee J.* 46(28) : 596

61. DEMUTH, G. S. (1925) Giving bees water in cellars. *Glean. Bee Cult.* 53(2) : 102

62. DETROY, B. (1977) Personal communication.

63. DETWYLER, J. Y. (1885) Valuable points regarding temperature. *Canad. Bee J.* 1(42) : 659-660

64. DIETZ, A. (1975) Nutrition of the adult honey bee. Pp. 125-156 *from* The hive and the honey bee. *ed.* Dadant & Sons

65. DOOLITTLE, G. M. (1900) The importance of water for bees. *Am. Bee J.* 40(35) : 551-552; 40(42) : 662-663

66. DOOLITTLE, G. M. (1914) Is water for the bees or for the brood? *Glean. Bee Cult.* 42(22) : 887

66a. DOULL, K. M. (1976) The effects of different humidities on the hatching of the eggs of honeybees. *Apidologie* 7(1) : 61-66

67. DREAMER, (1891) Warm water for bees. *Am. Bee J.* 27(23) : 742-743)

68. DuBois, W. L. (1943) Watering bees. *Am. Bee J.* 83(2) : 70

69. DZIERZON, J. (1882) Rational bee-keeping. *London: Houlston & Sons*

70. FARMER, J. (1946) A good water trough for bees. *Am. Bee J.* 86(1) : 21

71. FARRAR, C. L. (1968) Productive management of honey-bee colonies. *Am. Bee J.* 108 (2): 228-230   132/69

122

72. FLANAGAN, E. T. (1888) Water for bees during shipment. *Glean. Bee Cult.* 16(11) : 441
73. FLOYD, L. T. (1925, 1930) Water in shipping bees. *Am. Bee J.* 65(8) : 385; 70(7) : 337
74. FOSTER, W. (1911) Bees need water, even when half-and-half syrup is given. *Glean. Bee Cult.* 39(1) : 6
75. FREE, J. B.; WILLIAMS, I. H. (1970) Exposure of the Nasonov gland by honeybees (*Apis mellifera*) collecting water. *Behaviour* 37(3/4) : 286-290   947/72
75a. FRISCH, K. von (1967) The dance language and orientation of bees. *Cambridge, Mass* : *Harvard University Press*   289/69
76. GARY, N. E. (1975) Activities and behavior of honey bees. Pp. 185-264 *from* The hive and the honey bee. *ed.* Dadant & Sons
77. GENDOT, G. (1907) Eau necessaire aux abeilles. *Apiculteur* 51(4) : 164-168
78. GLEANINGS IN BEE CULTURE (1909) Editorial, *Glean. Bee Cult.* 37(10) : 296
79. ———(1933) Moisture within the hive. *Glean. Bee Cult.* 61(2) : 75
80. ———(1955) [No title]. *Glean. Bee Cult.* 83(6) : 358
81. ———(1964) A waterer for honeybees. *Glean. Bee Cult.* 92(6) : 372
82. GOLDSBOROUGH, A. T. (1892) An artificial watering-place after nature's ways. *Glean. Bee Cult.* 20(19) : 737
83. GRIERSON, P. S. (1943) Watering the bees. *Beekprs Item* 27(12) : 382-383
84. ———(1945) Bee waterer. *Beekprs Item* 29(5) : 162-163
85. GROOT, A. P. de (1953) Protein and amino acid requirements of the honeybee (*Apis mellifica* L.). *Physiol. comp.* 3 : 197-285   88/54
86. HANSSON, A. (1965) [How much food and water does a colony of bees require?] *Bitidningen* 64(6) : 192-194 *In Swedish*
87. HARRISON, C. (1932) Salted water. *Bee Wld* 13(4) : 44
88. HEINRICH, B. (1969) Temperature regulation in the bumblebee *Bombus vagans*: a field study. *Science* , *N.Y.* 175(4018) : 185-187
89. HOLMES, F. O. (1964) Distance to water source. *Glean. Bee Cult.* 92(9) : 541, 572
89a. HUNT, C. (1973) Build a better feeder. *Glean. Bee Cult.* 101(5) : 198
90. JAYCOX, E. R. (1967) Water for honey bees. *Am. Bee J.* 107(7) : 254-255   321L/69
91. ———(1970) Collecting and counting honey bees with a vacuum cleaner. *J. econ. Ent.* 63(1) : 327-328   609/71
92. JOHANSSON, T. S. K. (1974) VITA Inquiry Service No. 25511
93. [JONES, D. A.] (1885) The pollen theory. *Canad. Bee J.* 1(12) : 182-183
93a. KEYES, D. R. (1907) A can feeder attached to the back of a hive. *Glean. Bee Cult.* 35(18): 1212
94. KIECHLE, H. (1961) Die soziale Regulation der Wassersammeltätigkeit im Bienenstaat und deren physiologische Grundlage. *Z. vergl. Physiol.* 45 : 154-192   360/63
95. KITTSON, D. S. (1937) Watering the combs. *Am. Bee J.* 77(6) : 280
96. KUEHL, J. (1977) Wintering in buildings. *Am. Beekeeping Federation Convention, San Antonio, Texas*
96a. LANGRIDGE, D. F. (1959) Some hints for the summer. *Beekprs Bull.* 4(3) : 6-9
97. LATHROP, H. (1898) Wintering in a dugout. *Glean. Bee Cult.* 26(10) : 390
98. LENSKY, Y. (1963) [Study on the physiology and ecology of the Italian honeybee in Israel.] *Hebrew University of Jerusalem*: Ph.D. Thesis 103 p. *In Hebrew; French summary and annotations*   324/64
98a. LENSKY, Y. (1964) L'économie de liquides chez les abeilles aux températures élevées. *Insectes soc.* 11(3) : 207-222   758/65
99. LINDAUER, M. (1955) The water economy and temperature regulation of the honeybee colony. *Bee Wld* 36 : 62-72, 81-92, 105-111   215/56

100. Long, C. (1900) Waterbees. *Glean. Bee Cult.* 28(7) : 264
101. Lunder, R. (1949) [Queens should have water when caged.] *Nord. Bitidskr.* 3 : 86-87
    In Norwegian   84/50
102. ———(1950) [Can bees be stimulated early in spring?] *Nord. Bitidskr.* 2(2) : 33-39
    In Norwegian   55/54
103. Lyle, N. I. (1927) Water for bees. *Am. Bee J.* 67(5) : 253
104. Lysne, J. (1956) Bees and salt. *Am. Bee J.* 96(12) : 477
105. M., R. B. (1930) County supervisors make it offense not to provide water for bees.
    Am. Bee J. 70(8) : 374
106. Martinovs, A. (1964) [Bees' water requirements in relation to the nectar flow.] *Nord.*
    Bitidskr. 15/16 : 38-40 *In Swedish*   99/66
107. McCord, D. A. (1879) McCord's candy and bottle feeder. *Glean. Bee Cult.* 7(4) : 131
108. McLain, N. W. (1885) Report on experiments in apiculture. *Rep. Commissioner Agric.*
    for 1885, U.S.D.A. : 333-343
109. Miller, C. C. (1899) Stray straws. *Glean. Bee Cult.* 27(12) : 458
110. ———(1907) Water for bees. *Glean. Bee Cult.* 35(23) : 1498-1499
111. Milum, V. G. (1938) Bees need water. *Glean. Bee Cult.* 66(5) : 288
112. Miner, F. H. (1868) Water for bees. *Am. Bee J.* 3(9) : 169
113. Moffett, J. O.; Morton, H. L. (1975) Repellency of surfactants to honey bees. *Envir.*
    Ent. 4(5) : 780-782
114. Moffett, J. O.; Stoner, A.; Wardecker, A. L. (1977) The Wardecker waterer. *Am.*
    Bee J. 117(6) : 364-365, 378; see also *J. econ. Ent.* 70: 737-741 (1977)
115. Morehouse, K. W. (1935) An adequate watering system. *Glean. Bee Cult.* 63(8) :
    472-473
116. Morland, D. (1931) A drinking fountain for bees. *Bee Wld* 12(5) : 50-51
117. Mosher, A. C. (1883) Water for bees. *Glean. Bee Cult.* 11(2) : 81
118. Núñez, J. A.; Fischbarg, B. D. de (1969) [Behaviour of the water-collecting honeybee.]
    Physis, B. Aires 29(78) : 185-196 *In Spanish*   795/74
119. Owens, C. D. (1967) Beehive and honey handling equipment. *Agric. Handb. U.S. Dep.*
    Agric. No. 335: 37-41   720L/67
120. Owens, C. D.; Detroy, B. F. (1968) New engineering developments in beekeeping.
    Am. Bee J. 108(3) : 104, 106, 108, 110   124L/69
121. Owens, C. D.; McGregor, S. E. (1964) Shade and water for the honey bee colony.
    Leafl. U.S. Dep. Agric. No. 530   338L/65
122. Owens, C. D.; Woodrow, A. W. (1964) A waterer for honeybees. *Glean. Bee Cult.*
    92(6) : 372
123. Pawletta, J. (1906) Bees carrying water at night. *Am. Bee J.* 46(47) : 968
124. Pering, A. H. (1942) Water for bees. *Am. Bee J.* 82(4) : 152
125. Phillips, E. F. (1924) Moisture within the beehive. *Glean. Bee Cult.* 52(1) : 17-20
126. Piscitelli, A. (1959) Über die Bevorzugung mineralstoffhaltiger Lösungen gegenüber
    reinem Wasser durch die Honigbiene. *Z. vergl. Physiol.* 42(5) : 501-524   785/63
127. Pridgen, W. H. (1899) Pointers on queen-rearing. *Glean. Bee Cult.* 27(24) : 932
128. Putnam, B. L. (1931) Watering the bees. *Glean. Bee Cult.* 59(5) : 297
129. Randolph, W. N. (1914) A rain-barrel cistern for the beeyard. *Glean. Bee Cult.* 42(22):
    909-910
130. Rea, G. H. (1931) Water needed for early breeding. *Glean. Bee Cult.* 59(5) : 308
131. Renner, M. (1955) Über die Haltung von Bienen in geschlossenen, künstlich beleuch-
    teten Räumen. *Naturwissenschaften* 42(19) : 539-540   86/56

132. Ribbands, C. R. (1953) The behaviour and social life of honeybees. *London: Bee Research Association* 8/54
133. Root, A. I. (1891) Water for bees; good candy for spring feeding. *Glean. Bee Cult.* 19(21) : 856
134. ———(1892) Notes of travel. *Glean. Bee Cult.* 20(13) : 512-513
135. ———(1926) A. I. Root's story of his own life. *Glean. Bee Cult.* 54 : 176-177, 245-246, 255
136. Ruddiman, P. (1897) Handy bee-watering. *Am. Bee J.* 37(25) : 395-396
137. Scholl, L. H. (1905) Water for bees. *Glean. Bee Cult.* 33(12) : 642
138. Seifert, L. (1958) Werden Tränken mit Zusatzmitteln von den Bienen bevorzugt? *Leipzig. Bienenztg* 72(3) : 70-72 101/60
139. Shallard, M. (1914) Excessive heat causes bees to carry an astonishing amount of water. *Glean. Bee Cult.* 42(20) : 817
140. Simpson, J. (1964) Dilution by honeybees of solid and liquid food containing sugar. *J. apic. Res.* 3(1) : 37-40 829/64
141. Skeels, W. H. (1937) Bro. Adam's feeder for water. *Am. Bee J.* 77(5) : 233
142. Snyder, P. G. (1933) Bees use large quantities of water. *Glean. Bee Cult.* 61(4) : 213-214
143. Southwick, A. M. (1938) Water vs. poison. *Glean. Bee Cult.* 66(3) : 167
144. Stanger, W. (1964) Water your bees. *Univ. Calif.* [*Newsletter*]
145. Swanson, R. A. (1976) Beekeeping in upper Volta. *Am. Bee J.* 116(2) : 56
146. Turnbull, W. H. (1958) One hundred years of beekeeping in British Columbia, 1858-1958. *Vernon, B.C.: B.C. Honey Producers' Association* 75/59
147. Visser, N. (1969) A Dutch feeder. *Bee-Lines* 32 : 10-11
148. Vuillaume, M. (1957) L'importance de l'approvisionnement en eau dans la ruche. *Insectes soc.* 4(1) : 31-41 189/59
148a. Warner, H. (1970) Bee feeders. *U.S. Pat.* 3,526,913 740/72
149. Watkins, S. I. (1887) Do bees store water in combs for winter use. *Glean. Bee Cult.* 15(12) : 470
150. Whitcomb, E. (1896) Importance of watering in the apiary. *Am. Bee J.* 36(43) : 673-675
151. Wilson, H. F. (1929) Proper amount of packing. *Glean. Bee Cult.* 57(12) : 780-781
151a. Witherell, P. C.; Laidlaw, H. H., Jr. (1977) Behavior of the honey bee (*Apis mellifera* L.) mutant, diminutive-wing. *Hilgardia* 45(1) : 1-30
152. Woodrow, A. W. (1941) Some effects of temperature, relative humidity, confinement, and type of food on queen bees in mailing cages. *Publ. U.S. Dep. Agric. No.* E-438
153. ———(1977) Personal communication
154. Worsley, B. J. (1908) A wet board for watering bees. *Glean. Bee Cult.* 36(8) : 510
155. ———(1910) Water required by bees. *Glean. Bee Cult.* 38(8) : 256-259
156. Wright, P. H. (1942) Best bee-waterer of all. *Glean. Bee Cult.* 70(8) : 477
157. Wuggetzer, A. (1977) Beekeeping in Mexico. *Am. Beekpng Federation Convention. San Antonio, Texas*

CHAPTER 9

SUBSTITUTES FOR BEESWAX IN COMB AND COMB FOUNDATION

The idea of using plastic materials in hives for honey storage and brood rearing may sound like a modern concept, but it is in fact quite an old one. This chapter tells the intriguing story of beekeepers' attempts to find a durable, tough and sterilizable substitute for beeswax. Although the search has been going on actively for a hundred years, the final solution has still not been found—largely because of the high cost of providing anything that the bees will accept. The bees may yet defeat the beekeeper in the battle for factory farming.

Introduction

The original motives for manufacturing "artificial comb" or foundation were to use cheaper substitutes for beeswax, and to provide the bees with as much constructed comb as possible, on the assumption they would then exert more energy in the production of honey. Recent work does not indicate that there is necessarily a significant increase in honey production with the use of comb foundation, but where the colony could be provided with fully built combs there was an advantage[21]. Current efforts to provide manufactured whole combs are motivated by the advantage of uniform, durable combs for automated manipulations, and which can be disinfected for disease control.

With the development of movable-frame hives, combs became a valuable capital asset to the beekeeper, since he could return them to the colony for re-use. It is now appreciated that this presents a hazard for the bees, if the combs are contaminated with pathogenic organisms such as *Bacillus larvae*. The only alternatives would thus seem to be to destroy the combs by burning, or render them into wax with adequate sterilization; there are, for instance, licensed wax-salvage plants in California[18].

When information spread that the "miracle drugs" such as sulphathiazole and Terramycin were useful in preventing, if not curing, American and European foul brood, it was not surprising that beekeepers adopted them enthusiastically. Unfortunately, the disease organisms have now been subjected to sufficient quantities of drugs to uncover some resistant mutations amongst them[20].

It would be useful if satisfactory substitutes for beeswax comb were developed which could be sterilized by heat, or boiling in water, or some other non-chemical technique to avoid reinfection. If disease threatens to make re-used combs too hazardous for profitable beekeeping, perhaps we shall see some modification of methods used with fixed-comb hives in which a portion of the combs or colonies are harvested annually[34].

126

Comb foundation

Beeswax comb foundation, embossed with the bases of cells, provides the midrib on which the bees can build or "draw out" complete comb. Worker foundation, first commercially manufactured and promoted by Frederick Weiss in U.S.A. in 1875, has become standard equipment for use in movable-frame hives, but there are serious problems with it[19]. The sheets of wax sag when warm, and occasionally break. Various contrivances have been used to support the foundation, but Hetherington's practice of embedding wires has become the prevalent method. This has its disadvantages: when a nectar flow ceases suddenly, the bees tend to chew along the wires, leaving ribbons of wax which may fall out—or bend towards neighbouring combs, to which attachment may be made when wax building is resumed. Defective areas are filled with drone comb, reducing the value of worker foundation as a means of population control for drones. This long-standing bias against drones has, however, been assailed by recent research in which the expected correlation between an excessive drone population and decreased honey yields has not been found[4,22].

Materials other than beeswax could be advantageous for making foundation. In 1902, A. B. Anthony pleaded for a substitute that could withstand boiling water (to kill foul brood organisms) and which the bees could re-use for building the wax cell walls [GBC* 30 : 987]. In 1918, E. F. Phillips of the U.S. Department of Agriculture sent the following "Memorandum to Field Men" [Mimeographed Series xxxii, July 1]: "Sechrist has been at work for some time on the problem of using Bakelite as a substitute for beeswax in making comb-foundation. Thin sheets of this material have been obtained on which the outlines of cells were embossed in wax, and it is found that the bees accept this material readily. Sechrist recently visited New York City to consult with the officials of the Bakelite Company and further experiments are now in process with the different combinations of this material. A patent has been applied for on this invention in the name of the Government and it is hoped that it will result in considerable good to beekeepers. The object of substituting Bakelite for beeswax in foundation is to prevent the sagging of cells at the top of the combs which now causes so much loss of space for brood-rearing and it will be unnecessary to wire frames in which this material is used as foundation. In case combs become infected with any of the brood diseases it will be possible to disinfect the Bakelite foundation and frames very readily and furthermore the wax moth will be unable to do any damage to this material. Further particulars will be sent to field men when available, but in the meantime no announcement is being made of this work".

A U.S. patent for Bakelite foundation was awarded to Sechrist in 1918 (1,282,645), with the option of including a frame of the same material. It did not receive further publicity, and the Bakelite Company (Union Carbide) has no record of the matter[13]. James I. Hambleton, who succeeded Phillips in charge of bee research, remembered the experiments but did not recall that combs were ever drawn on the Bakelite. Hambleton thought the odour of carbolic acid was not masked by the beeswax coating, and that when the bees gnawed through the wax they were repelled[16,31].

The Sechrist patent makes no reference to Samuel Wagner's patent (32,258)

---

* *ABJ, BW,* and *GBC* are abbreviations for *American Bee Journal, Bee World,* and *Gleanings in Bee Culture,* respectively.

awarded on 7th May 1861 for "a substitute for the central division or foundation of the comb built by bees, either with or without the whole or any portion of the walls forming the hexagonal cells projecting from the division, which substitute is artificially and suitably formed upon both sides or faces, and of any suitable material which is susceptible of receiving the desired and necessary configuration". The title "Honey comb frame" appearing on the drawing for Wagner's patent is more apt for Sechrist's combination frame + foundation; conversely, the title "Septum or base for honeycomb" to Sechrist's drawing is applicable to Wagner's. In 1963 W. Z. Covington of Texas was awarded a patent (3,088,135), also for a combination frame and comb foundation made of plastic†.

Plastic-based comb foundation coated with beeswax is now available commercially (Fig. 1)[5,24]. Many other materials have been used in the past, in an effort to find a suitable substitute for beeswax comb foundation[31]. The following list indicates the first known use of each material:

> Aluminium, by O. Schultz [1913], *Praktischer Wegweiser für Bienenzüchter* 42 : 108 (1936); see also many references in early volumes of *BW*. (Fig. 2, 3)
>
> Artificial resin* by H. Bansbach, *Westfälische Bienenztg* 66 : 168–169 (1953)
>
> Bristol board[31]
>
> Cardboard[31]
>
> Cellophane*, by H. H. Root, *U.S. Pat.* 1,882,938 (1932)
>
> Celluloid* *GBC* 31 : 160 (1903); F. K. Babaev, *BW* 32 : 71 (1951) (Fig. 4)
>
> Cloth[31]
>
> Hard fibre, by H. L. Settle, *U.S. Pat.* 1,672,853 (1928)
>
> Metal foil, by G. Barratt, *BW* 6 : 108–109 (1924)
>
> Mineral wax, by H. H. Root, *U.S. Pat.* 1,583,605 (1926)
>
> Paper[7,33]
>
> Tin[7], *GBC* 32 : 533, 583, 967, 1055 (1904)
>
> Vegetable wax[29]
>
> Wire cloth[31]
>
> Wood veneer[14]
>
> Zinc, by G. F. Jaubert, *Apiculteur* 72 : 193–196 (1928)

Whole comb

Beeswax

Despite the problems associated with beeswax combs, considerable effort has been directed toward producing artificial combs of beeswax. J. Steigel (1892) found that his combs were too fragile to withstand the rigours of shipping[32]. P. Warnstorf of Germany obtained a U.S. patent (495,572) in 1893 for a mould

---

† Plastics may be imprecisely defined as resins (usually polymers of high molecular weight, organic compounds) in their moulded form. Some are identified by name— as Bakelite, celluloid and cellophane—but the majority of recently developed materials of this nature (which technologists identify by their resinous components) are collectively called "plastic".

128

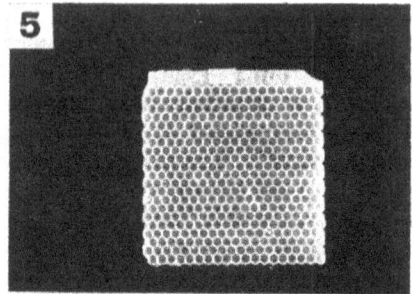

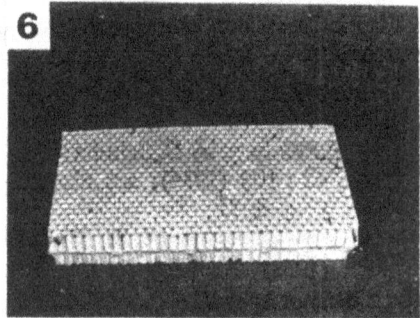

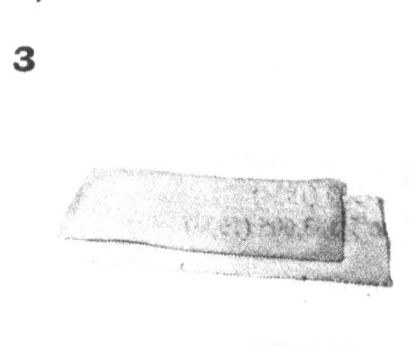

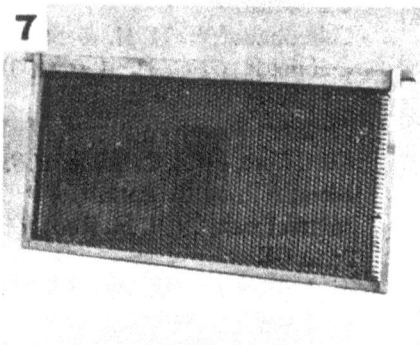

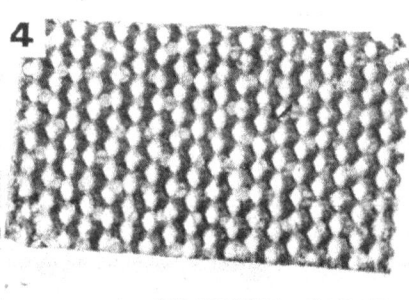

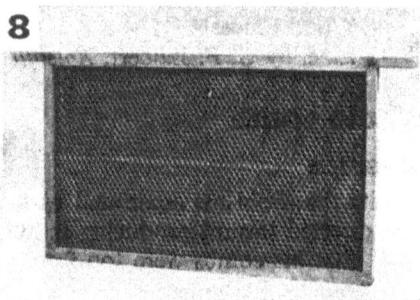

Photographs by F. G. Vernon; copyright Bee Research Association

to cast one side of a comb. In 1911, L. A. Aspinwall patented a comb with partial walls (994,559), and in 1922 W. G. Cook patented dies made of salt which was dissolved to remove the wax comb intact (1,427,149). W. Vincent is reported to have produced full-depth comb in 1928 [*BW* 9 : 70], and a U.S. patent for half-depth wax comb (Fig. 5) was awarded to A. R. Ellis and H. G. Marshall of South Africa in 1965 (3,182,339). A method for dipping cells and cutting to length was patented in 1892 (481,578) by E. T. Mason and M. H. Moskovits. In 1936 J. E. Walker patented a "former" for making honeycomb structures of any length desired; the wax or other material entered the die through hollow cores (2,061,295). G. W. Watson had developed a machine in 1925, in which a number of sheets were placed together and heated to produce cells (1,561,623).

Other waxes

A. Bonalda produced half-depth combs made of paraffin and carnauba wax, with cells somewhat larger than normal, to prevent the queen from laying in them. They were seven times the weight of natural combs, and this made them too heavy to be practical [*ABJ* 65 : 427 (1925)].

Paper

In 1870 comb was made from paper saturated with wax; it was said to deceive "almost any beekeeper"—but unfortunately it did not deceive the bees, which cut it into sawdust[8]. G. M. MacDonald of Pasadena (California) intended to market a paper comb in 1918, but the war cut off the German sources of suitable paper [*BW* 2 : 3-4 (1920/21)]. It proved impractical anyway, because the paper had to be "galvanized" to prevent the bees chewing it[3]. G. Johanson in Sweden has recently produced a paper comb which is reported to be successful [*Bitidningen* 68 : 64 (1969)].

A honeycomb made of Kraft paper treated with resin before conversion to

---

Fig. 1–8 (*opposite*) *show some examples of foundation and comb in the B.R.A. Collection of Historical and Contemporary Beekeeping Material. The Association would be pleased to receive other specimens, old or new, to strengthen this part of the Collection.*

Fig. 1.   *Plastic-based foundation coated with beeswax (U.S.A., 1967)*   B69/57

Fig. 2.   *Aluminium foundation in frame (England, 1920s)*   B52/115

Fig. 3.   *Modern aluminium-based foundation coated with beeswax (U.S.A., 1969)*
                                                                              B70/83

Fig. 4.   *Comb foundation of celluloid or similar, coated with beeswax (England, 1930s?)*
                                                                              B70/82

Fig. 5.   *Beeswax comb, half-depth : "Quick Comb" (S. Africa, 1965)*   B65/3

Fig. 6.   *Part of a plastic comb which incorporates the frame also (Germany, 1951)*
                                                                              B52/24

Fig. 7.   *Deep frame fitted with aluminium semicomb for brood, cells 5 to the inch, no mid-rib (England, 1920s?)*   B54/16

Fig. 8.   *Deep frame of aluminium semicomb for honey, cells 4½ to the inch and $\frac{7}{16}$ inch deep.*   B54/15

honeycomb form is described by G. May in "Plastics and the honeycomb structure" [*British Plastics* (June, 1952)] with the following conclusion: "But while honeycombs may be produced from a wide variety of different materials to serve in many fields, there is no type likely to be considered as being more economical or having wider scope than that made from resinated paper".

Celluloid

H. L. Cress of California invented a comb made of celluloid [*BW* 4 : 235 (1923)], and A. Z. Abushâdy promoted those made by MacDonald[17].

Rubber

The anticipated advantage of a comb built of India rubber was that the honey could be harvested by squeezing [*BW* 17 : 84 (1936)].

Plastics

Various attempts have been made to produce a complete comb of plastic[6,11]. Detroy and Owens currently contend that a frameless comb would avoid the difficulties that are caused in automatic uncappers by warped wooden frames which jam between the rollers. Their square frame has no top or bottom and can be rotated through 90° or 180° to relieve honey-bound conditions[25,12]. L. L. Esenhower observed that rotation of the frames opens the cappings slightly [*ABJ* 41 : 446 (1901)], and that it became a routine practice among beekeepers when hives with reversible frames (by Quinby, Heddon, Danzenbaker, etc.) became available[10]. Dr. E. Crane reports that plastic combs (Fig. 6) were in successful experimental use at the Bavarian Bee Research Institute in Germany in 1951 [see footnote, p. 153].

As these paragraphs are being written, a firm in California has placed advertisements for plastic combs, apparently to be used in honey supers only [*ABJ* 111 : 210 (1971)]. J. F. H. Perrachon developed a method of folding a stamped sheet of plastic to form the cells [*U.S. Pat.* 3,245,093 (1966)], as Dean and Robbin did for metal; see below.

The technology of manufacturing honeycomb structures, including those made by coating or impregnating paper, cotton, glass fibre and metal, has been described by G. May in *British Plastics* (June, 1952).

Metal combs made by a crimping technique

In 1870, Quinby showed the Northeastern Beekeeping Association a full-depth comb of galvanized tin coated with beeswax; he indicated that Wagner's inclusive patent prevented his obtaining one. The price of $1·50 per square foot was considered economical by some, as the comb could be taken apart, disinfected by boiling, and recoated with beeswax for use again. Quinby used a machine which produced crimped strips that could be assembled in a frame to form half a row of cells[31,33,8,28]. Steigel promoted such a tin comb in 1892, and estimated that a beekeeper could make 40–50 per day at home[32]. C. W. Christman developed a machine for making cellular cores from fluted stock [*U.S. Pat.* 2,933,122 (1960)].

The most publicized comb was developed in California by Hale Paxton, a practical mechanic, and George MacDonald, after they had met by chance in a cafe, and exchanged sad stories of colonies lost by American foul brood and combs melted in the sun. Their determination to develop an artificial comb resulted in *U.S. Pat.* 1,051,830 (1913) for a two-piece hinged aluminium comb that could be extracted without uncapping. The cappings were burned off with a torch, and the comb disinfected if necessary, after the honey had been removed. The comb marketed as "Moneycomb" in 1918 was a version with partial walls, made like Quinby's crimped comb and sold for 60 cents a frame (1,224,479). The use of tin was also considered. A fellow townsman, H. B. Dean, patented a method in 1921 (1,389,294) of bending a sheet of metal to form half-cells and folding it back and forth on itself to make complete cells— much like T. H. Robbin's comb [*Brit. Pat.* 26,856 (1921)].

A. Z. Abushâdy, editor of *Bee World* at its inception in 1919, became an enthusiastic promoter of metal combs and treated his readers to a blow-by-blow account of their development[9]. He was instrumental in introducing Adminson's "semicomb"[2,17] (Fig. 7, 8), and one of his own with square cells[1].

Although aluminium combs generated considerable enthusiasm among bee-keepers, bees did not use them freely for brood rearing in colder regions[15,27,30]. The need for using heavily insulated hives had not been made explicit, although Wagner anticipated this difficulty in his 1861 patent: "Thin sheets of metal, reduced to the tenuity of foils, may be used, though I prefer good non conductors of heat improved by being rendered waterproof if not so". H. A. Burch was quick to call metal combs a "humbug", almost as soon as they were conceived [*ABJ* 13 : 55 (1877)].

When Abushâdy moved to Egypt, he continued his experimentation with metal combs, and in warmer climates there was a growing acceptance of them. His sharp rebuttal to Morland's negative report published in 1926 came just before World War II interrupted normal peace-time communications[3,23]. In 1940, Abushâdy described his method of using aluminium combs [*Scot. Beekpr* 16 : 33], and confirmed Park's conclusion in 1925 that aluminium comb would be accepted by bees only when there was a heavy honey flow.

Other metal combs

The *American Bee Journal* [73 : 469 (1933)] reported that L. and G. Pensieri of Italy had produced metal comb with the appearance of having been made by honeybees, and that Angleri's comb, built up on a sheet of metal, was also ready for insertion into the hive.

Hives and combs for automatic honey extraction

Several inventors have designed combs that do not require opening the hive in order to harvest the honey—a "fatiguing and dangerous" operation. We list them below without comment—since they do not appear to be available on the market, nor are there any independent reports of their practicability. Except for the final three, numbers refer to U.S. Patents.

Avant, L. W.   890,397 (1908) uses hollow comb and partial vacuum

Babcock, G. W.   1,188,386 (1916), 1,407,244 (1922) continuously moving separators keep bees building "sticks" for comb honey sections

Sugano, G.   2,631,307 (1953) rotating knives uncap circular combs in the hive

Krause, I. J.   3,303,519 (1967) honey removed before combs are capped

Garriga, J. B. 2,223,561 (1940) comb spread apart to permit honey to drain out of the rear of cells
Mari, J. R. 2,779,037 (1957) knives cut a small hole in the rear of cells
Aesop *GBC* 44 : 15–16 (1916) an agitator in the hive
Cases, J. R. *Brit. Pat.* 592,090 (1947) combs softened by warming until honey flows out
Settman, T. *Bee Wld* 5 : 38 (1923) self-emptying comb

The technological extreme so far reached in practice has been produced in California and Australia [*Australas. Beekpr* 67 : 19–21 (1965)]. The following is Dr. Crane's description* from New South Wales: "In Roger Blackwell's apiary near Tamworth, the hives have Fox-Harrison fixed-frame supers. Above an excluder, on a normal ten-frame Langstroth brood box, is a stack of supers (about two-thirds as deep as the brood chamber), each containing seven frames fixed in it. The frames have identical top and bottom bars, but no side bars. Plasticore drone foundation with metal-bound vertical edges [as in Fig. 1] is fitted between the top and bottom bars, which are themselves clamped in place with a fillet of wood secured across their ends, two at the top and two at the bottom of the super. The extracting plant is at Kempsey, on the coast; it has a sophisticated uncapper with seven pairs of knives. These do not move to and fro as the comb drops past them, as in most mechanical uncappers; the knives are stationary and the *super* jiggles as it falls slowly past the 14 knives, each pair uncapping one comb. The extractor is simple in principle, but very large; twelve supers (or pairs of supers) are fixed in hanging cradles round the vertical axis; these swing away when the extractor gets going (like Hruschka's bucket), and the honey spins out. There is usually a second row of supers and sometimes a third—up to a total of 72. Since each can hold nearly 20 kg of honey, well over a ton can be extracted in a single operation, at a force of 80G, twice that in normal radial extractors. This is possible because of the strength of the plastic-based foundation."

A similar, vertical extractor was developed by A. F. Hodgson (Ontario, Canada) in 1923, and later modified to hold 8 special boxes; 12 uncapped frames were shifted from the honey supers into each of these, for uncapping and extracting.

Summary

Technology has a way of deriving sustenance from itself by demanding ever greater involvement to survive in the new modes. Beekeepers once manufactured only the clay cylinders, straw skeps, or wooden containers, in which

---

* We appreciate the inclusion of two reports by Dr. E. Crane which do not appear in the list of references, on plastic whole comb (page 152), and on Australian automatic honey extraction using fixed combs [see also *Am. Bee J.* 106 : 6–7, 19; 168, 173 (1966)]. In 1934 F. W. Lesser prepared 500 fixed-comb supers, and used a motorized auger to uncap between the combs; he extracted them in a machine holding 4 supers [*Glean. Bee Cult.* 62 : 156 (1934)]. His vision that further exploitation required much larger machines has now been realized. The Powers' Apiaries in western U.S.A. developed a 32-super model around 1955, which was manufactured by the Superior Honey Co. in Ogden, Utah.

captured or adventitious swarms were left to play out their predetermined chain of responses—building comb, gathering pollen and nectar, and rearing brood to renew their populations. The beekeeper provided the empty nesting place and was rewarded with surplus honey combs—to sell for cash and to make into mead or beer. In tropical parts of Africa these techniques still produce beeswax in sufficient quantity to influence world prices. And in parts of northern Europe some beekeepers still remain faithful to their straw hives for producing honey and swarms to sell. But generally the old ways were abandoned long ago in favour of devices which purported to restrain bees' ways and provide the ease of control we have over "barnyard" livestock.

Associated with the capital investment in furnished "bee palaces" is the price of labour and the cost of disease spread by combs re-used year after year. Ironically the increased productivity from movable-frame hives has been accompanied by a decline in honey prices (or absence of an increase during a general inflationary period). The search for ways to reduce production costs has produced sophisticated processing machinery for honey—and the concurrent requirement that hive furniture and combs conform to the tolerances imposed by the machines. Whether completely man-made combs will replace those made by bees will be determined first and foremost by economic factors: they must provide sufficient financial saving to compensate for the investment. Obviously they must be acceptable to the bees, preferably for both brood rearing and honey storage, and it must be possible to disinfect them easily and dependably. The array of modern plastics with diverse physical and chemical properties may yet provide comb acceptable to the bees, but the final decision will be made in the market place.

References

1. [ABUSHÂDY, A. Z.] (1919) Abushâdy's metal comb. *Bee Wld* 1 : 127–129
2. —————— (1920) Adminson's aluminium semicomb. *Bee Wld* 2 : 122–124
3. —————— (1938) Comments. *Bee Kingdom* 9 : 53–65 [See also 42–43, 270–271]
4. ALLEN, M. D. (1965) The effect of a plentiful supply of drone comb on colonies of honeybees. *J. apic. Res.* 4 : 109–119
5. *Bee Wld* 35 : 157 (1954); W. Laeis *Kunststoffe* 43 : 109–110 (1953); [*Apic. Abstr.* 213/55]; E. F. Smith *U.S. Pat.* 2,561,147 (1951); R. W Krekal *U.S. Pat.* 3,105,978 (1963)
6. *Bee Wld* 35 : 157 (1954)
7. B[ETTS], A. D. (1922) The press mirror. *Bee Wld* 4 : 18
8. BICKFORD, B. (1871) Artificial honey comb. *Am. Bee J.* 6 : 147–148 [Were full-depth paper combs made by Dr. Knaffee, Nashville[13], those mentioned by Bickford?]
9. CAMPBELL, D. J. & HENDERSON, G. P. (1962) The Bee World : Index to Volumes 1–30. *London : Bee Research Association* [see entry: Comb, artificial, metal]
10. CHESHIRE, F. R. (1888) Bees and bee-keeping: Vol. II. Practical. *London : L. Upcott Gill*
11. D., N. (1954) Sollen wir oder sollen wir nicht? *Landw. Wbl., München* (7) [*Apic. Abstr.* 199/58]
12. DETROY, D. F. & OWENS, C. D. (1971) Plastic comb and hive investigations. *Am. Bee J.* 111 : 220–221
13. DOWNES, A. W. (1 Dec. 1965) Personal communication

14. GEORGHIOU, G. P. (1955) History of beekeeping III. *Glean. Bee Cult.* 83 : 153–155 [Thin wood foundation sold by C. N. Abbot in 1872 (England); Root's was tested by A. Z. Abushâdy in 1922³.]

15. GIRAUD, E. (1927) Des rayons en aluminium. *Apiculteur* 71 : 48–50

16. HAMBLETON, J. I. (7 Dec. 1965) Personal communication

17. HARKER, L. S. (1938) Blazing the trail. Reminiscences of A. Z. Abushâdy. *London : C. W. Daniel*

18. JAYCOX, E. R. (1954) Wax-salvage plants. *Sacramento, Calif. : Bureau of Entomology* [Mimeo. A-18]

19. JOHANSSON, T. S. K. & JOHANSSON, M. P. (1969) The development of comb foundation. *Bee Wld* 50 : 61–65 [See also *Am. Bee J.* 16 : 524–525 (1880) for a last account of Weiss.]

20. ——— (1971) Antibiotic resistance. *Am. Bee J.* 111 : 56–57, 60

21. ——— (1971) Influence of comb foundation on comb, drone, and honey production in honey bee colonies. *J. econ. Ent.* 64 : 556–557

22. ——— (1971) Effects of drone comb on brood and honey production in honey bee colonies. *Ann. ent. Soc. Am.* 64 : 954–956

23. MORLAND, D. (1926) The Bee Research Institute at Rothamsted. *J. Min. Agric.* 33 : 33–38

24. NICHOLS, G. (1962, 1963) Plastic frame trials. *N.Z. Beekpr* 24 : 28–29; 25 : 47–48

25. OWENS, C. D. & DETROY, B. F. (1967) New engineering developments in beekeeping. *XXI Int. Beekeep. Congr.* : 324–334

26. PARKS, H. B. (1925) Experiments with aluminum combs. *Beekprs Item* 9 : 299–300

27. PELLETT, F. C. (1923) The metal combs. *Am. Bee J.* 63 : 508–509

28. QUINBY, M. (1872) "Artificial comb" in "Annals of Bee Culture for 1872" ed. D. L. Adair, p. 22–23

29. ROOT, A. I., Co. (1923) Root quality bee supplies [catalog]. *Medina, Ohio*; *Glean. Bee Cult.* [advertisement] 51(1) : back cover [Root's Three-ply foundation had a centre ply of beeswax and vegetable wax, *U.S. Pat.* 1,583,605 (1926)]

30. [ROOT, E. R.] (1920) Aluminum comb—What about it? *Glean. Bee Cult.* 48 : 330–331

31. ROOT, H. H. (1922) Wood base foundation. *Glean. Bee Cult.* 50 : 79–82

32. [STEIGEL, J.] (1892) Tin comb. *Glean. Bee Cult.* 20 : 924

33. WAGNER, S. (1876) [Comb foundation.] *Glean. Bee Cult.* 4 : 142–143

34. ZECHA, H. (1964) Bauerneuerung im Dienste der Gesunderhaltung und Leistungssteigerung unserer Bienenvölker. *Bienenvater* 85 : 185–190, 226–231, 267–272

CHAPTER 10

LORENZO L. LANGSTROTH AND THE BEE SPACE

Langstroth's place as the founder of modern beekeeping is so well established that any new information on his contribution to the development of the movable-frame hive is to be welcomed. The authors of this article have been able to study the notes Langstroth made in preparation for the fourth edition of his book, which was never published. These notes, and other material quoted, provide evidence which puts into rather a new perspective events which, a century ago, determined the course of world bee-keeping since then.

In 1955 we came across the footnote on page 98 of Edward Bevan's *The Honey Bee* referring to della Rocca's improvement of a Greek hive, which he described in 1790. We knew that Bevan's book, with Huber's, was among the first books on bees that Langstroth acquired. So it seemed reasonable to us that Langstroth also would have noticed the footnote, as well as other extensive statements in Bevan's text which point out the importance of spacing combs for ease of manipulation. This led us into deeper and deeper exploration of the circumstances in which Langstroth's name came to be associated with the 'discovery of the bee-space'.

When we read the elegant description by della Rocca of the bee space in the ancient Greek hives, it did not seem logical that Langstroth would have claimed this principle for his patent. We now have collected considerable evidence that he himself took pains to disavow such an assertion but somehow these generally went unheeded. The following excerpts, from two current texts and from *Bee World,* will serve to define the bee space and underscore the extent of the general persuasion that Langstroth 'invented' it.

'The discovery that bees would not fasten the frames or combs to each other or to the hive walls if a bee space of $\frac{1}{4}$ to $\frac{3}{8}$ inch was left between the frame and the hive was made by Rev. L. L. Langstroth in 1851.'—J. E. ECKERT and F. R. SHAW (1960) Beekeeping. *New York: Macmillan.*

'Mr. L. L. Langstroth, in the great invention which he gave to the world (the *first practical* moveable frame), made the discovery that bees recognize and keep clear passageways which are now called bee spaces. Taking advantage of this fact he made a frame for holding comb so that there would be a bee space all around between it and the hive, and a bee space between it and any other frame. All who preceded him had failed to grasp the fact that bees would leave such spaces unfilled with wax or propolis. . . . By bringing out his bee-spaced frame the "father of modern apiculture" solved, with one great master stroke, a problem that had been puzzling the minds of bee-keepers for centuries.' A. I. ROOT ET AL. (1950) ABC and XYZ of Bee Culture. *Medina : A. I. Root Company.*

'W. Herrod-Hempsall . . . maintains that Langstroth did not invent movable frames because the Stewarton hive was "adapted to take movable frames in 1849," and the unknown "J.A." designed a movable frame in 1683. [Surely neither of these frames had a surrounding bee-space? *It is the bee-space, and not the frame, that is the essential part of Langstroth's invention.* Britons are on the horns of a dilemma in this matter. If none of the early British frames had bee-spaces, then clearly it is useless to contest Langstroth's title to the invention of the movable comb. If, on the other hand, they had bee-spaces, we shall have to acknowledge that British beekeepers were very stupid not to have adopted the system : for its advantages must have at once become clear. We prefer to think that our countrymen were unlucky in not hitting on the bee-space, rather than they were so foolish as to neglect an obvious improvement; though, if Mr. Herrod-Hempsall is right, it would not be the first—nor the last—time that British—and most other —beekeepers have behaved like the mediaeval "bee-boy-cum-village idiot". If any Stewarton hive really had bee-spaces, it seems certain that someone in the early 1850s would have defended Britain's right to the invention. As this was not done, we think the accepted view must be the right one].'—[A. D. BETTS] *Bee World* 30(1) : 3 (1949).

Those outside beekeeping circles may regard the arguments that follow as a storm in a teacup, and some within the craft may accuse us of having a bee in our bonnets. But we feel that we have Langstroth himself on our side : 'I have never sought for more than my rights, and if any one can show that before my invention there existed any movable frame hive adapted to practical use, or any invention that used the essential and patented features of mine, I will try to be the first to acknowledge that although an *original* inventor, I was not the *first* inventor of such a hive.' (1861)

It is nearly a century since L. L. Langstroth's hive patent was contested and the *American Bee Journal* carried frequent articles and letters devoted to the semantic intricacies of patents jargon. Heated controversy raged in the pages of the *Journal* from February 1871 until June 1872, when a summary of the debate was promised as a separate supplement—there is no evidence whether this was in fact published. The death of the editor, Samuel Wagner, in February 1872 may have been a factor curtailing publication of the vehement comments, as he was an old friend of Langstroth.

Just prior to this (on 26th January), while Langstroth was on his way to visit Wagner, he fell and his foot was run over by the wheel of a street car. Langstroth's wife died in January 1873, and he is quoted in the March issue of the *Journal* as saying: 'I have made no application for an extension of my patent, and it will soon be public property (October 1873). Sickness, etc. has caused great delay in the prosecution of the suit, but it is not given up, and I am confident that the verdict will sustain my patent.'

Mr. R. C. Otis—who held a major interest in Langstroth's hive—had also become ill, and Langstroth took on the defence of the patent himself.

A hearing was set for 10th June 1873, but apparently illness prevented him from appearing in court. The chief 'infringer' of the patent, H. A. King, then 'donated' his own patents to the public in November 1873, when Langstroth's patent had run out; the contest was then over, except for periodical restatements of the arguments in bee journals down to the present time.

Langstroth's patent No. 9300 (5th October 1852) was not reprinted or excerpted then, nor during the intervening years, and no summary can do justice to the ten-page document. It does not claim the invention of the 'bee space' (bee corridor), as many textbooks state, but is based on: (1) the use of a shallow chamber with a perforated cover; (2) the use of movable frames; (3) a divider; (4) double glass set in a frame; (5) a moth trap. The advantage of this last feature is discussed elegantly in Langstroth's book. Many other contemporary patent hives claimed to have a unique method to control this scourge, and apparently Langstroth felt impelled to include a device to satisfy the demand for it.

In general European authors consider Langstroth's hive very successful, but give credit for the first movable 'comb' to Johann Dzierzon (1811–1906) who devised a bar hive over a period of years and published a description of it in 1847. His hive was adopted as a great advance, despite the breakage of newly drawn combs and the need to cut them from the sides of the hive. Baron von Berlepsch's addition of a frame around the comb was gradually recognized as a valuable improvement. Hives of a similar type, having frames removable from the back with tongs, are currently used in central Europe, usually stacked in a shed or bee house. Those who have not used such hives in bee houses may not appreciate their advantages, especially for some types of research, queen rearing, stock maintenance, etc. On the other hand the advocates of bee houses mostly live in countries other than those where the honey crop is 100–200 kg in a good year. This amount of honey, and the bee population needed to produce it, can only be housed in a hive whose size is increased according to need, and the easiest way of doing this is by adding more and more units from above—a facility not present in most bee houses. The idea of 'storifying' was first propounded by William Mew in 1649; in 1655 Hartlib published a drawing of such a hive by Christopher Wren.

Infringers of Langstroth's patent claimed that it was not original, and they prepared to defend their point in court. H. A. King went to Europe in search of evidence and secured statements from apiculturists such as Berlepsch. King complained that Langstroth had been able to secure copies of W. A. Munn's book, but that he could not. A copy of the 1851 edition of this book, with Langstroth's signature and his marginal notes, is now in the Mann Library at Cornell University. On page 17 there is a note to see page 16 of the first edition (1844, also Langstroth's personal copy), where an asterisk appears near Munn's words: 'a half inch space nearly all round them, which will to a certain extent maintain an equable temperature for the bees, both in summer and winter'. This point was a major assertion in Langstroth's patent: 'As there is a stratum of air always interposed between the combs and the sides and bottom board of the hive and bees are much more effectually guarded against extremes of heat and cold and the pernicious effects of condensed moisture than they can be in hives of the usual construction.'

Langstroth also marked the description of Munn's frame: 'The frames with their contents can be lifted out . . . whenever it is wished to examine the bees, etc., as the half inch spaces between the bee-frames will allow of a sufficient distance to be preserved between the lateral surfaces of the perpendicular combs formed in the "bee-frame" and this permits them to lift out by each other with facility.' This space also allows two bees upon opposite combs to pass easily.

Our own curiosity was aroused by Munn's remark: 'I should not be doing justice to Mr. R. Golding, if I did not particularly mention his "improved Grecian hive" by the use of which combs may be removed from the interior of the hive and inspected at pleasure. . . .'

As we studied the pages in the second edition of Bevan's book for a clue to Golding, we felt like shouting 'Eureka'—as Langstroth recorded in his journal that he could scarcely refrain from doing, when he thought of using a bee space in his shallow chamber between the walls and uprights on his bars. The quotations below will explain our enthusiasm, and we wonder why Mr. Golding has not been given his due. Standard sources refer to his *Shilling Bee Book* and state that he assisted in the preparation of Bevan's second edition. Why he has not been singled out for attention is all the more puzzling when we read Bevan's measure of the man in the advertisement to his own book (1838): 'Huber had the benefit of two pair of eyes in one Apiary; I have had the advantage of at least six or seven pair in as many different Apiaries; and over one of them has presided a scientific observer, who, together with a genius but little if at all inferior to Huber's, combines a courage and perseverance which place him quite upon a level with Burnens; I allude to Mr. R. Golding, of Hunton, near Maidstone.' On page 92 he describes Mr. Golding's improvements upon the Grecian bar hive and on page 96 and onwards describes his experiments in detail:

'In the former edition of this work, I took some notice of the Grecian hive, mentioned by Wheeler [*sic*] as in use about the neighbourhood of Mount Hymettus. This hive was designed to permit the removal of side-combs, by the use of loose bars placed on the top of it. I expressed my approbation of its principle, but stated my doubts of its applicability to general use. Since that period, however, my doubts have been completely dispelled by the success which has attended a series of experiments performed by Mr. Golding, and by a satisfactory repetition of similar ones by myself. This patient and assiduous investigator of the laws of the apiarian republic commenced with that particular modification of the Grecian hive recommended by Huish, [though Huish did not acknowledge this?] and the success of his first experiment afforded him much delight, but future trials convinced him that his success was merely casual; he thence suspected that there was some inaccuracy in the arrangement of the hive-bars; this he sought to rectify by attending closely to the proceedings of the bees when left to themselves. The result was what reason and philosophy would have suggested long since, had they been duly directed to the subject.

'The disposition of the bee, as has been known for ages, is to construct its *brood* combs of one uniform thickness, and at nearly one uniform distance from each other, whilst the thickness and relative distances of the *store* combs are subject to variation, the cells for the reception of honey being frequently so elongated as for a single comb to measure from two to three inches in thickness. Hence arises a difficulty in adjusting the bars of a hive or box to such distances as shall be uniformly applicable to practical purposes; for if the breeding distances were closely adhered to with respect to *all* the bars, (and it is impossible to determine how many will be required for brood,) some of the exterior ones would be found to approximate too much for the attachment of store-combs, and in all such cases the bees would be found to depart from the arrangement which is required for brood-combs. If, again, a full allowance were made through the whole range for the construction of honey-combs, these would deviate so widely from the breeding distances as to lead to equal disappointment from an opposite cause; the bars would some of them be too far asunder. Hence arises the difficulty, perhaps I might say the impracticability, of sur-mounting a hive or box with bars capable of easy removal under *all* circumstances. By compromising the two principles, (if I may use that expression), as applicable respectively to brood and to honey-combs, Mr. Golding has made a very near approach to this practical desidera-tum in the culture of bees, so near as to render the system completely available in a very great majority of instances. In *his* arrangement, he exceeded the breeding distances by the eighth of an inch, placing his bars so as for them to measure one inch and five-eighths from the centre of each bar to that of its immediate neighbour, a departure so small from the natural distances as not to be objected to by the bees for brood-combs, whilst it enabled him to meet the elongation of the honey-cells and the consequently increased thickness of the exterior combs.

'The ingenious application by Mr. Golding of a system of manage-ment, which, prior to his time, rested upon no definite principle, opens an entirely new field to the operations of the practical apiarian, wherein he will be able to work upon sure ground: to cottagers, when once inducted to its details, it must prove of incalculable value; and I avail myself of this opportunity, on their behalf and on my own, to express my acknowledgement to the indefatigable apiarian, who has thus enabled me to give publicity to this interesting and profitable mode of managing the bee-hive, which he has acquired almost entirely through the deduc-tions of his own reasoning faculties, his sole reward, the consciousness of becoming a public benefactor.'

We turned to the first edition of Langstroth's book to see what he had to say about all of this: 'There was nothing *new* in the use of movable *bars*; the invention being probably, at least, a hundred years old; and I had myself used such hives on Bevan's plan, very early in the commence-ment of my experiments. The chief peculiarity in my hives, as now con-structed, was the facility with which these bars could be removed without enraging the bees, and their combination with my new mode of obtaining the surplus honey.' It is interesting that in the second edition this is modified to include Golding's name: 'I had myself used such hives on Golding's plan, as recommended by Bevan. . . . '

In the third edition reference to both Bevan and Golding was deleted. It would be extremely interesting if our English colleagues could uncover additional information about R. Golding.

Mr. Roy Grout of Dadant & Sons kindly lent us Langstroth's interleaved copy of the third edition of his book, which contained the author's notes for a fourth edition (this was never published because of Langstroth's 'renewed and protracted illness'). We are thus able to include here those of the notes that relate to the subject at hand, and let Langstroth himself set some of the matters straight.

Langstroth intended to insert as a first paragraph to the *Introduction* (page 13) the following:

'Having spent much time for nearly 30 years in studying the habits of bees, and in devising hives for their profitable management, I submit to the public in a condensed form the results of my labors. In 1840 I procured a copy of Dr. Bevan's work on the Honey Bee, from which I made a hive after the plan of the celebrated Huber, and was thus enabled to verify some of his most important [observations?]. The accompanying cut taken from the original work of Huber will convey an accurate idea of his invention. The use of this hive even in its most improved form was difficult, the bees being constantly liable to be crushed between its close fitting frames. I learned from it however that complete control over the combs of bees might be presently obtained.'

He noted on page 15: 'Here state only Huber—Bevan—give some account of Munn and Debeauvoys—with plates—plates of Dubeauvoys 1st and 2nd hives—.' He planned to incorporate material on Dzierzon (p. 16): 'Short biography of Dzierzon A.B.J. Vol. X p. 38—born in 1811— and as neither of us knew of the labour of the other he was surprised at the similarity of our method of management. Give a cut of a Dzierzon hive. Hamet *L'Apiculteur* Vol. 5-6 p.147—Dzierzon hive anticipated.' Europeans concur that, prior to designing his hive, Langstroth was not likely to have been informed of the work of Dzierzon in view of the poor communication across the Atlantic during that time.

Page 17: 'History of movable comb Hives A. [B.] J. 169, 170, 172'; these are apparently the articles in Vol. 7 No. 8: 'Is Mr. Langstroth the Inventor' by H. A. K[ing]—which attacked the patent—and Langstroth's reply.

Page 15: 'Such comb bars had been used in Greece at least two hundred years ago, and the novel feature in my hive. . . .I found that with such hives natural swarming could be easly dispensed with. . .' This note makes it very clear that Langstroth did not intend to be given *credit* for more than he had done—certainly *not* for the discovery of the bee space, as this is the essential ingredient that makes the antique Greek hive manageable. Colonies could be divided, to secure the swarm control reputed to have been available since the seventeenth century. Additional evidence for a disclaimer by Langstroth can be found in his manifestly unequivocal statement published in the *Country Gentleman* (A.B.J. 1861, page 142): 'Since my application for a patent, I have ascertained that prior to my invention other movable frames besides those of Huber, were in use in Europe.' Here it is evident that he does not want credit for making the Huber frames practical, but only for producing his own particular variety of hive. In 1860 Langstroth offered to furnish George Neighbour with 'improvements' that would provide the basis for a British patent (Johansson, 1967).

As we read the charges and countercharges contesting the American patent, it becomes clear that an objective is involved other than simply to secure proper credit for the ultimate originator of a device, namely to establish that a particular device has some innovation (no matter how minute) which makes it different from devices described in previous patents. Immediately after Langstroth's book was published, and his patent hive promoted, there was a flood of other applications for hive patents. These hives were not essentially different, nor did they offer any basic revolutionary improvements, but there was some small change in design which hopefully would entitle the applicant to a 'patent'. Langstroth's frames hung from the top, so one inventor stood the frames on the bottom board, etc. We cannot expect a patent lawyer to document credits for innovations in the 'scholarly' tradition; to him, what matters is who first applies for an innovation that has not been patented before or offered to the public in an article, book, etc. An elaborate and delightful spoof, 'The art and mystery of patenting new and useful inventions', appeared in the *American Bee Journal* for April 1871.

As Langstroth prepared to defend his patent and searched through his old bee books, he could not but have been impressed by the quantity of ammunition available to his attackers. He owned both editions of Golding and Bevan in his extensive collection of books on apiculture. Della Rocca's work was also amongst them; he presented this to the Dadants in October 1885. This contains Langstroth's marginal notes on a variety of topics, and we were especially interested in those concerning the Grecian bar hive mentioned above:

Volume II on reverse side of the last page of errata:

465, 6 'Description of Grecian bar hives and how artificial swarms are made with them'

466, 8 'Description of his hive with close fitting bars on their top surfaces—but bevelled on sides so as to prevent bees from running their combs from one bar to another—first notice that I found of a triangular comb guide—'

499 'How he gets guide combs on his bars—'

469 'How he made an unsuccessful experiment by making the bars with the bevelled sides—and got each comb on separate bars not using comb as guides'.

Page 500:

'It would seem that Della Rocca is the father of hives with bars and side opening doors—and of close fitting bars which form the top of the hive and have below a sharp edge for a comb guide. . . .'

An asterisk in the margin of page 468 by line twelve of the second paragraph shows that Langstroth noticed the importance attached to keeping exactly the correct space between the combs of the ancient Greek bar hives. The manifest understanding of the principle of the bee space in the design of these hives can be judged from the following translations of passages on pages 467–469 of della Rocca's book published in 1790:

'This separation between the different bars inside the hive, and all the other dimensions I have just described, must be scrupulously observed, because everything stated with regard to the adoption of these practices, and to the selection of these dimensions, is directed towards making the bees construct each comb separately on a single bar, so that each bar has its own comb entirely detached from neighbouring combs, and any bar can be withdrawn at will, together with its attached comb, without disturbing the other combs. Now if our dimensions are observed with precision, I think that the bees will build their combs along the bars, which I have said must be as wide as the combs built by the bees. With regard to the separation between adjacent bars, this will serve as the space that bees normally leave for their movement between combs, so that they can work, store their provisions in the cells, attend to cells containing young bees, and carry out their other operations.

'For a better understanding of what we have been saying, and to make it easy to put it into practice, we give here the dimensions of the bars. Each should have a total width of 17–18 *lignes* [4·0 cm, 1·61 inches], and a thickness [depth] slightly more than half a *pouce* [1·4 cm, 0·54 inch]. Where the bars form the outside top cover of the hive, they must be in contact with each other all along their length; but on the underside each should be bevelled off so as to form an inverted ridge. Because of this double bevel, which forms an angular space, the bars are not in contact except at their top surface, and they keep between them a space of 3 *lignes* [0·68 cm, 0·266 inch] (each bevel taking up 1½ *lignes* on either side). The bees are therefore obliged to build their combs along the length of the bars, without encroaching on neighbouring bars, which infinitely facilitates the removal of each bar with comb attached.

'If one does not keep to these dimensions, and if the separation quoted is not left between the lower parts of the bars, then the bees, instead of constructing each comb along the length of a single bar, will build them slanting, or crossways, and take up several bars with one comb, in such a way that it will be impossible to withdraw one bar independently of the others, thus depriving us of all the advantage that we should naturally expect from this kind of hive.'

The fact that della Rocca designed a bar hive based on the Greek one has not been sufficiently appreciated. George Wheler described the Greek hive and its value for swarm control in *A Journey into Greece* as early as 1682, although he did not give the dimensions of the bee space. His statement that the comb could be removed 'without the least bruising, and with greatest ease imaginable' would catch the eye of anyone keeping bees in the skeps and primitive hives of that day. One man who reacted immediately was 'J.A.', who, in a letter written in 1683, gave specifications for a hive, prescribing that 'sticks must be laid cross the top, from Front to Rere, at the distance of half an Inch from one another'. The letter was included in a collection published later by John Houghton, F.R.S.; it was also reprinted by Walker (1928). J.A. refers to the advantage of these movable combs in swarm prevention as practised in Greece, and Walker suggests that the design was inspired by Wheler's book since entire sentences were borrowed from it. Walker's conclusions regarding Langstroth's patent may be useful to our narrative:

'Could Langstroth have maintained his patent if the record of "J.A.'s" hanging-bar-frame hive had been produced? It is arguable, but I think not. As he often insisted, it was not his frames alone, but the way in which they could be used in his hive that mattered, and in that respect I see no difference; in both hives they could be moved horizontally or vertically, or shifted into upper chambers. Minor devices, not easy to understand from the descriptions in his book, were included in his claims—a honey-board; the triangular, bevelled lower surface of his bars to induce bees to build straight combs; and movable dividers or dummy boards. It would be hard to find a better honey-board than the slotted one used by Prokopóvitsh; the second claim was afterwards abandoned when it was found that the device had been used and recommended by the celebrated surgeon, John Hunter, F.R.S. The dummy board was a useful invention, hardly good enough by itself to deserve a patent. I feel sure that, had not Langstroth's knowledge of bee history been so scanty at the outset, he would never have applied for one. It was limited, he himself said, to Huber and his leaf-hive. This was unfortunate. His hive, unpatented, might well have made him famous, and he would have been spared grievous trouble.'

Reverting to the battle of the patents, Herrod-Hempsall made the observation: 'had the Rev. Homer King known there was to hand in his own country a still more formidable weapon than the evidence of the hive designed by J.A., or even that of Major Munn, he need not have travelled to Europe in quest of proof to substantiate his claim against the Rev. L. L. Langstroth, for in "The Scientific American", of March 6th, 1847, p. 187, appear the particulars of a hanging bar-frame hive invented by Jacob Shaw, Junr., of Hinckley, Ohio.' In point of fact King *did* include this reference in his first article attacking Langstroth's patent! The defenders of Langstroth's patent turned aside this hive, as well as others, with the observation that the hives were 'impractical'. However, it is easy to misjudge the merits of a device if it is not tested objectively. Geo. W. Christians of Chattanooga, Tennessee, operated a sizable apiary using bars in the fashion of the earliest hives patterned after the ancient Greek hive; he manipulated them with no difficulty, and produced extracted and chunk comb honey. This system is adaptable to small-scale or medium-scale beekeeping; in areas where materials and capital are scarce, or where beekeepers are used to fixed-comb beekeeping, it may well prove more practical for commercial operations than the use of frame hives. It is being tried out, for instance, in Rhodesia. Georgandas (1957) described the recent use of the Greek bar hive (*anastomo cofini*) in Greece itself. He promoted the thesis that this hive was the forerunner of the modern movable-frame hive, and we are pleased to add to the evidence supporting such an attractive subject. The Greek hives are beautiful objects of hand-craft, and the bars are as accurately 'bee-spaced' as many factory made frames.

When Moses Quinby pointed out that Langstroth 'claims an improve-ment in movable combs—not the principle', editor Wagner expressed 'perfect amazement'. Some readers may feel similar amazement, since so many textbooks are emphatic that Langstroth invented the bee space, whereas what he did was to put sides and a bottom on the bar comb. Langstroth himself made it abundantly clear that others had preceded him in this also: 'I have repeatedly, in Mr. Wagner's Journal and else-where, stated that movable frames were used in Europe before my invention.'

Langstroth's eminent position as a promotor of rational beekeeping is not affected in the slightest by the facts submitted here. However, it would seem to be in keeping with his own striving for accuracy that the notes he made for the unpublished fourth edition of his book, and his statements elsewhere, should be published. They may help to correct the unnecessary carelessness with which his contributions have been designated.

The high value placed by Langstroth's contemporaries upon his contribution to the development of a practical commercial hive can be seen in the tributes published in a Memorial at the time of his death. T. W. Cowan, Editor of the *British Bee Journal* stated the matter concisely:

'. . . There has been a great deal of controversy as to who was the original inventor of the frame principle. It was not until 1851 that Langstroth invented his hive, and frames had already been in use some years previously. They were, however, not of any practical utility, for the hives containing them were complicated, or so exceedingly expensive that they could be looked upon only as luxuries for rich amateurs rather than hives to be used by bee-keepers for business purposes. (The single wall Langstroth as we know it today is patterned after his simpler Hive No. 1, rather than after his cumbersome designs using double walls, glass, etc.)

'. . . The opening of the hive at the top, the perfect interchangeability of the movable combs, and the lateral movement of the frames, have given the bee-keeper the most perfect control over his bees, and have more than justified Langstroth's expectations when he wrote the note in his diary in 1851, that "The use of these frames will, I am persuaded, give a new impetus to the easy and profitable management of bees." '

The ancient Greek hive opened from the top, but it most certainly did not allow for the interchangeability or lateral movement of combs, as did the frames in the hives of Munn and Dzierzon. Langstroth's design pro-vided a hive that could be exploited for large-scale commercial beekeeping in regions with heavy, rapid honey flows. It is on this substantial basis that his claim to fame properly rests, not on any priority in devising the 'bee space'.

We are not the first to sense a 'fault' in strata of accounts of Langstroth's work. The President of the Academy of Natural Sciences of Philadephia certainly did so, when he prepared his address for the dedication of the Langstroth Bee Garden in Philadephia in 1951. He had expected, but failed, to find 'this epoch making work on the "bee corridor" and its brilliant application to hive design' in the pages of the Academy's *Proceedings*, since Langstroth was an active member in 1851 when he invented his hive.

After all that has been said, we are understandably sympathetic with Alfred Neighbour's observation in 1866: 'May we not further speculate that the ribs of the carcase constituted the first *bar-hive*? Surely, "there is no new thing under the sun".' Munn stated in 1873 that it was indeed this fable of Samson feasting on combs of honey from the dry rib case of a lion (*Judges* XIV, v.8) that provided inspiration for his bar and frame hive!

REFERENCES

BEVAN, E. (1838) The honey bee, its natural history, physiology and management, 2nd ed *London : Van Voorst*

FRASER, H. M. (1958) History of beekeeping in Britain. *London : Bee Research Association*

GEORGANDAS, P. D. (1957) The forerunner of the modern hive. *Bee Wld* 38(11) : 286-287

GLEANINGS IN BEE CULTURE (1895) Langstroth memorial. *Glean. Bee Cult.* 23(24) : 927-940

GOLDING, R. (1847, 1848) The shilling bee book, containing the leading facts in the natural history of bees, with directions for bee management. *London : Longman & Co.*

HERROD-HEMPSALL, W. (1930, 1936) Bee-keeping new and old described with pen and camera. *London : British Bee Journal*

JOHANSSON, T. S. K. & JOHANSSON, M. P. (1967) Two letters from America to England. *Bee Wld* 48(3) : 110-112

LANGSTROTH, L. L. (1853) Hive and the honey-bee. *Northampton : Hopkins, Bridgman & Company* [2nd ed. 1857, 3rd ed. 1865*]

————Langstroth's reminiscences. (1893) *Glean. Bee Cult.* 21: 116-118, 160-161, 206-207, 250-251, 294-295, 338-339

LINTON, M. A. (1952) Langstroth and the Academy of Natural Sciences. *Morris Arboretum Bull.* 5(2) : 12-14

LUNDGREN, A. & NOTINI G. (1943) Boken om bina. *Stockholm : Albert Bonniers*

MUNN, A. (1844, 1851) A description of the bar-and-frame hive, with an abstract of [Daniel] Wildman's Complete Guide for the management of bees throughout the year. *London : J. Van Voorst*

NAILE, F. (1942) The life of Langstroth. *Ithaca : Cornell University Press*

PINGERON, J. C. de (1770) Les abeilles, poème traduit de l'Italien de Jean Rucellai...... *Amsterdam & Paris*

ROCCA, Abbé della (1790) Traité complet sur les abeilles...... *Paris : Chez Bleuet Père*

WALKER, H. J. O. (1928) The hanging bar frame hive. *Brit. Bee J.* 56 : 441-444, 453-457

WHELER, G. (1682) A journey into Geeece. *London*

WILDMAN, T. (1768) A treatise on the management of bees...... *London : printed for the author, and sold by T. Cadell*

* In the 3rd edition page 209 carries a footnote referring to Munn, and page 210 one referring to Wheler.

www.ingramcontent.com/pod-product-compliance
Lightning Source LLC
Chambersburg PA
CBHW081154270326

41930CB00014B/3157